Praise for

# DUDLEY PUBLIC LIBRARIES

The loan of this book may be renewed if not required by other readers, by contacting the library from which it was borrowed.

"Reading *Be Happy Without Being Perfect* allows women to exhale—finally. We women are so tough on ourselves that it takes a masterful advisor to get us to step back and think about changing our daily thoughts as well as our habits. Reading this book is like having a truly close friend whom you trust—and who just happens to be a psychologist, nutritionist, and coach.

"The book is wise, humane, and it goes down easy. I enjoyed reading it. What's more, I have Xeroxed a few of the pages and put them up in strategic zones (bathroom mirror, refrigerator door). There is something in this book for just about every woman I know."

—Pepper Schwartz, Ph.D., professor of sociology, University of Washington, and author of *Prime: Adventures and Advice on Sex, Love, and the Sensual Years*

"Giving up 'perfect' sets women on the road to true and sustainable health. If you feel trapped in any way by the need to have a perfect body, a perfect house, or perfect life on any level—you need this book. Now!"

—Christiane Northrup, M.D., author of *Mother-Daughter Wisdom, The Wisdom of Menopause,* and *Women's Bodies, Women's Wisdom*

"We strive for perfection in everything we do . . . work, the kids, the meals, and trying to be the dutiful spouse. But where does happiness fit into that equation? Not to worry. Dr. Domar tackles all the misconceptions (and misplaced pressures) and gets you back on the right track. *Be Happy Without Being Perfect* gives you permission to be you, to be good enough, and find happiness along the way. It's a must for each and every one of us."

—Nancy Snyderman, M.D., chief medical editor, NBC News

# Be
# HAPPY
# without being
# perfect

## HOW TO BREAK FREE FROM
## THE PERFECTION DECEPTION

## Alice D. Domar, Ph.D.
### and Alice Lesch Kelly

piatkus

PIATKUS

First published in the US in 2008 by Crown Publishers, an imprint of the Crown Publishing
Group, a division of Random House, Inc., New York
First published in Great Britain in 2008 by Piatkus Books
This paperback edition published in 2011 by Piatkus

Council for Spiritual and Ethical Education and Diana Baumrind: "Authoritative Parenting for
Character and Competence" by Diana Baumrind from *Parenting for Character: Five Experts, Five
Practices,* edited by David Streight (CSEE, Portland, Oregon, 2007). Reprinted by permission of
Council for Spiritual and Ethical Education and Diana Baumrind.

Gordon L. Flett: "Top Ten Signs Your (sic) a Perfectionist" by Gordon L. Flett. Reprinted by
permission of Gordon L. Flett.

Harmony Books: Excerpts from *Sacred Choices: Thinking Outside the Tribe to Heal Your Spirit* by
Christel Nani, copyright © 2006 by Christel Nani. Reprinted by permission of Harmony Books,
a division of Random House, Inc., and the author.

Mc-Graw-Hill: "The Ten Commandments of People Pleasing" from *The Disease to Please* by
Harriet Braiker, copyright © 2001 Harriet B. Braiker, Ph.D. Reprinted by permission of
McGraw-Hill, a division of The McGraw-Hill Companies.

National Eating Disorders Association: NEDA Eating Disorders Quiz. Reprinted by permission of
National Eating Disorders Association, www.NationalEatingDisorders.org.

James W. Pennebaker: Adapted text from "Writing and Health: Some Practical Advice" by
James W. Pennebaker (appearing on the James W. Pennebaker website). Reprinted by
permission of James W. Pennebaker.

A CIP catalogue record for this book
is available from the British Library.

ISBN 978-0-7499-2879-7

Typeset by Phoenix Photosetting, Chatham, Kent
www.phoenixphotosetting.co.uk
Printed and bound in Great Britain by
Clays Ltd, St Ives plc

Piatkus
An imprint of
Little, Brown Book Group
100 Victoria Embankment
London EC4Y 0DY

An Hachette UK Company
www.hachette.co.uk

www.piatkus.co.uk

*I dedicate this book to my beloved friends:*
*to Carolyn, my closest childhood friend, and to all the friends*
*I have made before and after. You humor me, you tolerate me,*
*you tease me, you nurture me.*
*I thank you all for your love and trust.*

—A. D. D.

*To Nancy and Kevin, for all of your support.*

—A. L. K.

# Authors' note

Although this book is a collaborative effort by Alice D. Domar, Ph.D., and Alice Lesch Kelly, for the sake of clarity and simplicity we use the pronoun "I" for Dr. Domar (Ali) throughout.

The names and identifying details of the patients and women who agreed to be interviewed for the book have been changed to protect their privacy.

The advice in this book is offered as a health recommendation, not as a substitute for standard medical care. We recommend that you use mind/body approaches in conjunction with mainstream psychological and medical care. Consult your physician, psychologist, or psychiatrist about any worrisome mental health symptoms you may have.

We use the words "husband" and "wife" in this book because it's the simplest way to write about male/female life-partnership without having to use clunky phrasing. The thoughts and advice apply whether you and your significant other are married or not. They also apply (minus the male-specific comments, of course) to same-sex couples.

# Contents

# Acknowledgments

There is no way that this book could have been written, let alone completed on time, without the support of my family. I don't know how many games of Risk my husband, Dave, played with our girls, Sarah and Katie, in order to give me some extra "book time," but it was enough to accomplish the task. Thank you to Sarah for agreeing to watch Katie at other times, even though it cost me $2 per hour plus fifty cents for Katie to "cooperate."

I also want to thank all of my colleagues at the Domar Center and Boston IVF for their ideas and flexibility. To Liz Rodriguez, thank you for your patience. You are a saint. And to Michael Alper and Ron Jones, thank you for your vision.

People often refer to children as sponges—they literally soak up everything around them. I think that therapists are the same way. I learn so much from my patients. From the problems they bring to my office, to the stories they tell, to the way they get well. I also learn from the talks I give to women around the country. These women ask really good questions and I learn even as I try to answer them.

I would like to thank my friends and colleagues at LLuminari. To Elizabeth Browning, Susan Love, and Nancy Snyderman, thank you for inviting me to join this most amazing group of health-care professionals. You invigorate me, you challenge me, and you make me laugh.

I would also like to thank Henry Dreher, coauthor of two of my previous books, who introduced me both to the magic world of publishing and to my agent, Christine Tomasino (more on her below). Thank you, Henry, for starting this journey for and with me.

And most of all, I would like to thank my coauthor, Alice Lesch Kelly. She is a word fairy. She has an unbelievable ability to transform my thoughts and experiences and anecdotes into logical, readable prose. She sprinkles her own humor and expertise into the mix and—presto—a book. This book.

—*Alice D. Domar, Ph.D.*

———

I would like to express my deepest thanks to my family and my husband's family for being so supportive of my writing. Thanks also to my writer friends and members of my electronic village who constantly offer support, encouragement, Red Sox talk, advice, and comic relief: Tim Gower, Carol Hildebrand, Kim Nash, Sarah Bowen Shea, Kathy Hollenbeck, Barb Bilodeau, and Amy Jones.

Love and hugs go to my husband, Dave, and my sons, Steven and Scott, who are so understanding when my work time expands out into family time. You are my perfect family and I love you so much.

This book would not exist without the determination of Chris Tomasino, our agent. Chris is with us from brainstorming to publication, helping us whip gaggles of thoughts into meaningful ideas. I feel so lucky to have Chris as my agent.

Finally, a huge bouquet of thanks and appreciation goes to Ali Domar, the most wonderful coauthor on the planet. Ali's sense of humor, punctuality, openness, trust, flexibility, ability to carve book time out of the busiest of schedules, and willingness to praise lavishly and critique gently made this book a pleasure to write. I hope that we'll be writing books together for many years to come.

—*Alice Lesch Kelly*

We both want to thank our agent and friend Chris Tomasino, whose humor (dry), expertise (widespread), and perseverance (stubbornness?) were the necessary ingredients for the launch of this project. Her faith in us is humbling.

Our editor, Heather Jackson, was with us every step of the way, with helpful e-mails, thoughtful phone calls, delicious Greek lunches, supportive editorial guidance, and wonderfully helpful advice and critiques. We cannot imagine any other editor doing a better job shepherding this book from proposal to finished product. We deeply appreciate Heather's enthusiasm and effort, as well as the tremendous efforts of the entire Crown team.

Finally, we want to thank most profusely the women who agreed to be interviewed for this book. We created a wave across the United States by contacting friends, family members, and Ali's patients, who in turn spread the word to their friends and family and coworkers (and so on and so on) that we were looking to interview women who have struggled with perfectionism. These women (many of whom were strangers to us) spent countless hours on the phone and at their computers opening up to us and sharing their personal stories of perfectionism—their challenges, their victories, and their hard-won advice. Thank you for welcoming us into your lives.

Sometimes it takes a village to write a book; in this case, it is a village of women helping other women. Thank you all.

# Be
# HAPPY
## without being
### perfect

# The Perfection Deception

A few years ago I met with Kim, a new patient. The first thing I do during an appointment with a new patient is to take a complete history, asking about physical and psychological health, family, relationships, career, stress levels, and health habits. Then I ask the patient why she has come to see me, and together we come up with a treatment plan.

Kim told me she'd been happily married for twenty years. She loved and respected her husband, Ted, and they took pleasure in each other's company. Over the years their sex life had decreased in frequency by mutual consent, but when they did make love, both felt satisfied. Ted had always been faithful to her.

Ted worked in the financial world and made a very good living. This allowed Kim to be a stay-at-home mom, which she preferred and enjoyed. They had four healthy, happy teens who were all doing well in school and participating successfully in sports and other activities. Kim volunteered at her children's schools, had many friends, and had an active and lively social life. Her father had died when she was a teenager, but she had a warm and close relationship with her mother, who lived close by and was always willing to help out with the children. Kim and her children spent summers at the family beach house, and Ted would drive up to spend the weekends with them.

Kim was slender and fit, ran regularly, and had recently started weight training. She did not smoke, and drank socially on the weekends. She had no history of depression or anxiety and no health problems. From what I could see, she appeared to be the model of physical and psychological health.

All the time I was taking notes on her health history I wondered what had induced her to make an appointment with me, a stress-management expert. She seemed to have it all. (Believe it or not, shrinks sometimes envy their patients.) What could possibly be bothering her? Finally, I asked her why she had come to see me. Her answer floored me.

"Because every time I open a drawer or closet and see the clutter, I feel like a miserable failure."

From my perspective, Kim's life seemed pretty perfect. But that's not what she thought. As she told her story, I saw a woman who was successful, lucky, smart, healthy, and well-loved. But Kim saw only the mess in the closets and the drawers.

Kim's anxiety level was as high as that of someone with a diagnosable health condition or a major life stressor. She was as anxious as some of the patients I've seen with heart disease or who have been laid off from their jobs. But it was her doing—the problem was in her mind. The only thing wrong with Kim's life was how she looked at it. Her cup was quite full but the clutter in her mind made it feel half empty. She couldn't enjoy her nearly perfect life because she couldn't get past the small, imperfect parts.

I wrote this book because Kim's story was so striking to me. I think about her all the time because nearly every patient I see does what Kim did—and what I do, too. We judge ourselves more harshly than we would ever judge someone else. We bring high expectations to our roles, and we are terribly hard on ourselves when we don't live up to them. We feel like failures, and we allow that feeling to color the way we look at ourselves and our lives. We torture ourselves over forgotten homework, wrinkled clothes, and too many nights of takeout. We let our few slipups overshadow our many accomplishments.

Be Happy Without Being Perfect

It's fine to want to be a good parent or keep a clean house or do an excellent job at work. There's nothing wrong with aiming high—it doesn't mean you have psychological problems. But if your expectations are so high that they detract from your quality of life, and if you can't be happy unless everything is 100-percent right, it's time to stop judging yourself and start appreciating what's going right in your life. This book will show you how to do that.

During our therapy sessions, I worked with Kim to help her find ways to step back and focus less on the drawers and the closets and more on what was wonderful in her life: the husband she enjoys, the children she adores, her good health, her success at staying fit, her good relationship with her mother, and her many friends. In this book, I'll do the same for you.

## Solving a Mystery

I've been working with women my entire career. My goal has always been to reduce their stress and help them be healthier physically and psychologically. During my twenty years of clinical practice, however, I've found that it's incredibly hard to convince women to take care of themselves.

This baffled me when I first started seeing patients. I knew that self-care and stress reduction produce solid, measurable medical results. Consider migraine headaches as an example. If you take a group of women who get migraines and teach half of them how to do mind/body stress reduction and self-care techniques, they'll inevitably feel better and get fewer headaches than the ones who don't learn how to do the techniques. The same is true with pretty much every health condition out there, from heart disease to anxiety to chronic pain. Many health conditions are *caused* by stress, and almost all are *exacerbated* by it. Study after study after study shows that if you teach people how to reduce stress and take better care of themselves emotionally, they're going to feel better and, in some cases, get better.

So picture me, twenty years ago, launching myself into the clinical world, full of ways to educate women about how to make themselves feel better. I began teaching patients a range of skills and was thrilled to see physical and psychological improvements in the women who incorporated these changes into their lives. But I discovered something else, too. Although my patients were willing to come in and learn these skills, many of them didn't practice them when they left the clinical setting. It didn't make sense: They knew a variety of simple, proven ways to feel better, but didn't use them.

After delving into this mysterious problem, I realized that part of what held women back was guilt: They felt guilty setting aside time to meet their own needs. They saw meditation, mini relaxations, mindful walking, yoga, journaling, social support, and all of the other proven techniques as being selfish acts because of the time they would take away from their families. Many of my patients considered self-care to be selfish—even when there was proof that it would improve their mood and their health and, by extension, their family's happiness and well-being.

But women are held back by more than just guilt. I give dozens of talks every year about how women can nurture themselves, and women attend in droves. I even wrote a book about it called *Self Nurture,* which was a bestseller. Women approach me after reading my book or hearing my talks and tell me wholeheartedly that they love the idea of self-nurturance, but they have trouble implementing it. It's hard to spend time with your friends when the laundry isn't done and the sink is full of dishes. It's hard to go out on a date with your husband when you feel like you're a bad mother who leaves her kids home with a sitter too much. It's hard to sit in a hot bath with a glass of wine when all you can think about is that your thighs are twice as big as they were when you were twenty.

Finally I understood what was causing the disconnect between these women's thoughts and actions. It isn't just that women feel guilty taking care of themselves. It's that, deep down, they feel that setting aside time to meet their own needs—even *having* needs, in fact—is a sign of weakness or failure, a sign of imperfection in a world that expects nothing less than perfection. Acknowledging that you need to work on something is acknowledging a failure, and that can be hard to do.

I've battled perfectionism all my life, and even though I teach and counsel women about it all the time, I sometimes continue to struggle with it myself. This morning I'm working on this book, and this afternoon I'm taking my daughter's Girl Scout troop Rollerblading—not because I have lots of extra time, but because of the occasional guilt I feel as a working mother. I live in a town where most moms don't work outside the home, and seeing all the things the stay-at-home moms do makes me feel that I must be a super-mom on the days that I'm home. I am trying to live up to my own expectations of what a mother should be. (I will of course not go totally overboard and actually Rollerblade. I want to be a good mom, but even I am not stupid enough to humiliate myself in the presence of dozens of coordinated preteens.)

It's impossible to acknowledge a need to take better care of yourself when you spend so much of your energy trying to live up to your and other's expectations. Even a woman who doesn't consider herself a perfectionist is constantly bombarded by perfectionist messages and expectations. It's impossible not to compare yourself to others in your life and in the media who you think are doing it better.

## Over the Years

Our world has changed so much during the past few generations and even since the time when I was raised in the 1960s and '70s. The expectations for mothers were different back then—if you kept your kids healthy and off the streets, you were doing your job well. Today, you're considered a neglectful mom if your kids aren't signed up for sports, flute lessons, ballet, karate, swimming lessons, extra maths classes, foreign language training, religious education and scouts. Even if you work full time, you also have to run the school fair, be a scout leader, teach Sunday school, coach basketball, bake brownies for bake sales, and sell at least

£500 worth of wrapping paper, popcorn, and cookies for the school fundraiser.

I'm exaggerating a little about all that—but not much.

After years of exposure to completely unrealistic expectations being passed off as attainable, we create an image of what we should be, how our houses should look, how we should raise our children, how we should do our jobs. Whether we realize it or not, we create a long list of expectations that we hold ourselves to every day. Acknowledging that we have needs, and that sometimes our needs deserve to come before those of our families, employers, and homes, goes against so many of the messages we've heard and internalized for decades. To embrace your own needs and commit to self-care, you have to commit to changing some of your expectations about your life.

I wrote this book for my patient Kim, whom I mentioned in the beginning of this introduction, and for all of the other women like her who have so much but can't enjoy it because they see only what's missing. It's for all of the women who feel, whether they realize it or not, that they can't be happy unless everything is perfect. Everything is *never* perfect, and if you expect it to be, true happiness and contentment will always be out of reach.

This book is about learning how to reset unrealistically high expectations and replace them with realistic, attainable ones that will result in success rather than failure. I'll show you how to create reasonable expectations for your home, your family, your relationships, your job, and your body. I'll share lessons I've learned as both a psychologist and a woman who struggles with perfectionism occasionally.

Throughout this book I'll pass along stories from more than fifty wonderful women—patients, friends, friends of friends, and even complete strangers—who agreed to open up their lives and be interviewed for this book. Their experiences are enlightening, and their advice is priceless. Some of their stories are also heartbreaking; seeing the impact that perfectionism has on their lives can make you cry.

I'll demonstrate how to do dozens of simple, effective, and clinically

Be Happy Without Being Perfect

proven techniques that will help you reframe the way you think and feel about your life. (Don't worry, you won't have to learn to do *all* of them. Different mind/body skills appeal to different people, and I offer a wide variety so that no matter what your personality, there will be something that works for you.) I'll help you decide what really matters in life—and how to let go of what doesn't.

Finally, I'll show you how to use your most powerful ally—your mind—to find the balance, contentment, satisfaction, and happiness you crave.

You can be happier. You can take better care of yourself. You can feel healthier, more content, and more satisfied. These may sound like pie-in-the-sky goals, but you can achieve them far more easily than you realize. You can be happier by reframing your expectations and embracing an imperfect life. You can be happy without being perfect.

# Quiz: How Much of a Perfectionist Are You?

The following quiz will help you determine how much of an influence perfectionism has in your life and which parts of your life are most affected by it.

*Rate each question on a scale of 0 (doesn't describe me at all) to 3 (describes me perfectly). Tally your points at the end of each section.*

## Section 1: Your Body

1. I'm constantly aware of what I eat. _____
2. When I interact with an attractive woman—at work or in a store— I feel intimidated and inferior. _____
3. I say negative things about my appearance and point out my flaws when I talk to others. _____
4. Shopping for clothes is a very frustrating experience because I feel that nothing I try on looks good on me. _____
5. Friends have told me that I exercise too much. _____
6. When people tell me I look good, I don't believe them. _____
7. I get angry at myself when I gain weight because I feel that I should have better self-control over what I eat. _____
8. The thinner I am, the better I like myself. _____

9. My anxieties about how I look interfere with my ability to enjoy sex. _____

10. I cringe whenever I see a picture of myself because I'm unhappy with how I look. _____

11. I feel disappointed with my body when I get sick. _____

12. I feel that if I try hard enough, I should never develop any kind of physical ailment or chronic illness. _____

13. If I feel depressed, I get angry at myself because I can't pull myself out of my bad mood and feel better quickly. _____

Section 1 score: _____

## Section 2: Your Home

1. I cannot go to bed until the house is neat and the dishes are washed. _____

2. There have been times that I haven't invited friends or family over because I felt ashamed of my house. _____

3. Visiting a friend whose house is bigger, newer, or better decorated than mine puts me in a bad mood. _____

4. I get very stressed when I'm having people over for dinner because I plan elaborate menus or cook difficult new recipes. _____

5. When friends drop by unexpectedly, I apologize several times if my house is messy. _____

6. Reading home-decorating catalogs and magazines depresses me because I feel my home is so much less attractive than what I see in pictures. _____

7. I think less of people whose homes are cluttered. _____

8. I am very concerned with germs in the kitchen and frequently wipe down the counters and table with disinfectant. _____

9. I get angry with myself when I am baking or cooking and accidentally burn something. _____

Be Happy Without Being Perfect

10. I feel pressure to do elaborate holiday decorating inside and outside my house. _____
11. It annoys me when my neighbors don't keep their yards looking as nice as I feel they should. _____
12. When I go grocery shopping I make a detailed list and follow it closely. If something I want to buy is sold out, I feel frustrated and annoyed. _____
13. I feel that my house will never be as well-decorated, clean, or organized as I would like it to be. _____

Section 2 score: _____

## Section 3: Your Job

(Note: If you are not employed, skip this section of the quiz.)

1. When I have a performance review, I am very upset if I don't get the top ranking. _____
2. I have trouble meeting deadlines because I get so wrapped up in doing projects perfectly. _____
3. I feel that my workplace is full of people who don't try hard enough to do a good job. _____
4. I put way more effort into projects than my coworkers do. _____
5. If my boss says something critical of my work, it bothers me for days. _____
6. I worry about making a mistake at work because I feel that if I do, I will be fired and my career will be ruined. _____
7. When I look at a project I've done, all I can see are the imperfections. _____
8. I don't like to delegate work to others because they don't do as good a job as I do. _____
9. I get upset when someone gives me suggestions on how I can

do a better job at work, even if the suggestions are on the mark. ____
10. My fears of doing a project poorly sometimes prevent me from getting started. ____
11. I don't like to ask my boss or coworkers for help, advice, or assistance. ____
12. I dislike working in teams because my coworkers don't work up to my standards. ____
13. I don't like my job, but I'm afraid to look for a new one. ____

Section 3 score: _____

## Section 4: Relationships

1. I want everyone to like me. ____
2. I can be very critical of my friends and family when I feel they don't hold themselves to the same high standards that I do. ____
3. I feel hurt and disappointed if a friend forgets to send me a birthday card. ____
4. I feel uncomfortable asking my family and friends for emotional support. ____
5. When something goes wrong in a relationship, I blame myself.
   ____
6. I feel guilty because I feel like I can never do enough for my parents. ____
7. Nobody I date seems good enough, or my husband says I criticize him too much. ____
8. I am very disappointed at how much work is involved in maintaining a good marriage and/or relationships with other people. ____
9. I am frustrated that my husband's parenting and housekeeping standards are much lower than mine. ____
10. I feel that if I make mistakes I will be rejected by my friends and family. ____

Be Happy Without Being Perfect

11. I have had arguments with family members and have not spoken to them for days, weeks, or months afterward. _____
12. I find it difficult to forgive people who have wronged me. _____
13. I feel that if my friends and family knew what I was "really" like, they would reject me. _____

Section 4 score: _____

## Section 5: Parenting

(Note: If you are not a parent or have adult children,
skip this section of the quiz.)

1. When I was trying to conceive, I felt that if I did everything "right," I would have gotten pregnant when I wanted and my baby would have been perfectly healthy. If anything had gone wrong, I would have considered it my fault. _____
2. I feel ashamed of myself when I feel bored playing with my children. _____
3. I feel that if I make a mistake in my parenting, my children will be irreversibly damaged. _____
4. I am constantly reading parenting how-to books. _____
5. I don't always trust my instincts as a parent. _____
6. I find it difficult to forgive myself when I make a mistake in my parenting. _____
7. I blame myself when my child misbehaves or shows poor manners. _____
8. I consider it a personal failing on my part when my child doesn't make the baseball team, win the spelling bee, or get into the college of her choice. _____
9. I feel guilty taking time away from my children to do something special for myself. _____
10. I feel that my children should excel in everything they do. _____
11. I feel that no babysitter is ever good enough. _____

12. If I lose my temper and yell at my children, I am angry at myself for hours. \_\_\_\_\_
13. No matter how hard I try, I can never be as good a mother as I would like to be. \_\_\_\_\_

Section 5 score: _____

## Section 6: Decision Making

1. I find it very hard to make big decisions. \_\_\_\_\_
2. I find it very hard to make small, everyday decisions. \_\_\_\_\_
3. I have trouble making decisions because I am afraid of making the wrong decision. \_\_\_\_\_
4. After making a decision, I often second-guess myself. \_\_\_\_\_
5. I often procrastinate on making decisions. \_\_\_\_\_
6. In general, I doubt my ability to make good decisions. \_\_\_\_\_
7. I regret some of the major decisions I've made in my life. \_\_\_\_\_
8. It takes me a long time to make decisions because I do excessive amounts of research and fact gathering beforehand. \_\_\_\_\_
9. I have trouble forgiving myself when I make a decision that turns out to be poor. \_\_\_\_\_
10. I let peer pressure influence my decisions more than I would like. \_\_\_\_\_
11. If I am in a group that is making a decision, I find it difficult to disagree with the people in the group. \_\_\_\_\_
12. If I make a bad decision, I tell myself that I'm stupid and criticize myself for a long time afterward. \_\_\_\_\_
13. When I make decisions, I rely heavily on the opinions of others, such as my spouse or my parents. \_\_\_\_\_

Section 6 score: _____

**Total score:** _____

Be Happy Without Being Perfect

# Scoring

First add up your scores in the individual sections of the quiz. The highest score (or scores) indicates where perfectionism causes the most trouble for you. Quiz sections correspond to the chapters in this book, so it's easy to know which chapters to read first.

Then add up your scores from all the sections. This is your final score. Use your final score to determine how much of a perfectionist you are. (If you skipped the "Parenting" or "Your Job" sections, see alternate scoring on next page.)

**0–40:** Perfectionism isn't a big problem for you. You may feel some-
**(1)** what perfectionistic in some parts of your life, but overall, you're able to forgive mistakes and accept when things don't go your way. (Maybe there's a perfectionist in your life you could pass this book along to!)

**41–91:** Most of the time perfectionism doesn't cause you trouble.
**(2)** You tend to set realistic goals, although you are sometimes rigid in your expectations. There may be one area in your life—for example, your career—where perfectionism is more prevalent, and you are sometimes hard on yourself.

**92–142:** You expect perfection in some, but not all, areas of your
**(3)** life. You occasionally get sidetracked by unreasonably high expectations. You have strong ideas about the "right" way to do things, but you're able to be realistic and flexible sometimes.

**143–193:** You find it quite difficult to accept failings in yourself and
**(4)** others, and this can interfere with success in your career and personal relationships. You set rigid standards and become very frustrated when they are not met. Perfectionism some-times impedes your ability to be happy.

**194–234:** Perfectionism is preventing you from enjoying life. Your
(5)    belief that everything should be—and can be—perfect could
       be leading to low self-esteem, depression, guilt, inflexibility,
       and anxiety. You may become immobilized by your fear of
       failure. If your score is in this range, your perfectionism is
       probably getting in your way and you might want to con-
       sider getting professional help.

## Alternate Scoring

If you skipped one quiz
section, scoring categories are:

(1) 0–34
(2) 35–76
(3) 77–118
(4) 119–160
(5) 161–195

If you skipped two quiz
sections, scoring categories are:

(1) 0–27
(2) 28–61
(3) 62–95
(4) 96–129
(5) 130–156

# CHAPTER 1

# In a Perfect World

*I*'m sure some people would look at me and never guess that I am a perfectionist. I don't keep a perfect house, I'm overweight, and my career path is bumpy, to say the least. I am always looking for another job, something more challenging and better paying, something that is more rewarding. I have had a rough time getting to a place where I could perform my best and enjoy what I do.

*I think my attitude stems from the perfectionist ideal I was raised with. My mother was very concerned with outside appearances—house, clothes—while Dad focused on his accomplishments. I take after him in that respect. When I was in school, it was imperative that I receive straight A's. If I got an A-minus or, heaven forbid, a B, I would be very upset with myself. In graduate school, I got sick and was hospitalized shortly before midterms. I felt awful and didn't do well on one of my tests. I got a B for my final grade. It was the only B that I received, but I still think about it.*

*I have always been overweight. Even though I try to talk myself into not worrying about what society thinks, I am still always thinking about it, trying to diet, and feeling disappointed that I can never get the weight off. My mom has always been a pain about my being* overweight. She has always been thin, and I take after my dad, who is also heavy. It bugs me less as I get older, but like most children, I want my parents to be proud of me and feel that they did a good job raising me. Now, at age forty-seven, it has become a health issue, which causes even more stress.

I suffered from postpartum depression when I gave birth to my third child—I was completely overwhelmed when she was born. We were moving to another state. My husband went ahead without me, and I had to take care of my two older children and sell the house. It was an extremely stressful time, and I was not happy about being pregnant because I had planned to go back to school after we moved. My husband loved his new job and was not home much. I was lonely and unhappy. I slept only a few hours a night. The PPD came upon me a few days after giving birth. It felt like the world was ending. After some rest and some meds, I was OK, but it took me a long time, about six months, to feel like myself. I hope I never go through something like that again.

When it comes to making decisions, I am the regret queen. I still think about mistakes I made when I was nineteen, and I wish I could do things over again. This is a problem I have dealt with for years and have had many long, expensive talks with my therapist about. My number-one decision that I regret is getting married when I did. I grew up in a very religious family and when I got pregnant, my mother and father felt the best thing for me was to get married. I am still married to the same man, but maybe my life would be different—better?—if I had married someone else, or if I had married him at a more convenient time.

I like to feel that I'm in control of things. That's why I don't drink much alcohol, because I don't like being at all out of control. I hate to drive with anyone else, too. I feel that I am the best driver, although I suppose that has to do more with control issues than with driving.

Be Happy Without Being Perfect

*Hoping everything will be perfect is an insane way to live. There is nothing perfect in this world, and continually trying to attain perfection leads to so many problems. I never quite feel that everything is OK, and I think that stems from my unreal perception of how the world should be.*

—*Cynthia*

A hundred years ago, a woman's job was clear: Have children, keep them alive, get meals on the table, and take care of the house. If your house was clean and your kids were fed, people thought you were doing a good job. Now, in addition to those responsibilities, today's women have numerous others. Many work outside the home. We worry about our jobs, the quality of our relationships with our husbands, how our kids do in school, how our homes look, how we look, how much volunteer work we do, how much money we give to charity, how well our kids behave, and so much more. We're even responsible for our kids' social lives. A generation ago, our mothers didn't arrange play dates. Mom booted you out the door and it was your job to find someone to play with while she did her housework (or invited a neighbor over for coffee).

No wonder we're unhappy! We want to excel at everything. But with so much to do, that's unattainable. It is impossible to do a great job with your marriage, your home, your kids, your career, your body, your friendships, your health habits, and everything else. Yet that's our goal—to do everything well. And when we can't, we feel like failures.

Remember my patient Kim, whom I mentioned in the introduction? She had almost everything going for her, but she felt depressed because her house was cluttered. That demonstrates the sinister nature of perfectionism. When Kim reflects on her life, instead of listing the many things she's got, she looks at herself and says, "You're a failure because your house is cluttered." If you can't learn to let go of a feeling like that, unless you can get the perfectionist monkey off your back, there's always going to be something wrong in your life.

# A Perfect New World?

In 1620, the first American colony was established by Pilgrims who had such strong ideas about how to practice their religion that they sailed all the way to a new continent to do things *their* way. Ever since the Mayflower brought this idealistic group to America, immigrants have flocked here hoping to find the freedom, opportunity, and happiness that had eluded them in their home countries.

By the early 1800s, American Puritanism and its angry God began to give way to individualism, with its emphasis on people's power to determine their own salvation through good works and proper behavior. "By the turn of the nineteenth century, Americans became rampant reformers with a certain righteous pride" that came from creating the largest democracy since the Roman Empire, writes Laura Schenone, the author of a fascinating book called *A Thousand Years Over a Hot Stove*. "American politics would be fairer than those of England. American people would be superior. Even the food in the new republic would taste better."

To reach these heights, reformists turned their attention to women. They found much that they wanted to reform. Until that time, most women couldn't read. But America needed strong, principled men to build the new nation, and for women to raise such men they would have to be educated. For the first time, large numbers of girls were taught to read; the number of literate white women skyrocketed.

As female literacy grew, so did the publishing industry. The 1800s brought a wave of cookbooks, women's books, and pamphlets that pointed out women's many failings and urged them to use the discoveries of the exploding field of domestic science to improve their lives, their homes, and their family's health.

In 1829 a writer named Lydia Child published a book, *The Frugal Housewife*, which became the bestselling standard of its time. This classic example of nineteenth-century women's books provided firm guidance

Be Happy Without Being Perfect

on a wide variety of tasks, including keeping house, devising home remedies, dyeing clothing, cooking, educating daughters, and enduring poverty. Child touched all of the domestic bases: She taught women how to make full use of a slaughtered cow (mix its brains with cracker crumbs and boil in a bag for one hour), cure constipation (drink dried huckleberry tea when the "digestive powers are out of order"), care for the eyes ("do not read or sew at twilight"), and arrange children's hair ("do not make children cross-eyed, by having hair hang about their foreheads, where they see it continually").

Like many other writers of the time, Child had rigid ideals about how moral women should run their homes and their lives, and she wasn't shy about offering dictates. For example, she warned that public amusements such as steamboats, taverns, and vacations would lead to a "luxurious and idle republic" that was destined to plunge the country into ruin. The message to women was loud and clear: They were responsible not only for their families' well-being, but also for the welfare, morality, and success of the entire nation. Talk about high expectations.

## Food = Health

In the kitchen, nineteenth-century women were taught that perfection wasn't just a goal, but a matter of life and death. "The person who decides what shall be the food and drink of a family, and the modes of its preparation, is the one who decides, to a greater or less extent, what shall be the health of that family," wrote Catharine E. Beecher and Harriet Beecher Stowe in a book titled *The American Woman's Home*, published in 1869. "It is the opinion of most medicinal men, that intemperance in eating is one of the most fruitful of all causes of disease and death. If this be so, the woman who wisely adapts the food and cooking of her family to the laws of health removes one of the greatest risks which threatens the lives of those under her care."

The Beecher sisters urged women to perfect their skills in making bread, butter, meat, vegetables, and tea. "If these five departments are all perfect, the great ends of domestic cookery are answered, so far as the comfort and well-being of life are concerned." Bad butter in particular aggravated them. Not ones to mince words, the Beechers condemned most of the butter in America as being "merely a hobgoblin bewitchment of cream into foul and loathsome poisons." They preferred the butter in England, France, and Italy—in fact, they extolled the superiority of French cooking so enthusiastically that American women must have felt the culinary deck was stacked against them simply because they were not French.

Nineteenth-century women embraced these books and mind-sets and applied their energy toward following them. They raised generations of healthy, well-fed, well-educated sons (and daughters). They helped build a nation, one healthy, moral child at a time.

But some of them wanted more.

## Voting for Power

As home economists and cookbook authors rallied for change in the kitchens, the fledgling women's rights movement sought change in the polls. In 1848 the first women's rights convention took place in Seneca Falls, New York. Participants called for equal treatment of men and women under the law and voting rights for women. Susan B. Anthony inspired women to wage state-by-state campaigns to allow them to vote, and in 1920 Congress amended the Constitution to give women voting power.

Meanwhile, in 1916 Margaret Sanger opened a birth control clinic in New York. Doing so, she took a first step toward giving women the reproductive freedom that would allow them greater than ever control of their childbearing.

The actions of home economists and women's rights activists moved in two very different directions—one leading into the kitchen and one out into the world. Each revolutionized a part of female life, and women would continue to feel their effects for decades.

In the 1940s, World War II drew women out of their homes and into the workplace. Millions of women, inspired by Rosie the Riveter (the famous World War II effort poster) did their patriotic duty and took jobs in factories and offices across the country. Not only did women discover that they could do the work their men had left behind, but many found they liked it. Working outside the home gave women a taste of the financial and personal freedoms that had been in a mostly men's-only world.

Like it or not, most women trudged back to their kitchens when the men returned from war. It was the 1950s, and women were expected to have large families and comfortable houses that their husbands could come home to after a long day at work. Women's magazines bombarded them with images of perfection, and their brand-new televisions showed June Cleaver and Donna Reed gliding effortlessly through a world where women ran the house and raised the children (in skirts, stockings, and high heels, no less!), but father always knew best.

## A Recipe for Everything

Magazine articles in the 1950s and '60s told women exactly how to dress, clean, cook, raise their children, and care for their world-weary husbands. A November 1956 issue of *Good Housekeeping*, for example, advised women on everything from manners to architecture: How to eat awkward foods (peel bananas by hand, then place on a plate and cut and eat with a fork), how to soften hard water (lease a water softening system for £2 a month), how to get rid of door-to-door salesmen who interrupt you while you're doing the wash (install an intercom system in the laundry room that "makes it possible to say a polite but firm no to salesmen without even opening the door"), the quickest ways to learn French, how to help your house plants grow ("rain water is especially good for all plants"), how to recognize the seven basic types of roof, how to spell the thirty most "mis-spellable" words (from "abbacy" to "therapy"), and how to recognize the words "no smoking" in Belgium, Denmark, Finland, France, and nine other countries. Articles on the proper way to set the table, restore chipped appliances, choose a spring hat, and launder a man's wash-and-wear suit appeared in other issues.

As for appearance, *Good Housekeeping* gave this advice to a woman entering her thirties: "The price of a lifelong good figure is a lifelong good diet. And the tab for an eternally comely face and coif is daily care. Pay both, no matter what. You cannot be an ill-groomed, gone-to-seed woman and keep your self-respect."

Meanwhile, advertising promised women that the only thing separating them from happiness was the latest labor-saving device ("many wonders are yours with a Ben-Hur Chest Freezer"), cleansers ("it's fun to cook with shiny pans"), personal care products (Veto Deodorant— "because *you* are the very air he breathes"), food (a Jell-O salad "*makes* the meal"), and lingerie (Maidenform: "the bra that makes your curves look more curvaceous").

## Occupation: Housewife

In 1963, Betty Friedan popped the balloon. Her book, *The Feminine Mystique*, described the dissatisfaction that percolated among middle class women forced into the narrow roles of mother, wife, and home-maker.

"The problem lay buried, unspoken, for many years in the minds of American women," Friedan wrote. "It was a strange stirring, a sense of dissatisfaction, a yearning that women suffered in the middle of the twentieth century in the United States. Each suburban wife struggled with it alone. As she made the beds, shopped for groceries, matched slip-cover material, ate peanut butter sandwiches with her children, chauffeured Cub Scouts and Brownies, lay beside her husband at night—she was afraid to ask even of herself the silent question—'Is this all?'"

Be Happy Without Being Perfect

Friedan saw the way a skewed expectation of female perfectionism had made its way into the American culture during the years after World War II:

> *Millions of women lived their lives in the image of those pretty pictures of the American suburban housewife, kissing their husbands goodbye in front of the picture window, depositing their station wagons full of children at school, and smiling as they ran the new electric waxer over the spotless kitchen floor. They baked their own bread, sewed their own and their children's clothes, kept their new washing machines and dryers running all day. They changed the sheets on the beds twice a week instead of once, took the rug-hooking class in adult education, and pitied their poor frustrated mothers, who had dreamed of having a career. Their only dream was to be perfect wives and mothers; their highest ambition to have five children and a beautiful house, their only fight to get and keep their husbands. They had no thought for the unfeminine problems of the world outside the home; they wanted the men to make the major decisions. They gloried in their role as women, and wrote proudly on the census blank: Occupation: housewife.*

## Freedom and Rights

After Friedan exposed "the problem that had no name," women's lives started to change. During the following decades, barrier after barrier fell. New laws and changing cultural beliefs gave women never before known freedom to attend college, have careers, and control when and whether they would have children.

Women headed for the workplace in droves. In 1960, 36 percent of women over age sixteen worked outside the home; by the year 2005, it had gone up to 60 percent. According to the U.S. Department of Labor, women represented just under half of the U.S. workforce in 2005, and the figure is similar in the U.K.

But a funny thing was happening. Even though women worked *outside* the home, expectations remained high for their roles *inside* the home. They'd come a long way, baby, but they still had to get dinner on the table, take care of the children, do the laundry, clean the house, remember to send birthday cards to relatives, and keep their husbands sexually satisfied. Society essentially told women that, sure, you can have it all— but if you're going to do it all, you'd better do it well.

Unfortunately, few men stepped up to the plate when it came to helping working mothers with grocery shopping, childcare, and cleaning. In her 1989 book, *The Second Shift,* sociologist Arlie Russell Hochschild pointed out that while men were free to relax after work, the story was very different for women. "Just as there is a wage gap between men and women in the workplace, there is a 'leisure gap' between them at home. Most women work one shift at the office or factory and a 'second shift' at home."

Hochschild calculated that because of housework and childcare, women worked an average of fifteen hours per week longer than men. Over the course of a year, they worked an extra month of twenty-four-hour days. Over a dozen years, it was an extra year of twenty-four-hour days. "There is no more time in the day than there was when wives stayed home, but there is twice as much to get done. It is mainly women who absorb this 'speed-up.'"

So, as women took on more and more roles—often with inconsistent support from the men in their lives—you'd think they'd get a break as far as expectations were concerned. But it didn't happen. Throughout the 1990s and beyond, the media continued to portray complete happiness in all facets of life as an attainable goal. You couldn't pick up a magazine without being told to improve yourself. Almost every article was about how to make yourself better: How to bake perfect cookies, how to remove stains perfectly, how to have a perfect pregnancy, how to be the perfect weight, how to discipline your children, how to dress perfectly. Nothing ever said, "You're just fine the way you are." The message that

Be Happy Without Being Perfect

magazines hammered in was that you had to improve yourself in every area of your life.

The most egregious example of this came in 1990 with the publication of the first issue of a magazine that would raise perfectionism to a breathtaking new height and forever change the way women viewed their homes: *Martha Stewart Living.*

## Martha's World

Nobody is better at showing us what perfection looks like than Martha Stewart. In her magazine, books, and television shows, Martha sets the bar higher than ever. For example, the November 2006 issue of her magazine promises "The Perfect Thanksgiving—a Classic Feast at Martha's." And perfect it is. A ten-page spread (plus six pages for recipes) shows Martha serving dinner to twenty-three people in her stable in Westchester County, New York. Her seventeen-and-a-half-foot-long mahogany dining table groans with picture-perfect food, including rolls shaped like turkey tails, mushroom soup with chervil cream and tiny croutons, a photogenic turkey with quince glaze, seven side dishes, three sauces, and two desserts—all made from scratch, of course.

Photos show Martha and her adult guests relaxing at the candlelit dinner table while the children sit happily at a kids' table made with plywood planks set across hay bales and covered with linen cloths. Five handsome thoroughbred horses stand in their stables nearby, adding ambience. A trough filled with bottles of wine and sparkling water sits beneath a large wreath made of real carrots. Martha even seems to have control over the weather: A light snowfall has "powdered trees, frosted rooftops, and coated the ground like a plush blanket."

What's wrong with these pictures? I'll tell you what's wrong with them. You see perfection, but you don't see the army of people—chefs, recipe testers, food stylists, editors, clothing stylists, lighting experts, horse trainers, and kitchen helpers, to name a few—who worked endless hours to create this fantasy. What you see in the pictures is Martha pulling off this immense, amazing dinner by herself, with the only help coming, in one picture, from a burly guest who helps her carry the perfectly browned twenty-six-pound turkey to the table. But one person can't pull this off. To cook this meal, you'd need to make twenty-one recipes that call for about one hundred and fifty ingredients. You'd need a restaurant-size staff to serve a Thanksgiving dinner like Martha's.

All this is fine as a fantasy, but when real women look at it and compare their Thanksgiving dinners to Martha's, theirs don't stand a chance. There is no room on Martha's table for canned cranberry sauce, green bean casserole with French-fried onions, and sweet potato–marshmallow bake. Martha's turkey-tail rolls would leave my ready-to-bake rolls in the dust, and her sweet tartlets made with "a variety of heirloom squashes chosen for their hues" would put my pie made with canned pumpkin and ready-to-bake pastry case to shame.

While ladling soup into elegant china bowls, Martha looks calm and fresh, without even a drop of basting juices on her apron. I don't know about you, but at my house, by the time I'm actually ladling things into bowls, I am sweating, splattered with gravy, and looking around anxiously for my next glass of wine. If a real family ate at Martha's, the kids would be fighting ("I don't *wanna* sit at the kids' table! I don't care if it's made of hay!"), the men would be searching the stables for a television, and the horses would be making a meal of the carrot wreath.

And don't get me started on what Martha does for Christmas.

## The New Normal

Even if you don't buy into Martha's fantasy world, it affects you. Having Martha in our culture raises expectations to unrealistic levels for all of us, whether we buy into it or not. It changes what our society thinks of as "normal." And it's not just Martha, although she is by far the most fun to pick on. Rachael Ray sells fantasy, too, but in thirty-minute packages. Sure,

Be Happy Without Being Perfect

her recipes take half an hour to prepare—provided you have a vegetable fairy to wash the celery, chop the onions, slice the mushrooms, dice the tomatoes, pulverize the garlic, and salad-spin the fresh herbs. What you see on television is perky Rachael making a pizza from scratch in half an hour. What you don't see is the shopping and preparation that go into having all those ingredients ready to use in the refrigerator.

Stores and catalogs sell fantasy, too. Selfridges, John Lewis and Littlewoods are some of the most egregious purveyors of daydream-as-reality, but even discount chains perpetuate the perfect party fallacy: For example, I recently saw a discount store refer to a football-themed serving dish as an "entertaining essential." I'm here to tell you that it is *not* essential to have a football-themed serving dish, no matter how many Super Bowl parties you host. People will not speak unkindly of you if you serve pretzels in a non-football-themed bowl. Most people won't care if you serve them pretzels in a bag. As long as the beer is cold, your guests will think well of you with or without a football-themed serving dish. And if there's enough beer, they won't even remember if there was any food served at all.

The most insidious part of all of this is that not only does the media tell you what to do to live a perfect life, but, through advertising, it tells you what to buy in order to have a perfect life. It's easy to forget that the media has a vested interest in making us feel like we need to be more and buy more. Having a country full of women who won't accept anything less than 100 percent is just what the media wants—you can spend an awful lot of money chasing perfection.

It's not just the middle class that feels perfection pressure. The media makes materialism and upper-middle-class perfectionism a goal for *all* classes. Judith Warner describes this phenomenon well in her book, *Perfect Madness: Motherhood in the Age of Anxiety.* "The influence of the upper middle class is disproportionate in American culture. It is upper-middle-class homes that we see in movies, upper-middle-class lifestyles that are detailed in our magazines, upper-middle-class images of desirability that grace the advertising destined for us all. *The upper middle class is our reference point for what the American good life is supposed to look like and contain."*

Until recently, the American dream was to attain financial security, intellectual freedom, and material comfort. It meant going a little further in life than your parents had. But that's not good enough anymore. Today, the American dream is to look and live like a television star.

## Do and Don't

While Martha and the pie-in-the-sky stores peddle perfection in the home, women's magazines set unreasonably high standards for how we should look. For example, *Glamour* magazine offers up "10 New Flattery Rules" in its *Big Book of Dos and Don'ts.* These rules cover everything from dressing to showcase your favorite physical feature to practicing the art of camouflage, choosing figure-flattering fabrics, using patterns wisely, and knowing that the A-line is your friend.

These rules make sense—you can't argue with someone who's recommending that a woman with trailer-width hips and a jelly belly avoid crop tops and pencil skirts. But *Glamour* pushes perfection a little too far when it tells women what they should do with these 10 rules. "Memorize them, believe in them, follow them, and you *will* leave the house fashionably every day." That's an awful lot to ask—I'd be happy to leave the house fashionably once a week. Plus, each rule is illustrated with a photo of a celebrity example—Jennifer Aniston, Beyoncé Knowles, Salma Hayek, and other stunningly beautiful women that the average reader wouldn't resemble no matter how many fashion rules she followed.

What these rules and the magazines that publish them really are saying is: Be thin. Be young. Have large breasts and a small waist. Spend hours and hours a week thinking about what you should wear so that you look the way you should. Do what we tell you (and buy what our advertisers are selling) and you can look like Salma or Jennifer or Beyoncé, and

Be Happy Without Being Perfect

if you don't, you're just not trying hard enough or memorizing our rules well enough.

*Glamour* does make a commendable nod to larger body sizes with rule number 10, which tells you that any body is a good body, whether you're a size 4 or 24. Standing beside this rule is Queen Latifah, who, yes, is a lot closer to a size 24 than a size 4. But even if she is a size 24, she's a beautiful 24. Few 24s can look like Queen Latifah no matter how they dress.

Again, if you view all this as entertainment, it's fine. But if you're feeling bad about yourself because you don't look the way the media says you should, that's a problem. Whether we want to or not, we let the media and cultural beliefs set our standards for how we should live our lives.

## Messages for Today

So where does all this leave us, the women who are trying to carve out a happy life for ourselves today? In the latter part of the twentieth century, the forces that had been building for nearly two centuries—excellence in the home and freedom in the world—came together and landed squarely on women's shoulders. Women could go to college, get married, have children, and have careers. We could have it all. The only thing we couldn't have was the extra time and energy we needed to do all of these things as well as we and society expected. So we took on two full shifts— one at work and one at home.

What we didn't shift was our expectations. We want our homes to look as nice as the homes of our friends who don't work. Working mothers try to do our jobs as well as male coworkers or female peers who don't have children. And even if we work full-time, we expect to be better mothers than the stay-at-home mothers who raised us, as Judith Warner points out in *Perfect Madness*:

> *Even if they had the inclination or the encouragement to do so, there wasn't time for our mothers to raise us with the exclusive*

*intensity we put into our mothering efforts today. Families were larger. Children didn't necessarily attend school before first grade. . . . Mothers did more housework. They didn't have time to religiously get in their sessions of "floor time" with each child. They stuck their little ones in playpens and did the ironing.*

Today's stay-at-home moms are not exempt from perfection pressure. Most find that as stay-at-home moms they are also supposed to be supermoms. Because you don't go out to work, there's even more pressure on you to keep the house clean, the kids creatively challenged, the swimming lessons scheduled, the play dates arranged, and the meals healthy and homemade. "Since being a mom is my job, I feel I have to take it more seriously and do better at it than my friends who work," a stay-at-home friend told me. "I feel guilty if I don't plan art projects and educational outings for the kids. And I do loads of stuff at their school—I help the librarian, I'm a class parent every year, I chaperone field trips, I paint bookcases on school appreciation day. Since we live on one income and not two, I spend a lot of time bargain hunting. I find lots of toys and kids' clothes at thrift stores and yard sales. I shop the sales at two or three supermarkets. It takes a huge amount of time, especially when you've got a toddler with you. But it's my job to do all that. I'm not sitting at home eating bonbons and reading romance novels."

Whether or not we work outside the home, we hear little voices—from ourselves, from society—reminding us of what we "should" be. From the minute we drag ourselves out of bed in the morning till the minute we fall asleep at night, we are inundated with messages that tell us we should be thin, beautiful, successful, and sexy while being exceptional parents, supportive spouses, superlative employees, and cheerful volunteers. Oh, and we're supposed to get a restaurant-quality Thanksgiving dinner for twenty-three people on the table without breaking a sweat. So, despite all the progress we've made, perfectionism is holding us back.

You can stop this perfection-based insanity. You don't have to be a slave to these messages. You can change the way you respond to the expectations set by others, and you can rescript the demands that you automatically place on yourself. But first let's dig a little deeper and look at where we are today.

# CHAPTER 2

# Why Can't I Do
# Everything Right?

*E*verything I do, I try to do perfectly. I am extremely competitive and have a great need to be right. This makes life hard sometimes. Recently I went though a difficult time with a project I was managing. The woman I hired to coordinate the project caused tremendous trouble. She told people we worked with that I was a terrible manager and that I snapped at her. Some of the top managers at the company seemed to believe her. This took place over the period of about a year, during which time I had insomnia and terrible back trouble. I was a wreck physically, mentally, and emotionally. I ended up leaving the job. I couldn't stand the idea of people thinking ill of me.

I realize that I spend a lot of time looking for permission to do things that are good for me but may affect others or their opinions of me. I am terrified of making mistakes, which makes me feel like I'm wound too tight.

When I was in college, my father's financial situation changed dramatically and he was no longer able to pay my tuition. During the ensuing three years, I variously wanted to transfer or drop out because our family could not afford to pay for it. Both of my parents convinced me to stick it out, maximizing loans and scrimping by.

I'd be called in to the finance office and pressured to pay the bills. I had no money and I had no control over my situation. This whole experience, aside from ruining college for me, left me wanting to control everything.

My college has a small ski area. It was very competitive to get on the ski patrol, and I really wanted to make it. I had a very busy semester, with a difficult course load and a varsity sport. I worked myself into a tizzy. When the ski patrol final exam came, I got the highest score on the test. I could not believe that I did better on the exam than all of those other (obviously more qualified) people. I wasn't capable of processing my successes in a healthy manner to boost my self-esteem.

When I graduated from college, my boyfriend of five years broke up with me. My mom thought it would be good for me to fly to California to visit my sisters, so she sent me the money for airfare. At the time, I was terrified of flying (as any good control freak should be!). When that plane took off, I experienced a rush of letting go that made me euphoric. I realized that I had to trust other people in this world (including that pilot). I let go of my dad and his controlling of my youth, I let go of the heartache of the terrible breakup I had just endured, and I touched the freedom of accepting the universe as it is for the first time in my life.

I still struggle though. Almost every big decision in my life has caused me undue stress. I don't trust myself, though by now I should have learned that once I make a decision, it's usually a very good one. About a year ago my partner and I decided to get married. The only way I could do it was last-minute in the privacy of our home. After we did it, I cried for four days, taking walks alone with my dog in the cold, gray, wet February weather. I felt trapped, claustrophobic. I think that I was clinging on to some image of myself that wasn't real, that somehow I was still single, even though we'd been together for fourteen years or so. Somehow that was wrapped up in

Be Happy Without Being Perfect

*my idea of youth. I never wanted to be a "wife." Having a relationship is a lot of work and very personal, and adding a layer of social definition was scary to me. Also, both my parents and my partner's parents are divorced, and there was always the fear that I'd end up like that. Giving my word is very important to me. When I said "for better or worse" I meant it and had to be very sure myself that those words were real for me, that I wasn't getting married just because everyone else was. So I'm glad we waited and I'm glad that we did it on our own terms.*

*When I compare myself to other women, I either think I am way better or I think I am at the bottom of the barrel. There does not seem to be a middle ground and I do not have a clear sense of where I fit into the big picture. There are very few women with whom I connect; however, when I do I tend to have long and deep friendships.*

*Sometimes I lie awake at night worrying about whether I will be able to keep my commitments to others. I worry whether I will actually do what I've said I'd do the next day. I've always gotten things done, but still I doubt that I will be able to.*

*—Angela*

Wanting things to be perfect *seems* like a good thing. We live in a pretty flawed world—who can blame us for wanting to make our little corner of it perfect? The trouble with perfectionism is a matter of degree. A dash of perfectionism here and there can be constructive; greater levels can whip up feelings of distress, anxiety, depression, low self-esteem, guilt, and disappointment. In extreme cases, it can contribute to marital problems, alcoholism, overworking, drug abuse, and suicide.

But let's not get ahead of ourselves. Before I go into detail about what perfectionism does, I'll clarify what it is and where it comes from. Then I'll explain some of the damage out-of-control perfectionism can cause in a woman's life.

# What Is Perfectionism?

Canadian researchers Gordon L. Flett and Paul L. Hewitt wrote the book on perfectionism, so to speak. (Their textbook on the topic is called *Perfectionism: Theory, Research, and Treatment*.) They consider "normal" perfectionism as having a goal of flawlessness: "Normal perfectionism is defined as striving for reasonable and realistic standards that leads to a sense of self-satisfaction and enhanced self-esteem."

When perfectionism goes too far it is considered extreme, or "neurotic," according to Flett and Hewitt. "Neurotic perfectionism is a tendency to strive for excessively high standards and is motivated by fears of failure and concern about disappointing others." In other words, *wanting* to be perfect is normal; *expecting* to be perfect in all aspects of your life is extreme. A person who strives for perfection will work hard for an A-plus; a neurotic perfectionist will consider anything less than an A-plus a failure—in fact, she may even think of an A-plus as something of a failure if she had to work very hard to earn it. Flett and Hewitt have found that some of the following tendencies crop up among perfectionists:

- **Expecting people and situations to have no flaws or faults.** There are three types of perfectionists: People who expect perfection of themselves, people who demand perfection from others, and people who think others expect perfection from them.
- **Getting "stuck" on tasks.** Doubt and concern over mistakes can trigger procrastination.
- **Having perfection-oriented automatic thoughts.** Even when they don't realize it, perfectionists tell themselves that they have to be perfect.
- **Having a hyperawareness of imperfection.** Perfectionists notice and dwell on every flaw.
- **Feeling shame and guilt.** When a perfectionist makes a mistake, she feels ashamed of what others think and guilty because of her own unacceptable performance.

Be Happy Without Being Perfect

- **Making mountains out of molehills.** For a perfectionist, a minor setback carries more importance than it deserves.
- **Setting rigid standards.** A perfectionist sets unreasonably high expectations; success is black and white—either you're a complete success or a complete failure.
- **Expecting the impossible.** Perfectionists feel they should excel in every area—even those in which they have no training or experience or that are not important.
- **Making all-or-nothing judgments.** If a perfectionist can't do something well, she may write it off as being worthless.
- **Overstating what's at stake.** Perfectionists convince themselves that the world hangs on every decision and action.
- **Overreacting.** Perfectionists tend to cope with problems in an overemotional, reactive way rather than facing them head-on with problem-focused, task-oriented strategies.

## Perfectionism vs. OCD

Perfectionists often joke that they have OCD (obsessive compulsive disorder). But there's a big difference between perfectionism and OCD.

People with OCD become preoccupied with certain persistent thoughts (obsessions) and use rituals (compulsions) to control the anxiety these thoughts produce. For example, if you're obsessed with germs, you may develop a compulsion to sanitize the kitchen counter over and over again. If you're obsessed with neat handwriting, you may copy a letter over many times before being satisfied with the results.

People with OCD sometimes feel the need to repeatedly touch, count, or check things (such as the kitchen stove, to make sure it's turned off). Their obsessive thoughts and rituals may interfere with their daily lives.

OCD affects about 2.2 million adults in the US, according to the National Institute of Mental Health, and as many as three in a hundred people in the UK, according to OCD-UK, although it usually appears first in childhood, adolescence, or early adulthood. OCD can occur alone or can be accompanied by eating disorders, depression, or other anxiety disorders, such as panic attacks and general anxiety. Men and women are affected in equal numbers by OCD, which is believed to run in families. Severe OCD can interfere with every facet of your life. OCD can be effectively treated with medications and/or psychotherapy.

This book is not aimed at women with OCD or any other major psychological condition. It is intended for women who find that their perfectionist tendencies sometimes take away from the quality of their lives.

If you suspect you have OCD, talk with your GP, who, if necessary, will refer you to a psychiatrist. More detailed information about OCD is available from the National Association for Mental Health (www.mind.org.uk).

## What OCD Looks Like

Sharon, one of the women we interviewed for this book, was diagnosed with obsessive-compulsive disorder twenty years ago. She offers a glimpse into life with OCD:

"I have an obsessive neatness disorder that has affected my life drastically. My family makes a joke of it but it got to the point where I would come home after work and put all the kids' toys away before I would say hello to anyone. I would need to put everything in order before I could move to the next step. I couldn't eat breakfast before all of the beds were made perfectly. I had to put all of the laundry away before I could leave the house. My husband used to say if he got out of the bed to go to the bathroom, I would get up and make the bed.

"About four years ago I gave in and decided to take Prozac to see if it would help. The OCD almost destroyed my marriage and drove my kids crazy, so I thought it would be worth a try. It has made a difference.

Be Happy Without Being Perfect

I have successfully conquered the more drastic aspects of the OCD, but still must have things in perfect order. My nieces and nephews call me Mrs. Clean or the Windolene Queen. My husband and my kids have learned to deal with it better and the stress level in the house has definitely subsided.

"My husband is absolutely wonderful, but I frequently get upset with him because he does not do things quickly enough, efficiently enough, or up to my standards. He gets angry at me because I use my expectations of what is right to judge him. He frequently says that nothing he ever does can be good enough for me. At times he rebels against my type A personality and doesn't do what I ask. I have tried to reduce the level of stress in my marriage by doing most things myself and avoiding the arguments. It works for the most part, but I frequently freak out when I get overwhelmed.

"I find it really hard to settle, even as far as wrapping a birthday gift for someone. I feel like I can't just buy pretty paper. I need a special bow, a card that matches, or accessories that make everyone say 'wow' when they see the package. I put so much pressure on myself to get it 'just right.' I can't accept that something looks fine. This has always been an issue of mine and has caused me great stress in my life. This attitude extends to all aspects of my life—decorating, dressing, work, my kids, etc. I always feel like I can do something else to make things better."

## Emotions and Stress

Perfectionistic thinking can erode self-esteem because perfectionists tend to engage in all-or-nothing thinking when they evaluate their performance. If a perfectionist fails at a task—say, she gets a low grade on a test—she tends to enlarge that feeling of failure to include not just the test, but herself, too. Perfectionists quickly jump from the idea of "I failed at this task" to "I am a failure." When there are a few things out of place on the kitchen counter, they move very quickly from "my counter is a mess" to "my entire kitchen is a mess" to "my entire house is a mess" to "I am a mess."

Perfectionists struggle tremendously with stress, which is indelibly linked to feelings of sadness, frustration, disappointment, and depression. Perfectionists have unrealistic expectations about stress—they think that if they work hard enough to find "perfect" solutions to their problems, all of their stress will disappear. To a perfectionist, stress is a sign of failure.

## Sickness and Wellness

Perfectionists have an elevated risk for a variety of ailments that are caused or worsened by the stress and anxiety that perfectionism brings. For example, perfectionists are vulnerable to postpartum depression (PPD). Feeling sad, anxious, or depressed for a few days after childbirth is normal—doctors call it "the baby blues." But some 10 percent of new mothers experience PPD, a more serious mood disorder. Women with PPD have trouble performing ordinary daily tasks because of feelings of anxiety, depression, and despair.

PPD can have many causes: Lack of family support, previous psychiatric illness, recent stress (such as a death in the family), changes in hormone levels, irregularities in thyroid function, fatigue, and a troubled relationship with one's mother. Studies show, however, that perfectionism can contribute to PPD.

A new mother with perfectionist tendencies expects herself to be a perfect mother from the moment her baby is born. She assumes that she should know by instinct how to breast-feed and care for her baby. She feels guilty if she doesn't bond with her baby right away (many women don't), or if her baby is unusually fussy, she blames herself and her mothering skills. Perfectionist mothers hold fast to their image of what an "ideal mother" should be; whenever they fail to uphold that image, they feel angry and disappointed.

I remember that when I was pregnant with my first child, Sarah—a very wanted, long-awaited child—I was plagued with worries that I wouldn't be a good enough mother. I confided these thoughts to my mother. She very wisely told me that it was too late for such doubts, so there was no point in dwelling on them. (She also assured me I'd be a great mom.) When Sarah was six weeks old and waking up every two hours to eat I was so tired that I thought I wouldn't survive. I told my mother that I had changed my mind and didn't want to have a baby. She reminded me once again that I was a bit too late on that one, came over to my house, rocked Sarah to sleep, sent me off for a nap, and proved for the thousandth time that moms are indispensable, no matter what we said to them when we were fifteen.

Perfection plays a part in eating disorders as well. Some 10 million females and 1 million males in the United States suffer from the eating disorders anorexia nervosa or bulimia nervosa. Many of them have perfectionist tendencies in terms of diet, exercise, body image, and weight.

An international team of researchers led by investigators at the University of North Carolina at Chapel Hill and the University of Pittsburgh School of Medicine has identified the top six personality/behavior traits among women with eating disorders. The six traits include obsessionality (the psychological term for a form of perfectionism) and concern over mistakes.

Women with eating disorders have unrealistically high expectations in terms of weight, control over their diet, appearance, and exercise adherence. They restrict calories, binge and purge, or overexercise to reach their "perfect" weight; however, no matter how thin they get, they never feel they've reached their goal.

Perfectionism can also cause or aggravate insomnia, gastrointestinal symptoms, and other stress- and anxiety-related conditions, as it does for Dorothy:

*My daughter has special needs. I go in a million directions being a super-mom and trying to do the best I can for her. Then I get so* exhausted from running her to occupational therapy, physical therapy appointments, and everything else. I get short-tempered and also forget to enjoy my sweet angel. I realize how big she's getting and how much I've missed being saddled with the role of full-time therapist-mom that I just cry and grieve for what's been lost. Yet if I slack off and just enjoy, she stagnates and doesn't make progress. So either way I end up crying and unhappy and feeling like the worst mother in the world, even though I know logically how great I am and how no mother could do more for her.

It wears me out. I had postpartum depression. I have irritable bowel syndrome, and I teeter on the edge of depression now and again. I also have severe temporomandibular joint disorder. Stress does all of these things. I don't know if perfectionism is the main player or if it just fuels the fire.

## Ten Top Signs Your a Perfectionist

1. You can't stop thinking about a mistake you made.
2. You are intensely competitive and can't stand doing worse than others.
3. You want something either "just right" or not at all.
4. You demand perfection from other people.
5. You won't ask for help if asking can be perceived as a flaw or weakness.
6. You will persist at a task long after other people have quit.
7. You are a fault-finder who must correct other people when they are wrong.
8. You are highly aware of other people's demands and expectations.
9. You are very self-conscious about making mistakes in front of other people.
10. You noticed the error in the title of this list.

*Printed with permission from Gordon L. Flett*

Be Happy Without Being Perfect

# Where Does Perfectionism Come From?

Many of the women we interviewed for this book grew up under the shadow of perfectionism. Raised by mothers who placed great value on looks, they lived in immaculate homes, and learned by example how to use makeup, clothing, and weight control to look their best. Parents pressured them to excel in academics, sports, and careers. Success was assumed; failure was either punished or completely ignored.

I was raised by a perfectionist father and a very casual mother. During childhood this confused me sometimes, and I think it had a huge effect on who I am today. I feel sometimes like I have a split personality—there are areas where I really push a lot and others where I don't really care. I constantly catch myself being a perfectionist as a parent and in my career. But in other areas I'm happy to let things go somewhat—at home, for example, and with my appearance. I've taken on parts of my father, who drove himself relentlessly in his career, and my mother, who felt comfortable amid clutter and wore no makeup aside from an occasional daub of lipstick. My mom was no perfectionist when it came to clothing, and I've inherited that trait, too—I don't care much about clothes, makeup, and hairstyles, which is fine with me, but has been difficult for my agent. Prior to my first book tour Chris was so exasperated with my clothes that she flew up from New York with her one-year-old daughter and dragged me to Lord & Taylor to pick out some outfits for me. Picture four of us in a fitting room—Chris and her one-year-old, Nora, and me with my four-month-old, Sarah. (By the way, that was eleven years ago and I still wear some of those outfits.) A criticism about my work would sting, but a criticism about my appearance would roll off my back.

Are perfectionists made or born? Probably both. Obsessive-compulsive disorder has a genetic component, and although perfectionism differs from OCD, there may be a genetic connection. I think behavior modeling plays a huge part in passing along perfectionist habits and beliefs. Perfectionist parents tend to raise perfectionist children.

That's not always the case, though. I've also seen many cases in which perfectionist women emerged from chaotic homes. They use perfectionism as a way to seize control in (or escape from) an out-of-control situation, as was the case with Brittany:

*I think the roots of my perfectionism come from childhood. I was the oldest, I was smart—academically, things came easily. I wasn't athletic, so I had no sports to take time away from my studies. When I was growing up, my dad was an alcoholic. My parents were very young when they got married. My father quit drinking years ago, but he did drink while I was growing up. Back then my mother wanted everything perfect—the socks had to match the outfit. I think she was trying to control the things that she could control because when my father drank, everything was out of control. My father was not abusive, and his alcoholism didn't make him miss work. He was the life of the party, in fact—very funny, very social. But something was just not right. That's how I grew up. It's what made me who I am today. If things had been different, my life would be different. I'm sure I'd be less of a perfectionist.*

Many women grew up using perfection to make up for an imperfect sibling. I was surprised at how many of the women we spoke to told stories of older siblings who had been born with disabilities, had died, or had disappointed their parents in some way. Whether or not their parents exerted overt pressure on them, these women felt they had to carry the torch that their older siblings could not or would not carry. Growing up, these women felt pressured to be twice as successful in school, in their careers, with marriage, and in producing grandchildren—as was the case with Donna:

*My sister died in a car accident when I was twenty, and I definitely felt that after her death I had to be more perfect. That's part of why I got married—I had to be the perfect daughter, not leave town, not go out on my own, just be there for my parents. I had to be the strong*

Be Happy Without Being Perfect

one. I married a perfectionist, and it was awful. We just picked at each other all the time. We both expected things of each other that were not possible. It was not a good situation. Looking back, I see that we were both being too rigid—it was my way or the highway and there was no other way to do it.

I felt very guilty getting divorced. I felt like here I had picked someone who on paper was perfect—he had just graduated from law school—we wanted to have the storybook life where I stayed home and raised kids and he worked—a real Leave It to Beaver lifestyle. But a couple of years into the marriage I said, "This is boring, I don't want to do this." We started to grow apart, nitpicking. I realized I had gotten married for the wrong reasons, and I had to get divorced. My family and his family were totally supportive of him, but not of me. They thought I'd gone off the deep end. I remember my dad saying, "You can't do better than him." I had a lot of inner strength to get through it, but I really felt guilty that I was disappointing all these people, especially my parents.

## In the Rearview Mirror

Some of the women we spoke to were older siblings who feared—either because of what their parents said or what they told themselves—that if they didn't work hard enough, their younger siblings would catch up with them or, God forbid, do better. Others used their achievements as a way to stand out; high grades and school prizes attracted the kind of positive attention for which they yearned.

Even a single comment made by a parent or family member can trigger perfectionist behavior. When I was a child, my father told me I was lazy. To this day, that's the label I fear most. I hear that comment when I sit down after a long day of work. I feel like I still have to prove to someone that I'm not lazy even though my father died ten years ago.

My coauthor had a similar experience when she was in elementary school. On the way home from her cousin's high school graduation,

Alice's grandmother observed that all of her cousins had won awards at their high school graduation ceremonies. The remark terrified her. What if she failed to win an award at graduation? Alice imagined the shame she would feel if she won no awards. She imagined her disappointed grandmother reeling from the discovery that one of her grandchildren had broken the chain of award success. Failing would reflect badly on her and her parents. But what could she win? She was a good student, but was she good enough to take top honors in a subject? She wasn't sure. Desperate not to break the winning streak, Alice started high school with her eye on the only award that she could control: the perfect attendance award. She never missed a day of high school, no matter how sick she was. She had to win that award. And she did. Her grandmother died during her sophomore year of high school, but Alice still felt relieved when she heard her name announced at graduation. Not surprisingly, she felt no pride in the award as she'd just done what she'd expected of herself.

As the mother of two daughters I am hyperaware that the comments I make about food or weight could affect them. I know my kids see that my husband and I push ourselves pretty hard in our jobs, so I point out any errors I make—I want to be a healthy role model, and I want them to see that it's OK to make mistakes. I don't make any comments about weight or food around them because I know it could affect their body image. Words have tremendous power over vulnerable women.

## The Desire to Control

Perfectionism is an act of control. If things are perfect, they feel more ordered, more in control. Let me tell you—every iota of stress, everything that brings people to psychologists' offices is related to a feeling of being out of control. Some people tolerate a lack of control; perfectionists feel overwhelmed by it.

Perfectionists may have uncontrollable chaos in their lives—an alcoholic parent or spouse, for example—and because that part of their life is in chaos, they try to wrest control by exerting super-control in

Be Happy Without Being Perfect

other areas of their life. Maybe they can't do anything about the alcoholic parent, but they can make sure to never gain a pound, that their house looks beautiful, and their kids have all the latest gadgets. It gives them a false sense of control—if everything *looks* good, it must *be* good.

As a psychologist, I have learned that so many people's lives look perfect from the outside but are troubled inside. But as a human being, when I meet someone who is beautiful and successful and has her act together, my first assumption is that she must be deliriously happy. Then I put my psychologist hat back on and remember how many of my patients, many of whom are struggling with major life problems, have lives that look perfect from the outside. Many people work frenetically to have their lives look perfect in order to mask massive underlying issues.

One of the women we interviewed illustrates this point perfectly. Her life appears to be a perfectionist's dream come true—she's stunning, she has beautiful kids, a gorgeous house, lots of money, the whole she-bang. But behind the scenes, her family is falling apart. The police arrested her honor-roll son for shoplifting. She and her husband barely speak. Her daughter needs therapy for anger management. Her neighbors know none of this—they think she has it all.

When you're feeling envious of someone else, trust me, her life probably isn't as great as it looks. The people who appear to have the most going for them often have major problems, but you don't see them because they are working so hard to appear perfect. It's their way of grasping for control.

It's OK to let go. Giving up some control can be a liberating, satisfying experience. It's hard to do, I know—but not as hard as you think. As with any job, you need the right tools to succeed. In the next chapter, I'll tell you about one that can change your life.

CHAPTER 3

# What Was I Thinking?

There's no doubt about it: How you *think* can powerfully impact how you *feel*. This intimate link between mind and body is the centerpiece of what's known as mind/body medicine.

Mind/body medicine is not really "medicine" per se. It's a set of tools and techniques that pave the way for the mind to alter behavior or physiology. Mind/body techniques can be used in sickness and in health. They can lessen the symptoms of disease and, if you're healthy, help you feel even better and actually keep you healthier.

When you can no longer cope with the stress in your life you feel anxious, angry, terrified, helpless, overwhelmed, and depressed. You can't always stop the causes of your stress, but you can change your reaction to them by using certain techniques.

If I've heard it once I've heard it a thousand times: Women with perfectionist tendencies want to be in control. When they lose control, they feel deeply unsettled and unhappy. Mind/body techniques can't give you control of what's going on around you, but they can help you regain control of how you respond to the challenges of life. You can't control the ocean, but these techniques make it easier for you to steer your boat through any kind of storm.

Throughout this book, I'm going to share the many techniques that can allow you to cope with stress and take control of your own emotional responses. I'll start with a tool called cognitive restructuring, which can start delivering positive results immediately. In the next chapter, I'll teach you some other critical skills. Then, I'll give you advice on how and when to apply these skills, as they can benefit you in every part of your life.

The information in this section is pretty serious stuff and may seem a little dry. It may feel a little more digestible if you think about it this way: To battle perfectionism, you have to start with the basic ingredients. If managing perfectionism is bread, then cognitive restructuring is flour. It's the primary ingredient that you'll use throughout the rest of the book. Start with the flour, and in the following chapters I'll give you the yeast, water, and salt to turn that flour into a delicious loaf of bread.

## Retrain Your Brain

Two women have completely different things happen to them on the same day. One wins a million dollars in the lottery. The other is diagnosed with early-stage breast cancer. Who do you think is happier?

Of course you'd think the lottery winner would be happier—it seems obvious. But that's not necessarily so. To answer this question accurately, you have to look at timing. A week after these events occur, the lottery winner would almost definitely be happier. But a year later, all bets are off, so to speak. The woman with the cancer diagnosis could be as happy as—or happier than—the millionaire.

Here's why. Researchers who study happiness have found that we all have a baseline for happiness. Having something very good happen may lift you above your baseline for a while, but you'll eventually return to your previous happiness level. The same is true if you suffer a trauma—you'll struggle for a while, but you'll probably return to your pretrauma happiness level. People are amazingly resilient that way.

That doesn't mean you're stuck with your current happiness level—it's not set in stone. You can raise it. If you think negatively about yourself—as so many women do—you are dragging down your ability to feel happy. If you can teach yourself to focus on the positive rather than the negative, if you can learn to curb your perfectionist tendencies and be less critical of yourself, I firmly believe you can feel happier on an everyday basis.

The best way to change how you think about yourself is cognitive restructuring. It is the most important mind/body technique for women whose perfectionist tendencies interfere with true happiness.

## What Is Cognitive Restructuring?

What you're thinking can determine your emotional state. Cognitive restructuring allows you to change the way you feel by changing the way you think. It is a psychological process in which you replace irrational (emotionally damaging) beliefs with more accurate (emotionally beneficial) beliefs. It allows you to challenge and replace thought patterns that trigger or reinforce depression, anxiety, and other negative emotional states.

We all have automatic thought patterns, or auto-thoughts. I think of these as tape loops that are running through the background of your mind, influencing what you do and say without your conscious knowledge. These auto-thoughts have been with you for years—many start in childhood and remain forever. They are so familiar to you that you take them as fact. Some are beneficial: "Always wear a seat belt," for example. But some are distorted and unrealistic, and they can cause stress, anxiety, depression, and dissatisfaction.

Let me give you an example. Kimberly, one of the women we interviewed for this book, has always struggled with her weight. In an effort to keep her weight under control, she works very hard to follow a healthy diet. When her daughters came along, she was determined from the very start to feed them nutritious foods and to keep them away from junk food.

One of Kimberly's automatic thoughts is that McDonald's is a bad place to eat because it serves unhealthy food. You can understand why she thinks this—McDonald's is certainly not a health-food restaurant, and its menu items can sabotage any diet. So when her daughters were old enough to go to McDonald's, Kimberly's original feeling, based on her auto-thought of "McDonald's is bad," was to forbid it. The thought of her daughters eating at McDonald's upset her because she equates junk food with weight gain, and she wanted so much to protect her daughters from developing weight problems that could plague them for the rest of their lives. So when her husband said he wanted to take her daughters to McDonald's, her auto-thought was to say no, because "McDonald's is bad." But then she stopped to think about it and realized that it made sense to restructure this thought:

> On a recent Sunday, my husband took my daughters to see his mother so I could have some time to myself. He planned to take them to McDonald's for lunch. When he said that, I thought of going to the grocery store and making lunch and sending it with them. But that would have defeated the whole purpose of the outing, which was to give me more time to myself. So I let it go. They had lunch at McDonald's and had a great time. If I had said, "No, you have to eat more healthfully," the whole visit would have been less fun for them and less helpful to me.

Cognitive restructuring teaches us to stop, reflect, and appraise situations accurately. That's exactly what Kimberly did—instead of acting on her auto-thought, she stopped, analyzed it, restructured it, and acted accordingly. Kimberly's thought was irrational—having one McDonald's meal would not destine her daughters to a lifetime of weight trouble. We call this kind of thought a cognitive distortion. If she had acted on that thought, she would have lost some important self-time and her daughters would have gained nothing. Instead she told herself that occasional junk food would not harm her daughters—a rational thought—and everyone was happy.

And I'll add my two cents about this: I've found that when parents don't allow their kids to eat any junk food, their kids become obsessed with it. We have lots of junk food in our house (usually left over from parties or from my husband, Dave's, poker nights) and my kids pretty much ignore it. But when kids from homes without junk food come over, they go crazy over it. Forbidden fruit is always so enticing. If you are taking a black-and-white approach to junk food with your kids, consider backing off. Allowing some junk food may actually make your kids want it less.

## HOW TO DO IT

Cognitive restructuring is a three-step process. I find that writing is one of the best ways to get the hang of it. Consider buying a purse-size notebook for this work.

### Step 1: Identify Detrimental Thoughts

What are some of the auto-thoughts that cause you stress? It can be hard to identify them because they are such an integrated part of the fabric of your mind that you take them as fact rather than distortions.

Start by looking at a problem and backing up to find its root. Say you're totally stressed out because your sister and her husband are arriving tomorrow and staying for the weekend. Go backward. Why is this stressing you? Maybe because you have a lot to do before they come and not much time to do it. Go backward again. What do you have to do before they arrive? Maybe you have to clean the house and shop for groceries. Go backward again. Why do you have to clean the house and shop for groceries? Maybe because you feel your sister will think less of you if the house is messy and you serve takeout instead of cooking a gourmet meal. Go backward again. Why would you feel this way? Maybe because you want to impress your sister. Why do you want to impress your sister? Because you've always felt that your sister thinks she's better than you. There's your auto-thought, buried under layers of cooking and cleaning: You feel inferior to your sister. Now that's a thought that's worth challenging.

A good way to become aware of these problematic thoughts is to write them down. Whenever you feel stressed, unhappy, or dissatisfied, jot down what you're thinking in your notebook. When you go back and look at your notes, you'll probably start to notice patterns that will help you gain awareness of stress-inducing thoughts.

Here's a helpful tip: Pay extra-close attention to any thought that contains the absolutist words "must," "should," "shouldn't," "always," "never," "have to," and "ought," because they often play a part in distorted thinking.

This is a list of some of the kinds of distorted auto-thoughts that plague women with a streak of perfectionism:

- If this report isn't perfect, I'll get fired.
- If I gain a few pounds, I will look like a fat pig.
- I'm a terrible mother because my kids don't always do what I tell them to do.
- If I don't bake brownies for the school bake sale, people will think I'm a lazy mother.
- I have to volunteer for every project.
- I can't go out with my friends because I shouldn't spend time on myself.
- Nobody ever appreciates me.
- If my child fails his spelling test, he won't get into a good college.
- I can never have anyone over to dinner because my house is messy.
- I will look terrible if I wear _____ because _____. (Example: I will look terrible if I wear shorts because they allow my spider veins to show.)
- Every project I do has to be 100-percent perfect.
- If people knew my true self, they would dislike me.
- I should put my own needs after everyone else's.

## Step 2: Challenge Your Thoughts

Once you are aware of your stressful auto-thoughts, put them to the test. Think of yourself as an attorney who's cross-examining a witness. Show no mercy—this thought could be causing you lots of trouble, so be tough with it and demand answers to the following 10 questions:

1. Is this thought really true?
2. Am I jumping to conclusions?
3. What is the evidence?
4. Am I exaggerating or overemphasizing a negative aspect of the situation?
5. Am I catastrophizing—that is, thinking of a small problem as a huge catastrophe?
6. How do I know it will happen?
7. So what if it happens?
8. Is it really as bad as it seems?
9. Is it to my advantage to maintain this appraisal?
10. Is there another way to look at the situation?

Sometimes you'll challenge an auto-thought and discover that it is indeed true. For example, if you are an airline pilot, making a mistake could not only get you fired, but it could put hundreds of lives at risk. But if you're a receptionist and you accidentally forget someone who's on hold, the world will not end. Most likely you won't be fired, either. The customer may be annoyed, but if you offer a sincere apology when she calls back, your mistake will most likely cause no damage.

## Step 3: Restructure Your Thoughts

Once you've identified an auto-thought as being irrational or detrimental, it's time to restructure it. To do this, examine the thought closely. Take from it any truth and push aside the distortions. Then, re-create the thought in a way that causes less stress.

To illustrate the three steps of cognitive restructuring with a real-life example, let's challenge a statement that we heard from many of the women we interviewed: **"I can't sleep if there are dirty dishes in the sink."**

## Step 1: Identify the Thought

One way to define this thought is to ask yourself if you feel this way. Another is to look at your actions. Is a sink check the last thing you do before shutting the lights off in the kitchen at night?

## Step 2: Challenge the Thought

Ask yourself the 10 questions on the previous page. Not all apply to every thought, but contemplate the ones that do.

- Is this thought really true? Probably not. It's highly unlikely that you would lie in bed tossing and turning in a haze of insomnia all night because there's a dirty coffee cup in the sink.
- What is the evidence? Have you ever left dishes in the sink at night? Were you awake all night? Probably not.
- Am I exaggerating or overemphasizing a negative aspect of the situation? Sure sounds like it.
- Am I catastrophizing? Ditto.
- How do I know it will happen? Unless you've actually suffered from a case of dirty-dish insomnia, you don't.
- Is it really as bad as it seems? Of course not.
- Is it to my advantage to maintain this appraisal? Not if it causes you stress, keeps you from getting enough sleep, and causes arguments with your husband because you're washing dishes instead of having sex.
- Is there another way to look at the situation? Absolutely. You really don't have to have every dish in the house clean in order to sleep.

Be Happy Without Being Perfect

## Step 3: Restructure the Thought

Look at each part of the thought and think about how you can restructure it. If you truly cannot sleep when there are dirty dishes in the sink, you should probably see a therapist. It would be more accurate (and beneficial) for most people to say, "I don't like to go to bed when there are dirty dishes in the sink." And think about the dishes. If there's one cup in the sink, it takes a few seconds to do what your auto-thought is telling you to do. But if there's a sinkfull and the dishwasher hasn't been unloaded yet from yesterday, then doing the dishes would take a good chunk of time—time that could be better spent sleeping, reading, having sex, or just unwinding from the day. In this situation, doing the dishes means that an empty sink is a more important priority than your having twenty minutes of downtime—perhaps the only downtime you would get all day.

A good way to restructure this thought would be: "I prefer having the dishes done before I go to bed, but it's more important for me to sleep than to wash dishes." Restructuring that thought removes a lot of stress and expectations of perfection. It gives you the space to do what you like—to wash the dishes if you have time and if it's not interfering with other important tasks. But it also gives you the freedom to put your own needs first sometimes. That's a big deal, because many women have the feeling that their needs always come last. Taking control and putting yourself first—even in small ways—can go a long way toward making you feel better. Even if you don't leave dishes in the sink most of the time, restructuring this particular thought may help you feel less stressed simply because you've given yourself permission to skip the dishwashing on nights when you really could benefit from some self-care.

## COMMON DISTORTED THOUGHT PATTERNS

Distorted thought patterns, also known as cognitive distortions, negatively affect the way you look at the world. They get in the way of clear thinking and can impact your life in a very destructive way. Certain distorted thoughts occur commonly, especially among perfectionists.

Frequently used cognitive distortions have been defined by a number of renowned researchers, including Aaron T. Beck, M.D. (the "father of cognitive therapy"), Albert Ellis, Ph.D. (the "grandfather of cognitive therapy"), and David D. Burns, M.D., author of a tremendously helpful cognitive-therapy self-help book, *The Feeling Good Handbook*. I've also noticed a few that come up over and over among my patients. Here are some of the most familiar negative thought patterns, along with examples and some ways to restructure them.

**All-or-nothing thinking:** You look at everything in extremes: Things are either good or bad, with nothing in between.

**Example:** If you find yourself in the slowest line at the supermarket you say, "I always pick the wrong line."

**Tell yourself:** "How nice to have a few minutes with nothing to do and nobody bothering me. I think I'll read a magazine."

**Overgeneralization:** When something bad happens, you conclude that it is one in a series of neverending miserable patterns in your life.

**Example:** A friend does something hurtful, and you decide that no one can be trusted.

**Tell yourself:** "Just because one friend says a hurtful thing does not mean others will. She's probably having a bad day."

**Mental filter:** You focus on the negative parts of a situation and ignore or discount any positives.

**Example:** You have a performance review. Your boss says nine great things about you and one negative thing. You ignore the praise and zero in on the criticism.

**Tell yourself:** "Nine out of ten is an A-minus, which is pretty darn good. I did nine things great and have only one to work on."

**Disqualifying the positive:** You refuse to acknowledge your own accomplishments, choosing instead to be overly self-critical.

**Example:** Someone compliments you for doing a nice job and you think or even say, "Anybody could have done it," or "They're just being nice."

**Tell yourself:** "It feels good that someone noticed my work."

---

**Jumping to conclusions:** You predict, either by mind reading or fortune-telling, that people will react negatively to you or that events will turn out badly.

**Examples:** You decide not to interview for a job because you believe you won't get it.

**Tell yourself:** "Even if I don't get the job, it's still worth going, because it will give me valuable experience that could help me with future interviews."

---

**Magnification or catastrophizing:** You exaggerate the importance of relatively minor issues (such as your mistakes).

**Examples:** "I have a cough—it must be cancer."

**Tell yourself:** "Colds are far more common than cancer—the average person gets eight to ten colds a year. It is highly likely that I have a cold, not cancer."

---

**Minimalization or belittling:** You minimalize your own accomplishments or someone else's appraisal of you.

**Examples:** Your boss raves about your performance on a task, and you tell yourself that he's just saying that to be nice.

**Tell yourself:** "Bosses don't rave about you unless you're good. He must mean it."

---

**Emotional reasoning:** You believe that your feelings are absolutely accurate.

**Examples:** "I feel inferior; therefore, I must not be as good as others."

**Tell yourself:** "Everyone feels inferior sometimes, no matter how successful they are. I'm just suffering from an attack of low self-esteem, just as everyone does sometimes."

**"Should" statements:** You use unproductive "should" and "shouldn't" statements to criticize yourself or others. Also "must," "always," "never," "have to," "need to," and "ought to."

**Examples:** "My house should always be neat."

**Tell yourself:** "I like my house to be neat, but if it's not, it's no big deal. There are worse things in the world than a messy house."

**Labeling and mislabeling:** You use inaccurate self-labels that are overly simplistic and overly critical.

**Example:** While on a diet, you eat a dish of ice cream and then say, "I'm such a fat slob."

**Tell yourself:** "Wow, that ice cream was really good. There's nothing wrong with an occasional treat as long as I eat well most of the time. I'll tack an extra mile onto my walk tomorrow to help burn it off."

**Personalization (the mother of guilt):** You take responsibility for things that are not your fault. Or you blame someone else for situations or events for which they are not responsible.

**Examples:** When your child fails an exam, you decide it's due to your bad parenting.

**Tell yourself:** "Wouldn't it be great if I had that much control over my child's performance! The truth is, there are many reasons a child fails a test. Instead of blaming myself I'm going to work with my child to figure out how to get extra help."

**Approval seeking:** You feel that all the significant people in your life must love and approve of you all the time and if they don't, it's awful. Because of this feeling, you consistently compromise your needs and desires to gain the approval of others.

**Example:** You opt not to buy a shirt you like because you think your mother might consider it too low-cut.

**Tell yourself:** "I like it and it looks good on me, so the heck with what my mother says!" (But as the mother of two girls, I'm with your mother on this one.)

**Self-righteousness:** You feel that people should always do what you think is right, and if they don't, then they're wrong.

**Example:** You give your sister advice, and you get upset when she doesn't follow it.

**Tell yourself:** "She probably asked several people for advice and is taking it all into account as she makes her decision. I'm flattered that I am one of the people she asked."

**Woe is me:** You regard yourself as a victim despite the ordinariness of a situation.

**Example:** Your car is in the shop and you interpret this as a personal human tragedy that challenges/tests your ability to cope. You fail to accept it as a normal part of life; rather, you become a victim of it.

**Tell yourself:** "Everyone has car troubles sometimes, and everyone thinks it's a pain. It's an inevitable inconvenience of modern life for everyone, not just me."

**Reductionism:** You fail to see the complex causes and potential benefits of a stressful experience by reducing it to one simple cause or consequence.

**Example:** You catch a cold and blame it completely on your exposure to your sick four-year-old nephew and not at all on your own degree of stress and lack of sleep.

**Tell yourself:** "There are a lot of things that predispose a person to catching a cold. Exposure to germs is one factor, but it's possible my immune system is weakened because of stress, lack of sleep, or poor diet. I'm going to take better care of myself and not waste energy on blame."

**Fallacy of fairness:** You judge a negative event as unfair when it really is just a twist of fate.

**Example:** You get sick despite living a healthy lifestyle and consider the illness to be completely unfair to you.

**Tell yourself:** "A lot of people who get sick have done absolutely nothing wrong. Bad things do happen to good people. Even though my health habits didn't prevent this illness or disease, they will help me get better faster and improve my chances of making a full recovery."

**Comparison:** You habitually compare yourself to others, which leaves you feeling either inferior or superior. These comparisons are based on little information or an isolated event.

**Example:** You compare the exquisite home-sewn Halloween costumes that your neighbor made for her kids to the run-of-the mill ones you bought for yours, and you decide that she's a better, more creative parent than you.

**Tell yourself:** "Yep, she's more creative. So what? She does some things better than I do, and I do some things better than she does. We all have strengths and weaknesses."

## Stop It!

Thought-stopping is a great way to halt the damaging thoughts that swirl uninvited through your head. When you find yourself thinking an automatic negative thought, immediately visualize a big red-and-white stop sign. Come to a shrieking mental stop. Take a deep breath. Ask yourself: What's going on here? What's making me so anxious? What's real, and what's fear? Then make a deliberate choice to reframe the thought and, if necessary, change the action that it is motivating. You can put the brakes on harmful auto-thoughts when you *stop, breathe, reflect, and choose.*

A patient of mine uses thought-stopping with great success. She is the mother of a small child, and she was recently diagnosed with breast cancer. Worries about dying plagued her constantly. However, once she started doing thought-stopping, she started to feel better. When she begins to worry about death, she stops, takes a breath, focuses on some of the cognitive-restructuring work we've done, and then points herself in a new direction.

Cognitive-restructuring techniques offer you a powerful way to change your destructive thought patterns. In the next chapter, I'll introduce you to an array of other great techniques to help you tame the perfection monster.

CHAPTER 4

# Taming the Beast

C ognitive restructuring, which we focused on in the previous chapter, is just one of many incredibly effective mind/body techniques
available for your use. In this chapter I'll tell you about some other tools
and techniques. These strategies can help you feel happier and alleviate
stress, anxiety, sadness, and guilt. They are valuable to anyone, but they're
particularly useful for perfectionists, who tend to feel stress keenly and
who frequently put their own needs last.

## Relax, This Won't Hurt a Bit:
## The Relaxation Response

You've probably heard of the "fight or flight" response. When you face
danger, your body prepares you to stay and fight or run away from the
danger by increasing your production of adrenaline and other hormones
that will help you become safer. During the fight-or-flight response, your
heart rate, muscle tension, respiration rate, and blood pressure go up.

The "relaxation response" is fight-or-flight's polar opposite. It's your
body's inborn capacity to calm down. When your body experiences the
relaxation response, there is a measurable decrease in heart rate, blood

pressure, breathing rate, oxygen consumption, stress hormone levels, and muscle tension.

You can bring on ("elicit") the relaxation response when you practice any one of a number of relaxation techniques, including meditation, yoga, visualization, and other methods that I will describe later in this chapter. Eliciting the relaxation response interrupts your body's physical and emotional reaction to stress, allowing it to return to a calm, relaxed state.

The relaxation response was first identified some thirty years ago by researcher and pioneer Herbert Benson, M.D., my boss and mentor for the first seventeen years of my career. Over the years, I have taught thousands of patients how to elicit the relaxation response. They have used it to find respite from the stresses of infertility, cancer, heart disease, depression, and other ailments. Regular elicitation of the relaxation response helps lighten the symptoms of many health problems, including insomnia, chronic pain, hypertension, the side effects of cancer treatments, hot flashes, irritable bowel syndrome, migraines, anxiety disorders, PMS, and eating disorders.

Eliciting the relaxation response makes most people feel good right away. But there's a longer-term benefit, too. People who consistently elicit the relaxation response for ten or twenty minutes twice a day for two to six weeks begin to notice a "carryover" effect: They start to feel better (and more in control of their lives) throughout the day, not just during and after a session.

You can elicit the relaxation response in many ways, including meditation, yoga, mindfulness, deep breathing, repetitive prayer, body scan, progressive muscle relaxation, and visualization. Which method you choose to elicit the relaxation response doesn't matter, although it is worth noting that many activities you may think of as being relaxing, such as reading a book or watching TV, do not trigger the relaxation response.

# Let Me (Not) Think on It: Meditation

Meditation is the process of letting go of your thoughts and turning your attention inward. People who practice meditation on a regular basis find that it can increase their sense of inner peace. It is an excellent way to elicit the relaxation response.

The basic tenet of meditation is simple: You put yourself in a quiet place, empty your mind, and focus on a single thing such as your breath or a mantra. Meditation works well for people who can successfully quiet their minds, but don't write it off if your mind is always buzzing: It may be the only way you'll find to calm it down. Try it several times, and you may find that it is a wonderful skill for you.

Audio guidance can lead you through a meditation session. You can take a meditation class at a local wellness center, hospital, or community education center. Or you can do it on your own, using the following guidelines.

## HOW TO MEDITATE:

- Find a peaceful, quiet place. Make sure that the phone is unplugged, the door is closed, and your pets or kids are in another room.
- Sit in a comfortable place. (Try not to lie down, because you may fall asleep.) You may sit in a chair, on the floor with a cushion against the wall, or on the bed with a pillow behind you.
- Choose a mantra (a word or phrase) for your meditation. Or you can opt to focus on your breathing. If you use a mantra, pick something that has meaning to you, such as "love and peace," "God heals," or "shalom."
- Close your eyes, if you're comfortable doing so. If not, keep them open.
- Starting with the number ten, count down to zero, one number for each breath you take. Notice that your breathing may get slower as you count down.

- As you breathe in, begin to concentrate on your mantra. Continue to concentrate on it as you exhale. Inhale through your nose and exhale through your mouth, if that feels comfortable.
- If your attention wanders, gently bring it back to the words on which you're focusing. If thoughts or feelings intrude on your practice, acknowledge them gently—don't encourage them or push them away—and then return to your breathing. Don't let yourself get frustrated or impatient if you have trouble emptying your mind. It is quite normal for thoughts to come and go. Simply note that your mind has wandered, passively ignore the thoughts, and go back to what you were focusing on. Remember, it's a skill that improves with practice.
- Gradually slow your breathing by pausing a few seconds after you inhale and again after exhaling.
- As your time for meditation comes to an end (a minimum of ten to twenty minutes works well), continue to be aware of your breathing, but start to be aware of where you are, the sounds around you, and where you are sitting. When you feel ready, open your eyes, look down for a few minutes, and get up slowly. If you are eliciting the relaxation on your own (i.e., not with audio guidance), do not set a timer. Sit opposite a clock and when you think that the time is up, open your eyes. If the time is not up, simply close your eyes and go back to what you were focusing on. If the time is up, slowly get up.

Becoming deeply relaxed can take some practice—it's hard for some people to let go—but it is a powerfully worthwhile skill to learn, particularly for stressed perfectionists. Don't worry about doing it perfectly—you benefit even if you manage to empty your mind for only a few minutes at a time.

There are a few practical steps you can take to make your meditation more successful:

- Choose the same place each day. If you reserve a place for your relaxation, you may automatically start to relax simply by sitting there.

Be Happy Without Being Perfect

- Choose the same time each day. This helps make it a habit.
- Connect it to exercise. If you exercise regularly, try eliciting the relaxation response immediately after a workout; the sense of deep relaxation should come more easily.
- Don't let your stomach distract you. Try not to elicit the relaxation response when you are very hungry or very full.
- Aim for twice a day. Two twenty-minute relaxation meditation sessions daily is optimal, but I know finding that kind of time isn't easy. If you don't have twenty minutes, it helps to focus on your breathing even for just five minutes. The only "bad" relaxation response is one not done.

## One Thing to Keep in Mind: Mindfulness

Mindfulness is one of the greatest gifts you can give yourself. We spend so much time planning or worrying about the future and regretting the past that we often forget to appreciate the present. Mindfulness allows you to learn to live in the here and now, rather than the past or future. You can be mindful anytime: while you're eating, walking, cooking, cleaning, making love, driving, and so on.

To practice living mindfully, set aside times each day when you consciously stop and focus on what's going on at that moment. (Some good times: while you're waiting for your train to work in the morning, before each meal, when you arrive at and depart from work, or when you're nursing a baby.) Take a few breaths and center yourself. Notice what's going on around you. Use all of your senses. By doing so, you begin to build a habit of appreciating what's going on in the present moment.

One of the best ways to learn to be mindful is to take a dog for a walk. Dogs are always in the moment. They can take the same walk every day for ten years and still experience grass in an entirely new way each day. They're not worried about the past ("Why didn't my people give me some of that chicken they had for dinner?") or the future ("I wonder if my people will give me any chicken when we get home?"). All they think about is what's right in front of them: the smell of the grass, the basset hound in the yard next door, and the squirrel in the tree across the street.

Practice your mindfulness skills the next time you eat at a nice restaurant. Focus on the delicious smell of food, the elegant décor, the taste of the wine, the sounds of satisfied diners around you, the feel of your partner's hand in yours. You can do anything mindfully.

Even when you're going through a difficult experience, mindfulness allows you to savor what's good and put suffering in perspective. A friend with cancer found that mindfulness helped her endure treatment. Several times a day, even when chemotherapy left her feeling nauseated and fatigued, she would stop, reflect, and be grateful. "I feel terrible," she'd tell herself, "but I'm alive."

Mindful walking is a wonderful way to practice mindfulness. To do a mindful walk, go outdoors and walk slowly, fully experiencing the sensations of walking one step at a time. While you walk, let your senses take over. Smell the aroma of grass and trees; notice the houses you pass and the people you see; really listen to the sounds of birds chirping, dogs barking, lawnmowers buzzing, or in winter the sound of snow crunching under your boots. If you walk in the city, be aware of the sounds of cars and buses, the smell of restaurants you pass, and the faces of the people you see. Try to stay present. When other thoughts enter your mind, gently acknowledge them and then let them go as you bring yourself back to the present moment. After your walk, try to carry that mindfulness with you for the rest of the day.

## Get Yourself Into a Knot: Yoga

Many of the women we interviewed say yoga is a lifeboat that saves them during stormy, stressful times. I usually recommend Hatha yoga because it is gentle, meditative, and relaxing, but some people prefer more athletic, invigorating yoga styles. If you have given yoga a try and don't think you care for it, experiment with another style or teacher, because they vary widely in their approaches to this ancient practice. Some focus more on the physical aspects of yoga, and others on its meditative side.

A daily yoga routine can stretch and relax the muscles, reduce fatigue and stress, and promote a feeling of tranquility. Before bed, gentle, meditative poses and breathing techniques can help you put aside the day's problems and fall asleep. (Keep in mind that energetic yoga poses can stimulate you and shouldn't be done at bedtime.) Yoga restores balance between mind and body—it quiets your mind and soothes your body.

## A Mental Vacation: Visualization

Visualization is an easy technique for perfectionists to learn because most of us do it already—but we do it in a damaging way. If you've ever lain awake at night picturing the horrible things that could happen to you, your family, or your friends—if you can close your eyes and *see* your gynecologist telling you that she found a huge tumor on your mammogram—then you know all about visualization. Chances are you're using visualization to your detriment all the time as you picture your boss yelling, your health failing, your children being injured, or a falling tree crushing your house into splinters.

Your body's stress-response system responds to tragedy whether it is real or imagined. If you create the mental image of a child molester abducting your daughter, your body's physical reaction will be quite real and quite dramatic even though the event is taking place only in your mind. Just picturing it would cause anxiety, trigger a release of stress hormones, and increase your muscle tension, heart rate, and blood pressure. Luckily, the opposite also holds true. If you visualize the positive, your stress-response system calms down. Imagining peace and tranquility can actually bring them about.

Visualization can also increase your chances of performance success:

Athletes visualize their techniques as a way of perfecting them. Before they compete, golfers visualize the perfect swing, skiers the perfect turn, baseball players the perfect hit. It's mental practice—visualizing excellent performance can actually enhance performance. (Make sure you don't let *visualizing* perfection lead you to *expect* perfection.) I remember a number of years ago, my coworkers and I gave a stress-management workshop at a private school. We taught the students about visualization, and it soon made an impact on them: At an important tennis match, their star player was playing poorly. During a break, he went courtside, closed his eyes, and visualized himself playing well. As soon as the break ended he sprinted onto the court, played beautifully, and won the match.

Perfectionists can use visualization as a coping tool. When you're in a situation in which you might fail, let yourself visualize it happening so you can prepare your response. While waiting for the results of a medical test, visualize what you will do if the outcome is unfavorable. Who will you call for support? What specifically will you ask of your supporter? What will you do for the hour or two after you receive the result? If the results are good, whom will you tell or how will you celebrate?

## HOW TO VISUALIZE:

- Find a quiet, comfortable place where you won't be disturbed.
- Close your eyes and take a couple of deep breaths.
- Imagine yourself in one of your favorite places—lying on a beach, hiking along a mountain trail, or floating in a pool on a beautiful summer day.
- Create mental images of everything you would see, feel, hear, smell, and taste in this favorite place. Feel the sights and sounds.
- Imagine yourself relaxing in this special place.
- Try to put everything else out of your mind.
- After several minutes of enjoying this visualization, take a couple of deep breaths and slowly open your eyes. You may find that you feel amazingly relaxed and refreshed from this "mental vacation."

- Don't be disappointed if you can't visualize perfectly the first time you try. It takes some practice.

## Little Breaks: Mini Relaxations

Mini relaxation exercises are focused breathing techniques that help reduce anxiety and tension immediately. You can do them with your eyes open or closed. You can do them any place, at any time; no one will know that you are doing them.

### HOW TO DO A MINI RELAXATION:

Breathe deeply. (This is called diaphragmatic breathing. If you are having trouble, try breathing in through your nose and out through your mouth.) You should feel your stomach rising about an inch as you breathe in, and falling about an inch as you breathe out. If this is still difficult for you, lie on your back or on your stomach; you will be more aware of your breathing pattern. Remember, it is impossible to breathe diaphragmatically if you are holding in your stomach. So relax your stomach muscles.

### Version 1

Count very slowly to yourself from ten down to zero, one number for each breath. With the first diaphragmatic breath, you say "ten" to yourself; with the next breath, you say "nine," etc. If you start feeling light-headed or dizzy, slow down the counting. When you get to "zero," see how you are feeling. If you are feeling better, great! If not, try again.

### Version 2

As you inhale, count very slowly from one to four; as you exhale, count slowly back down from four to one. As you inhale, say "one, two, three, four." As you exhale, say "four, three, two, one." Do this several times.

## Version 3

Inhale. Pause for a few seconds. Then exhale, and pause for a few seconds. Do this for several breaths.

## GOOD TIMES TO "DO A MINI"

You can do a mini relaxation anytime, anyplace. The only time that minis *don't* work is when you don't do them. Here are some opportunities to do a mini:

- While stuck in traffic.
- When put on hold during an important phone call.
- While in a doctor's waiting room.
- When you're about to undergo a medical test or procedure.
- When someone says something that bothers you.
- At all red lights.
- When waiting for a phone call.
- In the dentist's chair.
- When you feel overwhelmed by what you need to accomplish in the near future.
- While standing in line.
- When you're in pain.
- When you're about to yell at your kids.
- At the end of the day, right before you pick your kids up from school or day care.

# Take Good Care of Yourself: Self-Nurturance

We nurture so many people in our families, among our friends, and in our workplaces, but so often we forget to nurture ourselves. We push ourselves to the end of the line, and as a result, so many of our emotional, creative, and spiritual needs go unmet. The irony of this, of course, is that when we are unnurtured we feel stressed and anxious and have a far lower capacity to care for others.

Self-nurturing is not selfish. It is an essential life skill that can contribute to your happiness and overall satisfaction with life. Even a few minutes here and there make a difference. Self-nurturance doesn't have to be all-or-nothing—you can take care of yourself without spending a week at a spa. Try spending a half-hour a day doing something that you enjoy—listening to music, drawing, talking on the phone with a friend, or just snuggling down into a cozy sofa or a hot bath with a good book and a cup of tea.

If you're interested in delving more deeply into the topic of self-nurturance, consult my book *Self-Nurture*.

## Get Out Your Pen and Paper: Journaling

Writing about your thoughts, worries, fears, triumphs, and experiences can be an incredibly therapeutic experience. Journaling helps lessen the pain of traumatic experiences, aids in putting negative events in perspective, and offers an effective way to think through conflicts and decisions. Your journal is also an excellent place to do cognitive-restructuring exercises and practice active gratitude, which I'll describe later in this chapter.

James Pennebaker, Ph.D., a researcher at the University of Texas, Austin, has conducted extensive research on the benefits of writing about emotional upheavals. He and other scientists have found that journaling about disturbing topics can boost immune function, cause people to develop fewer illnesses, relieve pain, improve mood, and decrease depression and anxiety. For example, asthma patients and rheumatoid arthritis sufferers who wrote about the most stressful events in their lives experienced measurable health improvements: After four months, 47 percent saw a reduction in their symptoms; arthritis sufferers felt less pain and asthma patients had greater lung capacity. In HIV patients, journaling reduced lymphocyte counts and viral loads.

In your journal, you can explore your perfectionist feelings in a safe way. Ask yourself why you expect perfection, where that expectation came from, and what messages go through your head when you criticize yourself or dwell on your faults and failures. You can talk to yourself in your journal, and ask yourself why you don't treat yourself with the same love and compassion that you offer others. You can also give yourself permission in a journal—permission to make mistakes and to be imperfect.

Journaling can help you understand why a certain situation causes you stress. Even when you can't solve a problem, having a fuller awareness of what it is and why it's troubling you can go a long way toward removing its sting.

One of my patients, a woman who is married to a very difficult man, is thrilled with the impact that journaling has had on her life. When this patient first came to see me, she told me that her husband's various rants and raves made her feel like an incompetent wife and mother. I suggested that she write in a journal whenever her husband slighted her. She did, and over the course of a few weeks she began to see a very consistent pattern. Journaling showed her that in almost every case, her husband's complaints reflected a deep frustration with his own life that he projected onto her. When he was upset with himself he would criticize her. Journaling gave her a chance to step back and see his actions for what they were. It gave her the clarity to understand that the problem between them lay not in her competency, but in his dissatisfaction. As soon as she understood this, she stopped blaming herself for their conflicts. Her marriage remains difficult, but she continues to find that journaling makes it much easier to bear.

While you're journaling, write down the automatic negative thoughts you have about yourself. Seeing them in black and white can be shocking and embarrassing. When you write them, they seem so much less logical than they do when you think them. Getting these thoughts down on paper is a tremendous first step toward reframing them in a more positive, constructive way.

When you write in a journal, you benefit not only from the writing process but from rereading also. Sometimes when you reread your journal entries you have an ah-ha moment and something you've been struggling with becomes crystal clear.

## How to Journal

The following advice comes from James W. Pennebaker, Ph.D., a leading researcher in the field of journaling. Pennebaker says there are many beneficial approaches to journaling; you should use whatever feels right to you. Experiment to see what works best. Or follow Pennebaker's rough guidelines:

- Find a time and a place where you won't be disturbed, preferably at the end of the day.
- The best way to record your thoughts is writing by hand in a journal or notebook.
- Promise yourself that you'll write for a minimum of fifteen minutes a day for at least three or four consecutive days.
- Once you begin writing, keep going. Don't worry about grammar or punctuation or correct spelling. If you run out of things to say, repeat what you've already written.
- Some topics to write about include: Something that you're worrying about, dreaming about, or avoiding; something that is affecting you in an unhealthy way; or something difficult that happened in the past.
- You can write about the same thing each day, or different things.
- If you write about a traumatic event in your past, really let go and explore your feelings and thoughts about it. Delve into your deepest emotions.
- You may feel sad after you write, but usually the feeling passes within a couple of hours. If you find that you get extremely upset writing about a certain topic, write about something else instead.

- Be completely honest: What you're writing is for you alone. You can save your journal entries or throw them away. Saving them and rereading them in the future can help you see how you've changed and grown. Throwing them away can be cathartic, too. As Pennebaker recommends, you can burn them, erase them, shred them, flush them, or tear them into little pieces and toss them into the ocean or let the wind take them away.
- For a more detailed look at journaling, check out Pennebaker's book, *Writing to Heal: A Guided Journal for Recovering from Trauma and Emotional Upheaval*.

## Thank You: Active Gratitude

Gratitude is a powerful emotion that can have a compelling impact on your health. When you start noting what you're grateful for—not only the big things, but the small, everyday blessings as well—you're likely to feel happier, less depressed, and less anxious.

One of the best ways to practice active gratitude is to keep a gratitude journal. Every night before you go to bed, jot down a list of things from your day for which you feel gratitude. It takes only a few minutes. As you reflect on your day, you'll be surprised how much there is to feel thankful for.

Robert A. Emmons, a researcher at the University of California, Davis, has conducted extensive research on gratitude. In his studies, he and his colleagues have asked participants to keep daily or weekly gratitude journals. (Control subjects did not.) He has found that those who keep gratitude journals:

- Exercised more regularly, reported fewer physical symptoms, felt better about their lives as a whole, and were more optimistic about the upcoming week.
- Were more likely to have made progress toward personal goals.

Be Happy Without Being Perfect

- Reported higher levels of the positive states of alertness, enthusiasm, determination, attentiveness, and energy.

Practicing active gratitude helps you see how full your life is, and it allows you to put negative experiences into perspective. Perfectionists find that practicing gratitude focuses their attention on what they *do* have and *can* do rather than what they *don't* have and *can't* do.

The months after my mother died were very difficult for me, so I decided to follow my own advice and start keeping a gratitude journal. It made me pay more attention to good things that happened. I would do things during the day and think to myself, "This is going in my gratitude journal tonight." I found myself feeling thankful for the smallest things—the muffins at my local bakery, for example, or a particularly beautiful sunset on the way home from work. Then, at the end of each week I'd review my lists and see how very many things gave me happiness. Coping with my mother's loss was still hard, but my gratitude journal helped me see that even after her loss, so many good things remained.

Try writing in a gratitude journal every night for a week or two and see how it feels. Review your entries at the end of the week. I think you'll be surprised at how helpful this simple technique is.

You can practice active gratitude with your family by beginning a ritual called "news and goods." It's simple: When you are all together at the end of the day, each person takes a turn telling what new and good things happened during the day.

We do this at my house every night over the dinner table—my six-year-old, Katie, in particular is addicted to it. It's a way of inviting everyone to think about and share what they are grateful for. Typically when people get home from work they start unloading about what went *wrong* during the workday. This habit forces you to look at what went *right*.

# You Can Do It:
## Affirmations

Affirmations have gotten a bad rap from *Saturday Night Live*. People make fun of them, but they really are an effective cognitive strategy. An affirmation is a simple statement that you repeat to yourself—you say it over and over until you believe it. When you're thinking things like, "I'm not going to be able to do this," or "I'm going to fail," or "I'm going to look like a fool," replace them with affirmations: "I'm going to do the best I can," or "This is a learning process," or "Nobody is judging me." Before public speaking, some people concentrate on an affirmation such as, "I know more about this topic than anyone in the audience."

Choose one or two affirmations that ring true. Write them down, stick them on a mirror, program them onto your screensaver or iPod. The idea is to use the affirmation to wipe away the old negative (and damaging) thought.

# LOL:
## Humor

In Chapter 3 I told you about the main premise of mind/body medicine: That the way you *think* affects the way you *feel*. If you feel stressed and depressed, for example, your immune system is negatively impacted. So it makes sense that if you feel lighthearted, happy, and exhilarated, your immune system will be positively impacted. That's why humor is such an important coping skill. It's not for nothing that someone long ago came up with the adage, "Laughter is the best medicine." You don't need a scientist to tell you that it simply feels good to laugh.

When you laugh at something funny, you set off a physiological chain of events that are helpful to your body. Levels of stress hormones in the body fall. Muscles relax, the immune system gets a boost, and levels of virus-fighting immunoglobulin A go up. Natural killer cells, which destroy tumor cells, increase, as do the amounts of other immune system substances. Humor also helps reduce pain and distracts you from distressing situations.

You can take advantage of humor's health-boosting potential. The best way is to react to stressful circumstances by making fun of them, rather than being stressed by them. If, halfway through the workday, you realize you're wearing black shoes with navy tights, you could get upset and feel like a fool and become anxious because you think your coworkers must think less of you for making such a stupid mistake. Or you can react with humor, enjoying a laugh with others that you made the mistake in the first place, and talking about silly situations that could arise from it—high-heels with socks tomorrow, for example.

Finding the humor in everyday life helps head off negative reactions that can make you feel bad and, over time, weaken your body's ability to fight off illness. Boosting the humor in your life can help you stay healthier physically and psychologically. Here are some ways to do that:

- Spend time with funny people. You know the type—the ones who keep everyone laughing. Seek them out and make friends with them.
- Watch funny television shows and movies. Don't forget the oldies like Charlie Chaplin, Lucille Ball, and the Three Stooges.
- Watch videos or listen to CDs of comedians doing their routines.
- Choose entertainment that is humorous rather than tragic.
- Whenever possible, defuse stressful situations with laughter. If you're wrapped up in some kind of a perfectionist tizzy, poke fun at yourself. Some of the things we perfectionists do are pretty funny.

My friend and colleague Loretta LaRoche has taken this concept to a new level. Her specialty is how to reduce stress through laughter, and she is a master. I highly recommend her books and DVDs. All of my patient groups watch one of her DVDs. I have probably seen it fifty times, and yet I still laugh until tears roll down my cheeks.

The beauty of all of these techniques is that you can basically pick and choose the ones that work for you—there is no one technique that works for everyone. You might find, for example, that one approach helps you when you are feeling anxious while another is more effective when you are angry. I tell my patients that they should consider these techniques as tools in their coping toolbox. Whenever you are feeling out of sorts or stressed or unhappy, check the toolbox. Mentally review which of these approaches might be helpful in restoring you to your normal and healthy self, or at least getting you closer to that goal.

## In the Real World

Now that I've introduced you to these techniques, I'll show you what they can do for you. In the following chapters I'll tell you more about how to use these coping skills and many others to improve your life, enrich your relationships, and feel happier and more content. But first, let me share some wonderful real-world suggestions and advice that the women we interviewed for this book gave us when we asked them about how they relax and cope with stress:

> *I lie down and count to thirty or sixty. It's like pushing a pause but-*
> *ton. It's a quick fix—it only takes a minute. At the end of this pause,*
> *I'll realize what I should be doing at that moment.*
>
> —*Patricia*

> *My journal is my sanctuary—I write everything in it. I explain why*
> *I'm stressed in detail I don't always want to share with people in my*
> *life. I complain about issues that I know I rise above, I bitch, I gloat,*
> *I am obnoxious and whiny, smart and giddy. I am everything and*
> *anything I want to be and it's wonderful.*
>
> —*Stephanie*

Be Happy Without Being Perfect

*I try to live daily by a verse in the Koran: "Allah imposes not on any soul a duty beyond its scope." This helps me keep things in perspective and be more self-accepting. It gives me an out when I do not achieve my goals.*

—Margaret

*I have the opportunity to have chair massages two or three times a month. When you have regular massages, your body instantly falls into a relaxed state that is very rejuvenating.*

—Nancy

*When I got hypnotized as part of a school project, I learned the secret of falling asleep. I empty my mind and count backward from twenty. Everything gets darker, and I fall asleep. Sometimes I might need to do it a few times, because my mind is not truly clear.*

—Carol

*I like to take hot baths. I also play the piano. Sometimes I visualize scuba diving or kissing my husband to calm down.*

—Lisa

*When I go to bed I visualize my favorite place, which is in Utah. I can close my eyes and after five or ten minutes I really feel like I'm there. I see the animals in the woods, hear the sound of the water. I'm relaxed, life is good again, and I can fall asleep.*

—Laura

*I listen to show tunes while I walk. It allows me to completely escape, to daydream. I sing the songs in my head and act out the parts. I was a theater major in college, so I can visualize performing.*

—Betty

*I have a blog. It's a good outlet, although I try not to complain or rant about things too much. I try to capture special or humorous moments in my life. It also gives me a place where I have total control of the look, content, and so on.*

*—Nancy*

*I sit in a yoga pose for ten to thirty minutes at the end of the day. I focus on my breathing. I think, "into the ground"—my shoulders drop, my legs drop. I always carry my stress in my upper back. I also do mindfulness-based yoga with my teenage son. At first I think he agreed to try it just to avoid doing his homework, but now he wants to because it helps him sleep better.*

*—Jessica*

*Every other day I either run or do body sculpting, a class at our local gym. There's a lot of stretching, and it helps me get less tense. I've done yoga and Pilates, but I'm not very good at them—I'm so busy following the freaking instructions that I'm not getting the relaxation out of it. Running to me is way more relaxing.*

*—Susan*

*I do a lot of walking. It feels meditative to me. I walk briskly, but I'm not out of breath. I walk with my dog, but I don't listen to music—I just like to listen to the breeze, or a train go by. To me that's more relaxing than walking with music in my head. If I'm trying to think of ideas for work, I throw on my walking shoes and brainstorm as I go. A lot of times I come up with an inspiration even if I'm not thinking of anything. Walking helps consciously and subconsciously.*

*—Donna*

*I found a good, reputable therapist with whom I could be open and honest. I only go to her a few times a year, but she is a great sounding*

Be Happy Without Being Perfect

*board for me. She helps me sort out my feelings and always lowers my anxiety.*

—Cynthia

*I take painting classes at a local art center. The first class was landscape and still life, and it didn't work well for me as a perfectionist because it was all about getting things right. That's not what I wanted to do. I wanted to play with the paint. Now I'm taking an amazing class called supercharged painting. It's based on Jackson Pollock's style, and it incorporates collage, paper, wax, and experimental techniques with the paint. It's very much about exploring. You're not trying to make it look like anything, it's just about expressing what you want to express.*

—Melissa

*I find working on crossword puzzles to be a great distraction, especially before bed. I imagine that the focus and small-scale problem-solving stimulate a different part of the brain than the part that worries and obsesses.*

—Anna

*I talk with my husband, my mom, and my friends. If something is bothering me, I usually talk it out with a few people until I start feeling better. People often joke that you can tell how badly something is bothering me by how many people have to listen to the story!*

—Nancy

*I write mantras. I take a minute to write some sentences down while breathing deeply. I find that writing is more helpful than just saying them to myself, because when I do the latter I find that my mind just wanders.*

—Amanda

*When I'm in the car commuting, I sometimes shut off the news and start listening to classical music. There are times I'm overloaded and I tell myself, "You don't have to keep up with all the news." I still listen largely to talk radio, but when I'm feeling stressed it's a good switch to make.*

*—Elizabeth*

Be Happy Without Being Perfect

CHAPTER 5

# Celebrate Your Beauty, Not Your Flaws

*I*t doesn't matter how thin and toned you are—most women find
flaws in their body. I do, although I'm much more relaxed about
it than I was when I was a teenager.

I was never particularly heavy as a teen. My sister, who was
three years older, was on the heavier side—she weighed more than my
mother wanted her to. My mother wanted to get her on a good track
so she wouldn't become a heavy teenager. I took in everything that I
sensed was being directed toward my sister and used it to discipline
myself. When my breasts started developing a couple of years later, so
did my eating disorder.

I had all the classic symptoms of anorexia—weighing myself all
the time, adhering to a very strict diet, cutting food into small pieces.
Basically I was hearing all the dieting hints that my sister and mom
were using and becoming very good at using them myself. My weight
fell from 113 to almost 90. There was a sense of control that I
liked—I could control my appetite. I have a tendency to want to
have control, to keep order over things.

It was such a weird time—it was the late 1970s, and super-
skinny was in. As I lost weight, people actually encouraged me. I
don't know if my parents really recognized that I had started on a

dangerous track. I eventually saw it myself and got out if it after a couple of years. Now, I think I'm pretty healthy about it—I haven't dieted since I was a teen. I don't own a scale. But I'm still very weight-conscious.

I'm naturally on the thin side, but when I put on a couple of pounds—like when I'm getting my period—that little tummy starts to bother me and I cut back. But it hasn't reemerged as a disorder. I think I actually worry much less about my weight now than other women.

When I was pregnant I was much more concerned about stretch marks than weight. During my first pregnancy I gained only twenty-four pounds, but I got these horrible stretch marks. The second time, I gained less—when I began to get big I started cutting back on what I was eating. I didn't put my baby at risk, but I did restrain myself. I gained twenty pounds during that pregnancy.

After my children were born I got back to my previous weight pretty quickly, but I still have the stretch marks. I used to like my stomach, but I don't anymore. I'm trying to accept myself and have a sense of humor about it when my tankini rides up and the stretch marks show.

When I have time to exercise and practice yoga, I feel content with my body. When I am exercising and feeling strong and appreciating my health and what my body can do, I stop being concerned about prominent veins and stray hairs. I think I have come to terms with it much more in my older and wiser middle-age years.

As the mother of girls, I try to temper my perfectionism, although it's not always easy. I want to be good to them and to myself. I hope I am encouraging my girls to have a very healthy self-image.
—Elizabeth

A couple of years ago I spoke at an event that was cosponsored by Dove's "Campaign for Real Beauty." (You probably remember the campaign's ads—they featured full-length photos of groups of five or six ordinary women of various sizes dressed in plain panties and bras. These were not models, but real women with curvy hips and fleshy thighs and soft bellies.) During the event, Dove set up dozens of huge mirrors and invited attendees to look at themselves and use thick black markers to write something beautiful they saw in their reflections. Afterward I walked around reading the scribble-covered mirrors and loved what I saw: Comment after comment about beautiful eyes, gorgeous hair, strong bodies, sensuous lips, and sexy bustlines, all from real women with "normal" beauty. In other words, these comments were the polar opposite of what women usually tell themselves when they look in mirrors.

What I loved about this activity was that it encouraged women to examine themselves and—maybe for the first time—search for and celebrate the beauty, not the flaws.

When Dove launched its real woman ad campaign, it made headlines. It wasn't news that a company was using women in underwear to sell products—that happens all the time. What stood out was the fact that the women in the ads were not perfect. The ads "touched off a media furor," according to an article in *Women's Wear Daily*, a fashion publication. How messed up is a society in which it's normal for 5-foot, 11-inch, 8-stone women to prance around in underwear (and wings!) on a televised lingerie fashion show, but startling when an ad shows photos of everyday women?

I love what Dove has been doing for women these past couple of years. The company is promoting the beauty of people of all shapes and sizes and donating money to the Girl Scouts and other organizations that work to boost self-esteem in girls. I was horrified when I heard that people were criticizing Dove for photographing real women. Readers wrote letters to *People* magazine saying they didn't want to look at fat women in their underwear. Shame on them.

## Surrounded by Images

We live in a world that is obsessed with physical perfection. Magazine covers, movies, television shows, and catalogs flaunt nonstop images of

## Getting Real

No wonder the average woman feels imperfect.
Look at who she's comparing herself to!

| | AVERAGE WOMAN | BARBIE | STORE MANNEQUIN | BRAZILIAN SUPERMODEL GISELE BÜNDCHEN |
|---|---|---|---|---|
| **HEIGHT** | 5' 4" | 6' | 6' | 5' 11" |
| **WEIGHT** | 145 lbs. | 101 lbs. | Not available | 127 lbs. |
| **DRESS SIZE** | 11–14 | 4 | 6 | 4 |
| **BUST** | 36–37" | 39" | 34" | 34" |
| **WAIST** | 29–31" | 19" | 23" | 24" |
| **HIPS** | 40–42" | 33" | 34" | 34" |

*Sources: Anorexia Nervosa and Related Eating Disorders, Inc.;* Health *magazine; NEDIC, a Canadian eating disorders advocacy group; and Fashion Model Directory (FMD). *NB These are North-American statistics.*

gorgeous women. The message they send is that physical perfection should be everyone's goal, and if you're not perfect you should do everything possible to fix your flaws. If you don't look like a Victoria's Secret model, the photos imply, then get to work! Starve yourself, work out until you collapse, dye your hair, paint your nails, tan your skin, dress yourself in expensive new clothes, whiten your teeth, apply makeup. If that doesn't work, have your face lifted, your boobs enlarged, your lips pillowed, your wrinkles Botoxed, and your thigh fat vacuumed away—because if you don't look like Cindy Crawford, you're not trying hard enough.

The media sets ideals of beauty that only a miniscule percentage of women can attain. The rest of us—particularly the perfectionists among us—are left feeling anxious and inadequate because of our appearance.

Be Happy Without Being Perfect

In this country, telling people they look like they've lost weight is considered the ultimate compliment. But think about it: What does it mean when someone says you look thinner? That you looked fat in the past? That the only way to look good is to lose weight? What kind of compliment is that?

## What a Model

It's impossible, especially if you're a perfectionist, not to be affected by all the pressure our society places on thinness, attractiveness, and physical beauty. We are programmed to look for blemishes and dwell on what's wrong rather than what's right. The fact is, only 1 in 30,000 women have the body type to be a model, and yet somehow the other 29,999 of us feel like we're failing because we don't.

And let me tell you something about those models. I have treated models and professional dancers as patients. They are gorgeous women with incredible bodies, but many of them are not happy. Their careers depend on them staying thin. They are obsessed with food and about not being able to eat what they want. You simply cannot eat what you would like and look the way they do.

Quite a few of them have eating disorders. Their agents say they're naturally thin. Maybe, but not that thin. They look in the mirror and literally obsess about every real or imagined imperfection. I once had a size 4 model in my office, grabbing a tiny bit of her thigh, bemoaning her cellulite. I have to tell you that it is tough being a supportive therapist in situations like that. I know that she was anxious and worried—and indeed, her career depended on the state of her thighs. But my next patient was a young mom with cancer. It makes you wonder about the priorities in our society.

The messages we receive and give are so constant that sometime we don't even realize we are making or hearing them. Last year I was one of two moms chaperoning our daughters' Girl Scout troop cookie sale at our local supermarket. We were there for two hours. The first sad thing that happened was that I observed that virtually every woman (but not man) who was approached by one of the nine-year-old Girl Scouts made a comment about her weight. The women who refused to buy a box said something to the effect of, "Look at me, you think I need to eat cookies?" And each woman who did buy a box basically said, "I really shouldn't be doing this; the last thing I need is to be buying myself cookies."

The second sad thing was that at the end of the two hours, I mentioned this behavior to the other mom. She hadn't even noticed.

But isn't it scary that these little girls had just been exposed to two hours of negative self-talk from nearly every woman they approached? If messages like this are a constant in their lives, how can we expect them to grow up with a healthy self-image about their bodies?

You can escape the pressure to have a perfect body—I'll show you how in this chapter. I'll also help you discover how to tune out your self-criticism and make peace with your imperfect but beautiful body.

## Eating Disorders and Perfectionism

An eating disorder is a serious disturbance in eating behavior fueled in part by feelings of distress about body shape or weight. People with eat-

### Do You Have an Eating Disorder?

The following questions were developed by the National Eating Disorders Association (www.NationalEatingDisorders.org). According to the organization, answering "yes" to one or more questions suggests that your eating behaviors may be disordered and that you may benefit from seeking professional help. To be honest, if you're like many women I know, you'll answer "yes" to at least two. It may not mean you have an eating disorder, but it does suggest that you should question how much you pressure yourself in regard to weight and eating.

Be Happy Without Being Perfect

- Do you avoid eating meals or snacks when you're around other people?
- Do you constantly calculate numbers of fat grams and calories?
- Do you weigh yourself often and find yourself obsessed with the number on the scale?
- Do you exercise because you feel like you have to, not because you want to?
- Are you afraid of gaining weight?
- Do you ever feel out of control when you are eating?
- Do your eating patterns include extreme dieting, preferences for certain foods, withdrawn or ritualized behavior at mealtime, or secretive binging?
- Have weight loss, dieting, and/or control of food become one of your major concerns?
- Do you feel ashamed, disgusted, or guilty after eating?
- Do you worry about the weight, shape, or size of your body?
- Do you feel like your identity and value is based on how you look or how much you weigh?

ing disorders may starve themselves, exercise excessively, force themselves to vomit, or purge by means of laxatives, enemas, or diuretics. Eating disorders tend to develop during adolescence or young adulthood, although they are becoming increasingly more common during older adulthood. Women are much more likely than men to develop eating disorders. They can cause serious harm and, in extreme cases, can lead to death.

Eating disorders are far more common than most people know. Experts don't know exactly how many women in America have eating disorders, but they estimate the number at about 8 million, or 3 percent of the total population. Chances are someone you know has an eating disorder that you're not aware of—most women with eating disorders are of a normal weight. Unless someone is severely anorexic, they don't "look" like they have an eating disorder.

Girls and women with perfectionist tendencies are at an elevated risk for eating disorders. Numerous studies have found a connection between perfectionism and irregular eating and exercise patterns. It makes sense: When a girl or woman feels the need to be perfect, it's no surprise that she expects perfection from her body.

Eating disorders are not failures of will—they are medical illnesses, not character flaws. Anyone with an eating disorder needs treatment to get healthier as soon as possible. You can get help from doctors, nutritionists, and counselors who specialize in eating disorders. Ask your GP for a referral or contact the National Centre for Eating Disorders for resources in your area. The earlier an eating disorder is diagnosed and treated, the better the chances are for full recovery.

Many people who work in the field of psychology think the biggest cause of death among people with mental illness is suicide. But in fact, more people die from eating disorders than from any other psychiatric illness.

## What We Tell Ourselves

Perfectionist women have loads of body-related automatic thoughts looping through their minds. How often have you found these thoughts in your head?

- Look how fat my thighs are.
- My belly looks awful.
- I weigh too much.
- I'm so out of shape.
- My hair looks terrible.
- These wrinkles make me look ten years older than I am.
- All my friends look better than I do.

- My body is letting me down.
- I should be on a diet.
- I should have a higher (or lower) sex drive.
- What a pig I am, eating all those cookies.
- I'm lazy. I'm disgusting. I'm a mess.

We tell ourselves these things because of the disappointment and shame we feel as a result of not achieving the goal of physical perfection that we and our culture set. But they are so destructive. Telling yourself you're a pig after eating half a packet of biscuits won't help you eat less next time—but it does erode your self-esteem and deprive you of happiness.

## We Asked Women . . .

### How does perfectionism affect the way you feel about your body?

*I'm almost six feet and wear size 11 shoes. It was really hard in school—being tall and having big feet is terrible when you are a little girl. In fifth grade I was twice as big as the boys. But I got over it when I went to college and made the basketball team.*

*—Laura*

*I spend half my life trying to make my hair straight, and it just wants to do this frizzy curl thing. It's ridiculous to spend this much time on it, but I like it to look a certain way. A couple of times I've decided to just let my hair do what it wants, but then I see how it looks and I go back to straightening it. My daughter likes to walk by me and put her fingers in my hair to mess it up. She does it playfully, but it annoys me.*

*—Rose*

*I refuse to be intimate with a man unless I have shaved my legs and bikini area, even though I know most guys couldn't care less about such grooming.*

—*Anna*

*When I was a teenager I thought I was a really hairy person and I used to have fantasies about getting all the hair removed from my body. But now I look back and realize that I'm really not a hairy person, and the hair I have is very fine. That shows how skewed my perception was when I was a teenager.*

—*Elizabeth*

*I am rarely at peace with my body. My muscular legs show through my pants too much, my stomach isn't flat enough, my skin isn't clear enough, my hair is too thin. Although I notice these traits, I rarely do anything about them. I just feel a constant sense of dissatisfaction.*

—*Stephanie*

*I am awfully darn fussy when I go to a clothing store. I'll try on twenty pairs of pants and not buy any of them. I end up wearing the same pair of Levi's because I can't find pants that fit right. If things don't look perfect, I can't buy them.*

—*Patricia*

## Tools You Can Use

It can be difficult to accept physical flaws, but the mind/body tools described throughout the rest of this chapter really can help.

## BEWARE OF COGNITIVE DISTORTIONS

Cognitive distortions cause a huge amount of trouble when it comes to body-related thinking. We are so hard on ourselves! If we spoke to others the way we speak to ourselves, we wouldn't have many friends.

Black-and-white thinking is the most common cognitive distortion. It leads a perfectionist to think that if she can't do something perfectly, she shouldn't do it at all. Here's an example of black-and-white thinking as it relates to your body: You know you're overweight, and you know that losing a few pounds would improve your health. But you tell yourself that if you can't become a size 8, why bother even trying? (The fact is, if you're overweight, losing as little as 5 to 10 percent of your body weight can bring measurable health benefits. If you're 200 pounds (14 stone), shedding 5, 10, or 20 pounds won't turn you into Kate Moss, but it will reduce your risk of heart disease, type-2 diabetes, and other ailments.)

When I spoke to my older daughter's Girl Scout troop on body image and self-esteem recently, I asked them what their first thoughts were when they were offered a piece of candy. Most of them responded with black-and-white statements: "All candy is bad," or "You should never have chocolate," or "Candy makes you fat."

One of the best examples of black-and-white thinking is the "what the hell" effect. Perhaps you'll recognize it: You're watching what you eat, but at lunchtime you devour a delicious croissant. Instead of being careful for the rest of the day, the "what the hell" effect takes over and you eat junk all day. You've already ruined things with the croissant—so what the hell, go ahead and have a half-dozen cookies, three handfuls of chips, a plateful of cheese and crackers, and a big scoop of ice cream. You can start over tomorrow.

Another common example of black-and-white thinking is telling yourself that if you have only a few minutes to exercise, there's no point in bothering because a little bit of exercise has no value. In fact, short bouts of exercise can do as much as—or perhaps even more than—long workout sessions. A recent study found that people with hypertension who exercised for ten minutes six times a day reduced their blood pressure more than those who exercised for one sixty-minute block.

A little cognitive restructuring will remind you that doing a twenty-minute walk is better than *not* doing a forty-five-minute workout session. Carolyn knows all about that:

Celebrate Your Beauty, Not Your Flaws

*If I can't get to the gym every day for at least an hour, I sometimes think, why bother? And if that doesn't happen, then nothing will change and . . . then I get into the cycle of "if it's not perfect, I just can't."*

Another cognitive distortion that body-conscious perfectionists fall into is minimalizing. We find it so hard to take a compliment—if someone says something nice, we minimize it by discrediting the comment or the person who said it. Or we go for a twenty-minute walk and minimalize its importance because it's not as good as an hour of spinning. Again, some cognitive restructuring can help you reframe and enjoy compliments and accomplishments.

If cognitive distortions are twisting the way you think about yourself, grab your journal and do the cognitive-restructuring exercises described in Chapter 3. Here are some examples of common body-related cognitive distortions.

**Distortion:** All-or-nothing thinking

**Example:** If you have one piece of cake your diet will be ruined for the day; you might as well have three pieces of cake and start over tomorrow.

**Tell yourself:** "Congratulations on having only one piece of cake. Everyone deserves a treat occasionally."

---

**Distortion:** Mental filter

**Example:** You miss one exercise class out of ten and you criticize yourself for not being able to stick to a workout plan.

**Tell yourself:** "I'm doing great—I made it to 90 percent of my exercise classes!"

---

**Distortion:** Jumping to conclusions

**Example:** You don't even try an exercise class because you decide that it will be too hard or that everyone else in the class is much more fit than you.

**Tell yourself:** "I can't fail at something I don't try. I'm going to sign up for a beginner class, promise myself I'll go at least twice, and then decide whether to continue."

**Distortion:** Catastrophizing

**Example:** You think that eating one cookie will ruin your diet and lead to a lifetime of obesity.

**Tell yourself:** "Fifty calories can't cause obesity. Eating one is fine, if I stop at one."

**Distortion:** Minimalizing

**Example:** You tell yourself you don't have to quit smoking because loads of people smoke and don't get cancer.

**Tell yourself:** "Maybe, but most people who get lung cancer are smokers."

**Distortion:** Labeling and mislabeling

**Example:** After polishing off a big bag of chips, you label yourself as a "pig" or a "slob."

**Tell yourself:** "I probably shouldn't have done that. I'll write about it in my journal to see if I can figure out why I did it, and how I can prevent it from happening in the future."

**Distortion:** "Should" statements

**Example:** You tell yourself that you should never go out of the house looking anything less than perfect or people will think less of you.

**Tell yourself:** "If people are judging me solely by how I look, they're not very nice people."

**Distortion:** Emotional reasoning

**Example:** You wake up and find a big pimple on your forehead, and you are tempted to cancel a job interview because you feel the interviewer would be repulsed by you and not hire you.

**Tell yourself:** "They probably won't even notice the pimple—and if they do, they certainly won't hold it against me."

**Distortion:** Personalization

**Example:** You blame yourself for a physical flaw that you have no control over, such as being short or having a weak chin.

**Tell yourself:** "I need to forget about my chin and focus on my beautiful eyes and shiny hair."

**Distortion:** Approval seeking

**Example:** You choose not to swim at a pool party because you think people will disapprove of how you look in a bathing suit.

**Tell yourself:** "All the people at the party are so self-conscious about how they look that they're not even seeing me. Plus, I stand out more not swimming than I would if I just jumped into the pool."

## SET REALISTIC WEIGHT GOALS

Just about every woman wishes to be more slender. But perfectionists don't just wish it, they expect it—and if they are not, they blame themselves for being flawed and lazy and for lacking self-control and self-discipline.

Obviously there are health risks associated with obesity, and a healthy weight is a smart goal. But the fact is, you don't have to be reed-thin to be healthy. In fact, research shows that it's actually better to be overweight and fit than slim and sedentary. Using black-and-white thinking, overweight perfectionists tend to feel that if they can't whittle themselves down to a size 6, there's no point in trying to lose any weight at all. But there is a middle ground. And the best way to find your middle ground is by setting a realistic weight goal. Here are some tips on how to do that:

• **Be reasonable.** If you have a smallish number of pounds to lose, pick a weight goal that is reasonable, healthy, and attainable. Don't pick what you weighed in high school.

- **Set a series of goals.** If you have a larger amount of weight to lose, consider setting a series of weight goals. For example, if you weigh 13 stone and would like to weigh 9 stone, don't set 9 stone as your goal because losing 4 stone is just too daunting. Instead, set a goal of losing a pound a week or a few pounds a month. Losing even a few pounds will do wonders for you—it will lower your risk of disease, boost your mood, energize you, and allow your clothes to fit more comfortably. When you get to 12 stone, stay there for a while and practice maintaining it. Then you can set a new weight goal for, say, 11 stone. By breaking weight loss up into achievable chunks, you increase your chances of success.
- **Get moving.** Some women find it best to forget about the numbers on the scale and focus instead on moving their bodies. My friend Miriam Nelson, author of *Strong Women Stay Slim* and other books in the *Strong Women* series, has found that when overweight women concentrate solely on short periods of strength training just a couple of times a week, their strength levels improve noticeably in a very short time. What's more, they lose weight and inches. Then, as strength levels increase, women feel more energetic and are naturally more interested in exercising more. Once they've built an exercise habit, healthier eating seems to fall into place on its own. That's what happened with Lisa Delaney, an editor at *Health* magazine and author of the book *Secrets of a Former Fat Girl*. Twenty years ago, Lisa, a size 18, began a successful weight-loss journey simply by exercising. She changed her diet later, after the pounds started to come off. Lisa, now a size 4, maintains her weight loss with exercise and smart eating.
- **Change one thing at a time.** Another great approach is to forget about how many pounds you have to lose and concentrate on changing your eating habits. But don't change everything at once, or you'll become overwhelmed and frustrated. Instead, pick one eating habit—your nightly bowl of ice cream, perhaps—and make a change. Switch to low-calorie ice cream, cut your serving

size in half, leave off the hot fudge, or whatever it takes to make a small but definite change. Stick with it for a week or two, and then make another change—switch from half-and-half to whole milk in your coffee, for example. Sustain that change for a week or two, and add another. The idea is to pick small goals, achieve them, feel comfortable with them, and then add more goals. In other words, take baby steps.

The "baby step" approach is the complete opposite of what perfectionists are usually drawn to. We perfectionists don't like baby steps—we like big, giant steps. We like to leap! When we set out to lose weight, we pick a dramatic weight-loss goal, an unrealistic exercise plan, and the diet of a penitent monk. We start out full of excitement and purpose and stick to our goals like glue for three days. Then something happens—the babysitter calls in sick or a meeting runs long—and we have to skip a workout. Because we miss a workout, we dispense with our Spartan diet and gobble up a double cheeseburger at lunch. Then we give up on the whole thing because we weren't able to do it all perfectly.

It's a hard concept for perfectionists to buy into, but taking baby steps is an incredibly effective way to achieve weight loss or any other goal. Taking baby steps with exercise leads you naturally to weight loss and healthier eating—not on day one, but eventually. As opposed to thinking you have to lose one hundred pounds, think about taking a five-minute walk once a day. Next week, increase your walk to ten minutes. And so on. People who take baby steps can eventually run marathons. They can lose dozens of pounds. But it takes time and patience, two skills that tend to be in short supply among perfectionists. But don't worry—you can find time and develop patience.

*I struggle with my weight. I'm not overweight, but those last few pounds I gained when I was pregnant never go away. After my second child was born, I was at a weight I wasn't happy with for about a year. I went to Weight Watchers, lost twenty-three pounds,*

Be Happy Without Being Perfect

*and got to my goal weight. Then ten pounds crept back on. I managed to lose five pounds, but the rest wouldn't come off. I was disappointed, but I decided that weight is probably where I'm meant to be. This is who I am. I'm never going to have a flat stomach or be really thin. It's just not going to happen. I've accepted the fact that age, gravity, and two C-sections have changed me permanently. I try to wear good bras and clothes that cover my tummy pouch. Once you do accept it, it takes one more burden off your shoulders.*

—*Betty*

## SET REALISTIC EXERCISE GOALS

Many of the women we interviewed chose exercise as their top stress buster. And well they should: Studies show that exercise reduces anxiety, stress, and depression. In some cases, exercise is as effective as medication in treating depression.

In addition to toning and strengthening your body, exercise has a huge impact on your brain. Exercise triggers the brain's release of endorphins (opium-like substances that relieve pain and boost mood) and the neurotransmitters serotonin, norepinephrine, and dopamine, which act as antidepressants in the body.

Research shows that the best results come when you exercise five or six times a week for thirty to sixty minutes a day. But the reality is, anything you do is better than nothing. Walking down the block may provide just a few minutes of exercise, but it's more than you'll get if you do nothing. If you don't have lots of time for exercise, it's fine to break it up into ten-minute chunks throughout the day. That may not feel good enough if you're a perfectionist about fitness—several of the women we interviewed said that because of all-or-nothing thinking, they sometimes do not exercise at all if they don't have time for a full-fledged, sweat-breaking workout. Sure, a sixty-minute aerobics class is better than a ten-minute walk around the block, but the ten-minute walk is far better than nothing—and a daily ten-minute walk is better than an hour once a week.

Ten minutes here and there doesn't sound like much, but it adds up. In a 2001 study, researchers asked fifteen sedentary, postmenopausal women with high blood pressure to add an extra 4,000 to 5,000 steps a day by making simple changes in their daily routines—parking their cars farther away from their destinations, taking a quick walk during their coffee breaks, and so on. (It takes most people less than half an hour to walk 4,000 steps.) Six of the women saw their high blood pressure return to normal; another three reduced their high blood pressure to healthier borderline-high levels. After twenty-four weeks, the women brought their blood pressure down an average of eleven points.

Even occasional workouts help. Although following a regular exercise regimen provides the most mood-boosting benefits, sporadic workouts can deliver an immediate boost of good feeling, according to a study conducted at the University of Texas. Even a single bout of exercise—thirty minutes of walking on a treadmill—could lift the mood of a depressed person. "Many people with depression attempt to self-medicate with alcohol, caffeine, or tobacco to manage their daily routines," researcher John Bartholomew, Ph.D., said when the study was published. "Low- to moderate-intensity exercise appears to be an alternative way to manage depression—one that doesn't come with such negative health consequences."

Exercise can also help reduce the number-one complaint of women: fatigue. After my second daughter, Katie, was born, she decided to announce her presence by sleeping all day and staying awake all night. We tried everything to keep her awake during the day, but to no avail. So I was, of course, truly exhausted. I quickly realized that taking a midday walk made me feel far less tired than taking a nap. So until Katie finally reversed her schedule, I walked for an hour a day. And I have kept it up—when I am feeling tired, I take a walk. It always helps.

The take-home message? Next time you're feeling stressed or blue, go for a walk or jog instead of reaching for a cigarette or a glass of wine.

Be Happy Without Being Perfect

## Rewards of Exercise

In addition to reducing stress, anxiety, and depression, exercise provides some of the following benefits:

- Strengthens your cardiovascular system
- Improves your cholesterol levels
- Lowers blood pressure
- Controls blood sugar
- Helps with weight control
- Curbs insomnia
- Facilitates digestion
- Delays the disabling effects of arthritis
- Increases bone density to help prevent osteoporosis
- Builds muscle
- Boosts metabolism
- Decreases body fat
- Improves strength and flexibility
- Increases mental performance
- Enhances sexual performance

## SET REALISTIC EATING GOALS

*I've always struggled with my weight—I've always been on the heavier side. My weight is always on my mind. I almost wish I could stick my finger down my throat after I eat, but I love food too much. I joined Weight Watchers two weeks ago. I don't know if I'll get to the point where I stop obsessing about it, but I'd like to be healthy and be a good role model for my daughters. I don't want them to see me being miserable and having my self-esteem go up and down with my weight. Last week my husband was away on the night of my Weight Watchers meeting. I could have brought my daughters along, but I*

*just don't want my effort to lose weight to become a part of their con-*
*sciousness. So I called a babysitter. I feel hopeful, though—just last*
*night my daughter and I were at my neighbor's house visiting my*
*daughter's friend, and my neighbor gave them each three cookies. I*
*was thrilled; my daughter ate only one of her cookies and left the*
*other two. I would have eaten all three. It's a good start.*

*—Ashley*

It would be great if you could always eat well. But it's also impossible. If you feel angry at yourself for anything less than 100 percent compliance to a healthy diet, it's time to change the way you think about food and follow the 80/20 eating plan. With this plan, if you eat nutritiously for 80 percent of your diet, you can be less careful about the other 20 percent. The key to the 80/20 plan is that it is based on the realistic expectation that although you can't eat nutritiously *all the time,* you can do it *most of the time.*

Some women eat really well on weekdays and indulge themselves with some treats on the weekends. Others save their 20 percent for afternoons, when they crave snacks. The beauty of the 80/20 plan is that it fosters a healthy diet while allowing you some occasional extravagances. It doesn't come naturally to all-or-nothing perfectionists, but with some practice, you can make yourself comfortable with it.

How rigid are you with your diet? Are you already on the 80/20 plan, or do you sway between 100 percent nutritious and 100 percent junk? Take the quiz below to find out.

## Quiz: How 80/20 Are You?

The following exercise will help you determine how 80/20 your eating habits are. To complete it, check the food from each pair that you eat more often. Be careful not to check the food that you know you *should* eat more often, or the food that you would *like* to eat more often, but the food that you *do* eat more often.

# Which Do You Eat More Often?

Check one from each pair:

| | |
|---|---|
| _____ sliced chicken/turkey | _____ bologna/salami/ham |
| _____ fresh fruit | _____ canned fruit in syrup |
| _____ baked potato | _____ French fries |
| _____ low-fat cottage cheese | _____ cream cheese |
| _____ whole-grain bread | _____ white bread |
| _____ coffee with low-fat milk | _____ latte with whole milk |
| _____ grilled fish | _____ breaded chicken |
| _____ granola bar | _____ chocolate bar |
| _____ grilled chicken sandwich | _____ cheeseburger |
| _____ fresh vegetables | _____ canned vegetables |
| _____ Romaine lettuce or red leaf lettuce | _____ Iceberg lettuce |
| _____ salad | _____ roast beef sub |
| _____ vegetable soup | _____ cream-based chowder |
| _____ seltzer or diet soda | _____ full-sugar cola |
| _____ baked tortilla chips | _____ full-fat potato chips |
| _____ skim milk | _____ whole milk |
| _____ pasta with vegetables | _____ pasta with meatballs |
| _____ home-cooked dinner | _____ frozen dinner |
| _____ air-popped popcorn | _____ buttered popcorn |

Celebrate Your Beauty, Not Your Flaws

| _____ whole-grain unsweetened cereals | _____ presweetened cereals |
| _____ TOTAL (80%) | _____ TOTAL (20%) |

To score, count the number of checks in the right-hand column.

**0–3:**  You may be trying too hard to eat a perfect diet. Let go a little and enjoy an occasional treat.

**4–5:**  You're right on target with the 80/20 plan.

**6–10:**  You're indulging too often—try to replace a few of your 20 percent foods with 80 percent foods.

**11–20:**  Your diet needs an overhaul. For some great hands-on advice on planning a healthy diet, go to www.eatwell.gov.uk. This site, sponsored by the Food Standards Agency, helps you choose the foods and serving sizes that are right for you. Or, contact your local health authority.

## PRACTICE ACTIVE GRATITUDE

If all you see when you look in a mirror is flaws, practicing active gratitude can help. When you look at yourself, try to focus on what's good. Search for what's strong, beautiful, healthy, or unique. Write a list of these positives in your journal so you can reflect on them when you're feeling particularly critical of your body. (Or take a page from Dove's book and write on your mirror with a thick black marker!)

If you have trouble finding anything that meets your perfectionist standards, change the way you're looking at yourself. Pretend you're viewing someone else's reflection—your best friend, your sister, or someone else you love. Apply the standards that you use for your loved ones' bodies to your own body. Using those standards, choose at least five things about the image that are positive. Tell your image what you see, addressing her as a second person. "Your eyes are a beautiful green," or "You have strong legs." Speak to the reflection with the same love and compassion that you'd use when addressing a beloved friend or relative. I hope you'll find that when you speak to yourself as you speak to others, the words that come out will be far less harsh and you'll be better able to appreciate your body's merits.

I had a good lesson in practicing active gratitude recently while talking with my older daughter. We were having a conversation about how people's bodies change during adolescence, and I was telling her that it's normal that some kids mature earlier than others. With two girls in the house I try never to say anything negative about my body, but for some reason I told her that although most grown women wish for larger breasts, I would prefer to have smaller breasts. Her response brought tears to my eyes. "Oh, Mom," she said, "your breasts are perfect. Your whole body is perfect." It reminded me to be grateful for my body's assets and to try not to dwell on its imperfections.

## SHUT OUT THE MEDIA

Generations ago, women felt pretty satisfied with themselves because their comparison circle was small—the women at church, the neighbors, relatives, and photos in the occasional copy of *Life* magazine. Today, we see images of the world's most beautiful women on a daily, even hourly, basis. And most of the images we see are touched up, making nearly perfect women even more perfect. I remember reading an interview with a supermodel who said that when she looked at her own touched-up photo on a magazine cover, she felt intimidated because even *she* didn't look that good in real life. How can we compete with models when they can't even live up to their own published images?

Even the people on so-called reality shows are far from real. Maybe the people on these shows are not professional models or actors, but they're still far from ordinary. The producers of reality shows reject thousands of people to find a select few.

What we see in the media are the two extremes—the perfect women on magazine covers and the losers on daytime TV. We don't want to be like the losers, so we gravitate toward the perfect. Given the black-and-white choice, we'd rather side with the beautiful than the ugly.

I know that when I'm advising you to shut out media images, I'm asking the impossible. But, even though you can't block all of the perfectionist images from your life, you can eliminate some of them. Do what you can to take these images out of your line of sight: Cancel your subscriptions to magazines that fixate on beauty and perfection, avoid television shows in which women flaunt perfect bodies, turn your head when a city bus drives by with a fifteen-foot-long photo of a gorgeous actress lounging seductively. (If only they had shown a photo of her *before* it was touched up.) You can't cut it all out, but you can reduce your exposure.

Recently my daughter and her friends attended a seminar on body image and self-esteem for preteen girls. They viewed an online video that showed a team of makeup artists and computer experts transforming a perfectly ordinary-looking woman with pimples and bad hair into a gorgeous woman who, it turned out, was indeed a model. The video showed how Photoshop software can be used to raise cheekbones, thin the neck, remove blemishes, deepen eye color, improve skin tone, and basically make nearly anyone perfect. The next day, when my daughter noticed a picture of a beautiful celebrity on a magazine cover, she said, "Yeah right, that's what she really looks like. Sure." I wish every woman could see that video and understand how true it is that what we see in magazines and on billboards is not what these women really look like. Even the women whom most of us would consider perfect once the makeup artists and stylists are done with them are Photoshopped into ultra-perfection.

## GET REAL ABOUT SEX

The characters in movies, books, television shows, and magazines have mind-blowing sex all of the time. Real people don't. Perfectionists think

Be Happy Without Being Perfect

their sex lives should be as good as the sex lives of fictional characters. Expecting that is a recipe for disaster.

People are having sex a lot less often than we think, and they're not enjoying it as much as we imagine. Some 40 percent of women report having sexual dysfunction—they're not very interested in sex, they don't find it satisfying, or they can't climax. Millions of men are drugging their penises. So many of these people are doing what perfectionists do all the time: Trying to live up to an expectation that's not based in reality.

The truth is, a woman's sex drive waxes and wanes throughout her life. It's completely normal, at certain times, to have zero sexual desire—after the birth of a baby, at different times during your menstrual cycle, while your children are young, and at times of extreme stress and crisis. So if you're feeling like your sex life doesn't measure up and you're going through one of those life cycles, relax. It's normal.

However, some perfectionist expectations of a different kind can interfere with sexual fulfillment. It's much harder to enjoy your body in a sexual way if you dislike it, feel highly critical of it, and want to hide it from your partner. You will enjoy sex a lot more if you can feel less perfectionistic about your body. Consider this:

- Your body does not have to be perfect in order to turn a man on. Despite the way they gawk at stick-thin magazine models, most men prefer curvy women. If you want to have good sex, let go of the "only women with perfect bodies have good sex" ideal. It's ironic, but even the most beautiful women struggle with this. Many of the models whom I've seen as patients don't see themselves as beautiful and have as many self-esteem issues in the bedroom as ordinary-looking women.
- Your partner is probably a lot less critical of your body than you are. So what if your boobs are droopy and you gained five pounds—your partner most likely finds you attractive anyway. Men are visual—if they see a pair of breasts over a flabby stomach, what do you think they home in on? Not the stomach, that's for sure.

- Most men care far more about how you *act* in bed than how you *look*. Try to focus on *being* rather than *judging* your body. You will *look* sexier, no matter how you're built, if you *feel* sexy—and your partner will notice.
- Every sexual encounter isn't going to be perfect—sometimes you're turned on and your partner's mind is a thousand miles away, and sometimes vice versa. It's hard to get two people in the same place at the same time.
- Masturbation is such a good way for women to understand what turns them on. It allows you to explore fantasies in a safe way and helps you feel less embarrassed about using your imagination during sex. When you know exactly what you like, you can communicate it to your partner and work together to meet your needs and his.
- For more get-real advice about sex, read the book *Everything You Know About Sex and Love Is Wrong* by Pepper Schwartz. (All her books are great.)
- If intense feelings of shame, anxiety, or guilt hold you back from enjoying a healthy sex life, consider seeing a therapist who will help you explore where those feelings come from and how you can work around them.

## REWARD YOURSELF

A few years ago, a fascinating study examined why people who lose a lot of weight tend to gain most of it back. The researchers followed people during the periods of weight loss, weight maintenance, and weight gain. Why did the subjects regain their weight? The answer was loud and clear: While the subjects were losing weight, they received loads of attention and praise. However, when they reached their goals and stopped dropping pounds, all the support and admiration ended. Without all the positive reinforcement that had fueled them during their weight-loss period, the subjects regained their weight.

That study demonstrates two things: First, that rewards help reinforce positive behavior, and second, that we can't rely on the people around us to give us the acknowledgment we need. Rewards do work when you're trying to change a negative behavior. But you have to create your own reward system. The outside world isn't going to give you the acknowledgment you need, so you have to give it to yourself.

Set small, attainable goals and reward yourself when you reach them. When you fail to meet goals, don't beat yourself up. Accept that you've missed a goal, set a new goal, and decide what reward you'll work toward. It's a strategy that really works.

## PRACTICE SELF-FORGIVENESS

This is one of the most difficult skills for perfectionists to learn. We're not supposed to make mistakes—so why in the world would we forgive ourselves when we do?

Why is it that if a friend makes a mistake we can forgive her, but when we make mistakes we beat ourselves up? That's what perfectionists tend to do. We can't accept the fact that we are not perfect. When we slip up, it feels like a travesty. All or nothing thinking leads us to believe that if we mess up once, everything will fall apart and go to hell. For example, when a nonperfectionist on a diet eats an unplanned brownie, she forgives herself and simply decides to skip dessert tomorrow to make up for it. But when a perfectionist on a diet eats a brownie, she engages in catastrophic thinking—a common cognitive distortion—and panics because she feels that eating one brownie will lead to eating the whole tray of brownies, which will lead to uncontrolled obesity, heart disease, and an early death. When you lose control once, perfectionist thinking convinces you that you will never get it back. Once you cross a line, you fear that you'll keep on going.

Learning to forgive yourself isn't easy, but it's worthwhile, especially when it comes to diet and exercise. When you eat something you hadn't planned to eat or miss a workout, pay attention to the automatic thoughts that flood through your mind. Using cognitive-restructuring strategies, identify the thoughts, put them to the test, and then restructure them in a more constructive way.

Another great cognitive skill to use in this situation is thought-stopping. Say you eat too much ice cream. Automatic thoughts immediately start berating you for lacking self-discipline and losing control. When you recognize these thoughts, immediately visualize a big red-and-white stop sign. Take a deep breath and ask yourself why you're saying these things to yourself. Then deliberately and gently reframe the thought and, if necessary, change the behavior in which you are engaging. Remember the four steps of thought-stopping: Stop, breathe, reflect, and choose.

When you struggle to forgive yourself, try to imagine what you would do if your best friend called you and told you that she had made the mistake that you made. Would you berate her and call her names and tell her she's weak? Of course not. You'd support her and urge her to forgive herself and let it go. Try to look at it the same way when you mess up and be as gentle with yourself as you would be with a friend.

Also, as you concentrate on practicing self-forgiveness, think about the cognitive distortion known as "mental filtering" and ask yourself if it's something you engage in. For example, if you follow your workout schedule for two weeks and then miss one day, mental filtering blinds you to the days you did exercise and narrows your focus to the missed day. Using cognitive restructuring, you can put these thoughts in perspective.

## MAKE PEACE WITH AGING

Nobody wants to age, but when you consider that the alternative is dying young, aging isn't so bad. Nonetheless, perfectionists struggle with the physical changes of aging because they can't control them.

The best strategy for coping with age-related changes is to change what you can and accept what you can't. You can't stop the aging process, but you can, for example, wear loads of sunscreen to prevent wrinkles, eat in a way that reduces your risk of disease, take calcium and vitamin D supplements to maintain bone strength, and do aerobic exercise to boost your energy.

Miriam Nelson has done a lot of research on aging at Tufts University, and she's found that older women who strength train can stop or reverse age-related muscle weakness. In Nelson's strength-training studies, even women in their eighties and beyond increased their flexibility, strength, stamina, and ability to function well in their everyday lives. Women of all ages who begin a moderate strength-training regimen see results in a matter of weeks. (If you'd like to learn more about Nelson's work with strength training and aging, as well as descriptions of routines you can do at home, her book *Strong Women Stay Young* is a terrific resource.)

There's no doubt about it—as you get older, every cell in your body ages and your risk of cancer, heart disease, arthritis, and all kinds of other diseases goes up. It's your choice—you can sit back and let it happen or you can do as much as you can to protect yourself.

## Perfectionism and Illness

A twentysomething grad student I used to work with could have posed as the poster girl for healthy lifestyle choices. She was a vegetarian who ran marathons, she never smoked—basically she took excellent care of her body in every way. Despite all those healthy behaviors, she developed terminal cancer. This woman did everything right, and she still got sick.

An elderly man I know is the exact opposite. He has smoked for over fifty years, never exercises, eats whatever he pleases, and enjoys a cocktail or two every evening. Despite all of his decidedly unhealthy choices, at eighty he's still going strong. He has done everything wrong, and he's perfectly fine.

It's not fair. But the lesson these two people teach us is that there are some things in life that we simply can't control. That's a terribly hard concept to accept, particularly for perfectionists.

I'm not recommending that you take up smoking and abandon all your healthy lifestyle habits—you can absolutely reduce your *risk* of disease by making healthy choices. But ultimately you're not in control of your physical fate.

It's extremely difficult to be diagnosed with a serious disease and have to face the fact that your body isn't perfect. When it happens, you feel that you've lost all control over your life. (You know how hard it is for us perfectionists to admit that we're not in control!) You feel like your body has let you down. It's normal to feel that way.

If health problems develop, you can use some of the strategies in this book to deal with your disease.

## SEARCH FOR MEANING

One coping skill is to look for meaning in your misfortune. That's what some of the parents of kids killed at Columbine did—they started foundations to prevent, detect, and treat youth violence. And an attorney I know who was paralyzed in an auto accident used her experience in the medical trenches to become a patient advocate for the disabled. These people have taken a crisis and used it as an impetus to change their lives or create something meaningful, as Pamela did:

*I used to be a perfectionist, but after breast cancer, several years of therapy, and daily life with three kids, four cats, a large dog, and a husband who travels quite a bit, I'm not anymore. You can write in the dust on my dresser, I sometimes go to bed with dishes on the counter or in the sink, and the garage has only a small walking path now because it's so in need of cleaning out. I no longer feel the drive to do laundry every day, I leave garbage cans at the curb for my kids to bring in, and they make their own lunches half the time and iron their school uniforms if I can't do it for some reason on any given day. When I'm tired, I rest instead of pushing like I used to, and I miss almost every birthday that requires advance mailing (which is a large chunk of them). I can't say none of this bothers me, but it is my reality.*

*When I finished my last chemo treatment, my doctor released me to go on vacation. His parting words were, "Don't do anything you don't want to do." I will never forget that. All my life, I had done what other people wanted, even if I resented them while I was doing it, for "guilting" me into it. I did what I wanted with my life and my morality—no one could change that—but the little things, like babysitting for other people's kids when I had enough of my own, not wanting others to see a dirty counter, chastising myself for not being able to keep up with ironing or housecleaning or making meals—it was endless.*

*Having cancer gave me permission to choose what was best for ME, heedless of what other people wanted me to do. At first, I began to make choices based on my health. In time, it became a way of thinking, a way of giving myself permission not to be perfect in terms of exercise, keeping up with other people's ideals, and following the urge to do, do, do, which had been driving me crazy.*

*So did cancer reduce perfectionism? Most definitely. Am I free from all guilt at never again being able to keep up with everything? No. But I am working full time and I have a family, and I can't do it all. Too bad for those who think I can; my kids are living in a reality-based household where people have to pitch in, and when they don't, dishes sit there. I do more than some mothers and less than others, but my main concern at this point is not where I fit in among them. It's when will I make time to pray, to knit, and to exercise in addition to what I do now. I'm not doing enough of any of those, and my goal is to increase them—not for perfectionism, but for my own pleasure and growth.*

After a diagnosis you experience an acute phase during which it's tough to adapt, and then you start adjusting. If you don't, explore the possible reasons behind it. Are you getting adequate support? Are you doing what you need for yourself? Would it help to see a therapist? Are you rushing yourself and expecting to return to "normal" too quickly? Don't bottle up your emotions about serious health problems. Allow the emotions to be there, and allow yourself to feel them. It's healthy to grieve. Give yourself time, and seek whatever support you need from friends, support groups, or a therapist.

## AVOID BLAME

Ask yourself if you're blaming yourself for your disease. Perfectionists tend to blame themselves even for occurrences that they have no control over—most diseases have significant genetic components. Playing the self-blame game gets you nowhere—in fact, it can cause emotional harm. A recent study by researchers at Baylor College of Medicine found that breast cancer patients who blamed themselves for their disease reported more mood disturbance and poorer quality of life than those who did not blame themselves.

It's normal to imagine that you've caused your own illness, says Jessie Gruman, Ph.D., author of the book *AfterShock: What to Do When the Doctor Gives You—or Someone you Love—a Devastating Diagnosis*. It is especially common among perfectionists. Gruman describes some of the self-blame that can occur in the days after a diagnosis:

> *Many people spend hours going over their past behavior to establish the cause of their condition. They are often joined by family members and friends in their attempts to come up with an explanation for the sudden appearance of this disease. "I know I should have gotten that colonoscopy!" "I'm sure I got this disease because I have been so depressed and angry for so long." "I smoked for thirty years." . . . Such speculation about the cause of a disease has roots in the very human need to see the world as a place that is governed by rational laws. If you can identify something you did to cause your condition, it affirms that this situation is predictable and, by extension, that*

Be Happy Without Being Perfect

*the world is predictable—as opposed to random, as it feels right now. Others, by identifying behavioral causes, can convince themselves that they can avoid your fate.*

As odd as it may sound, a perfectionist may feel like she's in familiar emotional territory if she blames herself for her disease. Why? Two reasons. First, most perfectionists are so accustomed to blaming themselves for things that it is a natural reaction when just about anything goes wrong. Second, if a perfectionist can blame herself, the world feels safer for her—perfectionists hate being out of control, and they hate knowing that fate can toss curveballs that they have absolutely no control over.

For perfectionists to get sick after doing everything "right" really makes their card houses tumble down. It is a breach of trust. They begin to question everything in their worlds. They blame themselves. Self-blame is destructive, however. It erodes feelings of self-worth, which are usually already fragile in perfectionists. It may prevent you from making responsible treatment decisions. And finally, self-blame will dampen your spirit and lower your chance of being happy and coping well with your disease and treatment. As Gruman writes:

> *The most important matter for you now is not how you may have contributed to your condition but, rather, what you do now that you know about it. Your past behavior may have influenced your health, but that is irrelevant to the challenge before you: How can you make decisions about health care and your daily responsibilities to contain or minimize the impact of this disease on your life?*

Even if your lifestyle choices have contributed to your disease, you can't waste energy beating yourself up about it—you need that energy to fight your disease. Forget about the past and ask yourself what you can do to take control in the present.

If you're healthy and you fear disease, try to put your fears in perspective. Most people don't develop serious health problems while they're young. And those who do resiliently adjust. Healthy people believe that people with an illness have a poor quality of life. The truth is, after an initial period of anguish, most people return to their predisease happiness level and their quality of life is just fine.

For my whole life I lived in fear of my mother dying. I thought that if she died I'd just fall apart. But you know what? When she died, I got through it—and I got through it a lot better than I thought I would. Anticipating a terrible event is often worse than actually experiencing it. Yes, it's awful, but the human condition is that we return to baseline relatively quickly. We are far more resilient than we realize.

## PRACTICE ACTIVE GRATITUDE

You can practice active gratitude even when you're struggling with your health. Spend some time each day thinking about what is *not* wrong with you. While you're writing in your gratitude journal, list what's going *right* with your body. Concentrate on how easy it is to breathe when you don't have a cold, how wonderful it is when your bum knee isn't acting up, how clearly you can think when you don't have a headache, how carefree you feel when your monthly menstrual cramps are weeks away. Look in the mirror and celebrate the fact that today you have no pimples and your hair came out well. Everything could fall apart tomorrow, so appreciate, enjoy, and be thankful for what's great today.

Practicing active gratitude works even if you have physical limitations, chronic illnesses, or other health problems. I've spoken to breast cancer survivors with mastectomies who practice active gratitude by enjoying the beauty of their remaining breast. Or they express gratitude for their scar because it is a physical sign of their triumph over the disease—a battle scar, so to speak. Likewise, a friend who has food allergies makes it a point to actively appreciate all of the foods she *can* eat. By practicing active gratitude, you can begin the process of moving your attention away from flaws and toward all of your body's good points.

Be Happy Without Being Perfect

## HOLD ON TO YOUR SEXUALITY

I'm seeing a young patient now with a serious illness that causes severe pain in all of her joints and restricts her ability to move. When she was diagnosed, she thought her sex life was over. I sat down with her and helped her understand that just because you have a chronic illness doesn't mean you stop being a sexual person. There are still lots of sexy things she and her husband can do together. Sex does not mean intercourse only. Use your imagination. Be creative. And have some fun.

I received an e-mail from her yesterday. The day before, she and her husband hired a babysitter for their young child, went to a hotel (without any luggage), and got a room for the afternoon. They had a truly good time together. Her husband called her three times yesterday and they could not stop giggling about it. My e-mail back to her simply said, "hubba hubba." I guess using their imaginations worked. . . .

## REALIZE THAT YOU'RE STRONGER THAN YOU KNOW

Years ago I met a woman whose mother died of breast cancer. This woman was terrified of developing the disease herself—it was a massive cloud hanging over her life. Eventually she did get breast cancer. After she finished treatment, she told me she was relieved. All her life she had feared cancer, and she felt that if she received a cancer diagnosis she would surely fall apart. But she said it wasn't nearly as bad as she thought. My point is not that cancer treatment is easy—it certainly is not. But if you have to face a difficult diagnosis or grueling treatment, have faith in your ability to handle it.

CHAPTER 6

# Make Peace with Your Dust Bunnies

*W*e have a very lovely old house that needs a lot of work. Right now we're having an issue with the driveway. Most of it is asphalt, but part of it is concrete. The concrete needs to be repaired or replaced, but if I replace the concrete with asphalt, the driveway will be two different colors. That would drive me crazy. So I'm looking into all kinds of ways to reseal the asphalt or use a color to seal the concrete so it matches the asphalt. I'm calling all over the place getting estimates. I should just get the concrete replaced with asphalt so the driveway is functional—I shouldn't be so concerned about having the colors match. But I want everything to be perfect.

It's like that with everything. Every summer I put pots of flowers out front. I usually get them at Home Base. I stopped there yesterday and bought some of what I needed, but they didn't have the small purple flowers I wanted. So I went to a nursery, and they didn't have the right color and I ended up leaving empty-handed. I told myself to just pick something, but I didn't. So I stopped at another place. I found what I needed, but it took three trips. At least I didn't go to sixteen places. I could have settled on a different kind of flower but if I had, I would have looked at the pots every day and been unhappy with the color.

*Having the lead paint removed from the outside of the house was a nightmare. It took me several years to figure out how to get the paint removed without my kids being exposed to even a single speck of lead. I bought a paint remover tool that stripped off paint and sucked it into a vacuum with a special HEPA filter. I hired painters to use it, but they had a lot of trouble with it. I complained to the company that the painters could not get the device to work properly, and they sent a representative from a couple of states away to show them how. This dragged on for years.*

*The house is very beautiful, but I've learned I don't have the time or the skill to renovate it, especially because I want everything to be perfect. I always wanted an old house, but I'm not very happy with it. We talk about selling it, but we'd have to do a lot of work on it before we could even put it on the market.*

*—Barbara*

Your home should be a haven—a peaceful, comfortable place where you can set aside your world-weariness and relax.

For perfectionist women, however, the home can be a source of stress rather than a place to relax. Every speck of dust, every dirty glass, every unmade bed is a blatant, unavoidable imperfection. You crave serenity and calmness, but the stress caused by dog hair on the carpet, fingerprints on the walls, baked-on crud in the oven, and leaves in the yard can turn your home into a giant anxiety pit. For thousands of years the home offered protection from the elements—it kept families warm and dry. Home was a shelter, not a showplace—your average cavewoman didn't need to have matching curtains and sofas.

Perfectionism at home sets you right in the middle of a vicious circle. You long for peace and order, but you can't relax until the dishwasher is unloaded and the trash is taken out. No matter how hard you work, the to-do list never ends. The more you chase the unattainable goal of perfection at home, the more stressed you become.

# Our Mother's Culture

A big part of our problem is that we hold ourselves up to expectations that made sense fifty years ago but really don't fit our lives today. Arlie Russell Hochschild, author of the book *The Second Shift*, suggests that modern-day women work feverishly to stay connected to the outdated and ill-fitting "domestic culture" of the past: "Women of every social class and in every kind of job are faced with a common problem: How shall I preserve the domestic culture of my mother and grandmother in the age of the nine-to-five or eight-to-six job?" (Or eight to eight!) Hochschild believes women stay true to their old-fashioned domestic ideals by spending their first shift of the day laboring at work, and their second at home. "On weekends and holidays, most working women revert to being housewives," she writes. Women fight an often-losing battle to "carry forward a domestic culture"—a culture of baking from scratch and sewing Halloween costumes.

Pride complicates matters further. Your home is a reflection of you—and if it doesn't look good, it reflects poorly on you, rather than your husband or kids. So if the paint is chipping and the furniture is dusty, if guests have to push aside piles of old *People* magazines in order to find a place to sit, you can't help feeling that it makes you look pretty bad. "If my house is a mess," the perfectionist tells herself, "then I must be a mess." And if there's anything we perfectionists don't like, it's messes. That's why perfectionism causes more trouble at home than almost anywhere else.

Working women are particularly prone to perfectionist struggles at home. Research has shown that when the average woman compares her house to others, she judges it against her mother's house or the houses of her stay-at-home friends. This basis of comparison can be unfair, since most women who work outside the home have less time for housekeeping than women who stay at home.

What it all comes down to is control. The more a woman is feeling out of control elsewhere in her life, the more control she tries to exert at home. Perhaps she can't control her work, her husband, her kids, her health—but she can darn well make sure there's no cat hair on the draperies. When a woman crosses the threshold between keeping the house relatively clean to obsessively clean, she needs to look at what else is going on in her life to see if there's a deeper problem that is causing her to feel so consumed by housecleaning.

## We Asked Women . . .

### How does perfectionism affect how you take care of your home?

*I'm a baker, not a cook. The idea of just throwing things into a pot is a little scary. I want a predictable result.*

—Linda

*I can never leave the house with dirty dishes. I have to have a certain amount of order. I can have piles of magazines next to the bed, but I can't have dirty dishes or laundry strewn all over. I make my bed every morning. I tell myself, "You don't have to do this, just get out the door," but I can't. I'm sometimes a little late dropping my daughter off at school because I'm tidying things up.*

—Elizabeth

*I feel less stressed when I'm organized. My husband laughs at me when I'm running around picking up toys at the end of night. He asks me why I don't just sit down and read the paper. But I feel better when things are in order, the refrigerator is stocked, the grocery list is made. I can't nap—I'm always thinking of the things that need to be done.*

—Denise

Be Happy Without Being Perfect

*We recently bought a farm and have been working on rehabbing the place. I started painting the outside of these true-divided light windows, and oiling the insides of them. Each window has about four to six hours' work in it. Oiling the windows is a messy job, and the cleanup takes forever. My husband keeps telling me the windows look fine as they are, that I'm being too anal, but to me they are a mess.*

*—Carol*

*Chaos makes me crazy. I cannot stand clutter. My house is very clean and kept up—there's nothing on the coffee table. It's very organized. I do it for myself. I'm not worried about other people. Clutter bothers me more from an order standpoint.*

*—Laura*

*For years, I wouldn't do dinner parties if I didn't think everything was perfect—my house, my cooking, and so on. If things weren't under control I wasn't going to do it, and I wasn't going to settle for potluck or a pot of spaghetti or a pot of soup. That really held me back socially.*

*—Linda*

*I get so concerned with making the house perfect on weekends that I often forget to "schedule" some fun into my limited free time with my fiancé. I need to start adding that to my weekend checklists. That being said, I feel very happy when the things on the list start being checked off.*

*—Janet*

## Tools You Can Use

The good news is that mind/body techniques work as effectively at home as they do anywhere else. If you want to stop stressing about your home and start enjoying it, you can. Drop your dust cloth, curl up in an unmade bed, and read on.

What are you telling yourself about your house? What criticisms jump into your mind when you cook, clean, or entertain? What cognitive distortions have taken root in your automatic thoughts?

Of all the cognitive distortions, the ones that seem to crop up the most often among women who are perfectionists about their homes are: mental filter, disqualifying the positive, approval seeking, all-or-nothing thinking, and "should" statements. Here are some examples:

**Distortion:** Mental filter

**Example:** You make a huge dinner for twelve. You forget about the rolls and they burn in the oven. Everything else is great, but you feel the dinner was a failure because the rolls burned.

**Tell yourself:** "Look at all the carbohydrates I saved my guests by not serving rolls."

**Distortion:** Disqualifying the positive

**Example:** A neighbor comments on how nice your house looks and you think to yourself, "What does she know? Her house is always a mess."

**Tell yourself:** "It's nice she noticed. Maybe she'll use my house as an inspiration."

**Distortion:** Approval seeking

**Example:** You're redoing your kitchen and although you prefer oak cabinetry, you are thinking of choosing cherry because a friend told you that oak cabinetry is hokey.

**Tell yourself:** "Who's going to be living in this kitchen, my friend or me? I should pick what I like—besides, other friends may not approve of cherry, so why not just pick what suits me?"

**Distortion:** All-or-nothing thinking

**Example:** When you see some dust on a table and you think, "This house is filthy. I am such a slob."

**Tell yourself:** "I wouldn't say that to a friend, so I why am I saying it to myself? I deserve to be treated better than that."

**Distortion:** "Should" statements

**Examples:** You tell yourself: "I should be able to keep the house looking clean and neat all the time. It should never be messy."

**Tell yourself:** "Maybe my house is messy, but at least it's clean."

As you think about your perfectionist tendencies at home, be aware of what you're telling yourself. Jot down your thoughts in your journal. Once you've identified your auto-thoughts, put them to the test using the cognitive-restructuring strategies in Chapter 2. Ask yourself: What are the thoughts and expectations that cause me stress? Are they accurate? How can I restructure the thoughts in such a way that I will feel less stressed?

## ASK YOURSELF: IS IT WORTH IT?

This strategy works for any kind of perfectionist thinking, but it's particularly effective at home, because our actions have such impact on the people we live with. The problem with perfectionists is that we always think we're right, and we never stop to think that there are other ways besides ours that may work just as well.

Sit down with your journal and make a list of the benefits of being a perfectionist. Then, list the benefits that would result if you loosened your standards somewhat. Here's an example:

Some of the benefits of being a perfectionist at home:
- The house always looks great when people visit.
- I feel good about my house—it looks nice and is organized and neat.
- When people have dinner at my house, they are impressed by the food.
- When everything is the way I like it, my house lives up to my expectation of what a house should look like.

Make Peace with Your Dust Bunnies

Some of the benefits of loosening perfectionist standards at home:

- I would have more time to spend on myself and with my partner, children, and friends if I spent less time on housework.
- I could go to bed earlier if I worried less about cleaning up at the end of the day.
- Mornings would be less hectic if I didn't insist on having all the beds made perfectly.
- Entertaining would be more enjoyable—and I would do it more often—if I didn't insist on serving an elaborate meal made from scratch.
- My partner and I would argue less.

After you've made your list of pros and cons, ask yourself what matters more. Compare each point and choose your priorities. For example, what's more important: cleaning up at night or getting an extra half hour of sleep? Does enjoying a dinner party matter more than impressing your guests with gourmet food? Only you can answer these questions. They're definitely worth asking, though, because you'll feel less stressed even if you can find just a few ways to loosen your perfectionist expectations at home. I always used to make homemade rolls or bread when we had friends over for dinner. That all changed when we went to a friend's house for dinner—everyone raved over her rolls and polished them off. Afterward, she told us that they were ready to bake, from a packet! That's what I serve now. It's one more way to reduce the stress when folks come over for a meal. It's a start . . .

Be sure to consider the impact your perfectionism has on others when you do your cost-benefit analysis. Perfectionism can cause a real strain in a household, especially when nonperfectionists and perfectionists live under the same roof. Perfectionism goes hand in hand with criticism, bossiness, irritation and anger; loosening perfectionism's hold can help you and your family feel better and enjoy life more.

*When my son was in Montessori school, the children were asked to write about their families. I will never forget what my son wrote:*

*"My father plays baseball with me, and my mother makes chicken."*
*When I read that I thought, maybe I should be out there playing*
*baseball and ordering pizza.*

*—Susan*

*I always go to my son's soccer games, but I had to miss one because of*
*a work commitment. My son said it was his best game ever, and*
*when I asked why, he said it was because I wasn't shouting advice to*
*him while he played. He said he was kidding, but I don't think he*
*was, because I do shout advice from the sidelines. I had thought of it*
*as cheering, but I don't think that's how he sees it. Now I keep my*
*mouth shut.*

*—Tammy*

## PUT YOURSELF FIRST

Let's face it: It feels good when the house is clean and in order. I've been
on a rampage lately to de-clutter my house, which has been in a state of
chaos since my mother died and I inherited half a houseload of stuff. I do
my organizing on a room-by-room basis, and I have to say, when I walk
into a newly organized room I feel great. Is it a sense of calm? Pride? A
sense of control? A lack of angst? Probably a little of each.

I don't like clutter. I like to be able to find things easily. But sometimes I need to put my family's needs or my own needs first. When time
is short and I feel stressed, and I have a choice between sorting through
my cereal cabinet or putting my feet up and reading a book, the book
should win even though I would like the cereal cabinet to be more organized. There are days that I need downtime more than I need the house
to look good.

I'm not telling you to let your house go to hell, but I am suggesting
that you make conscious choices rather than just doing housework by
rote. It's fine to organize cabinets, but if you've had a long day and you
need a hot bath, let the cabinets wait.

Here are some signs that you need to work harder to put your own needs before those of your house:

- You bake brownies at 10 p.m. after coming home from a three-day business trip.
- You hold your annual holiday open house party two weeks after having a C-section—with the same number of homemade dishes that you served the year before.
- Your children ask you why you spend so much time cleaning up for the cleaning lady.

Here's one way to put yourself first while doing housework: Invite a friend over to help. I did that recently—an old friend was visiting, and we spent the day organizing my family room. The work got done and we had a great time gossiping, reminiscing, and drinking tea. I did most of the sorting, but having her there to talk to while I worked made it so much less of a chore. When my friend needs help at her house, I'll be happy to return the favor because I know we'll have another great day.

Housework takes time, as you well know. Whatever time you're spending living up to an unrealistic expectation is time taken away from friends, family, hobbies, sleep, self-nurturance, self-reflection, sex, exercise, meditation, going to the movies, reading, and so many other good things. Again, I'm not telling you to let your house go—but I hope you'll start putting more emphasis on your own needs and a little less on the needs of the house, as Linda has:

> When I did some traveling and left most of my "stuff" at home, I realized how little thought I gave to the things I left behind. I thought that these possessions were very important to me—that in some ways they defined me—but I realized that all I really need is some money in my pocket and the clothes on my back and the goodwill of the people I'm with. I'm letting go of old stuff,

*clearing out to make room for new opportunities. If you're so consumed with the house and your stuff, there isn't room for anything new.*

*—Linda*

## LOCATE THE SOURCE

An important step toward adjusting your perfectionist expectations at home is to understand where the feelings come from. Most of us carry an image in our minds of what our homes should look like. This image has many influences, primarily our mothers, families, friends, and the media. Where do your images come from?

Look at how your family influenced you. Were your parents perfectionists? Were they sloppy? What about your partner's family? Simply understanding and acknowledging these influences can be helpful.

It's also helpful to understand what kind of perfectionism (or lack thereof) lurks in your partner's past.

I grew up with—how can I put this diplomatically?—a nonperfectionist mother, who was raised in a wealthy home full of servants in pre-Hitler Germany. When she fled her country, nearly penniless, and came to America, she had little interest in learning how to keep a perfect house. Unfortunately my father was an extremely neat person, so the discrepancy caused conflict. Even though I was closer to my mother than to my father, I'm more like my father when it comes to clutter—I'm much less tolerant of it than my mother was.

It's always interesting to me to ask perfectionists where their mothers fell on the perfectionist scale. Most of the time a perfectionist has either a very neat, orderly mother or a very messy, disorganized mother. We either copy our mothers or go in the opposite direction. Perfectionists don't often spring from middle ground. I'm surprised at how often I find very neat people who grew up in messy houses, and vice versa. It reminds me of adolescent rebellion.

Recognizing the source of your perfectionist expectations at home helps because it gives you some of the insight and perspective you need to change.

> *My daughter considers me a perfectionist. I think she's probably not the only one. My house is very neat and organized. I pay attention to the details and I don't think most people are like that. I suspect it bothers her a little bit, because I don't have two little kids running around and the kinds of demands on my time that she has. In comparison, it may make her feel like she's not together. I've noticed people get a little intimidated by my home because it's neat and clean and I keep it very nice. But they don't understand that I do it for myself.*
>
> —Rose

## SEPARATE MEDIA FANTASY FROM EVERYDAY REALITY

Our images of what we think our houses "should" look like are often shaped by media-generated fantasies. Do you expect your house to resemble a movie set or a magazine spread? Are you spending too much time with Martha Stewart? (Yep, we're back to Martha again.) No one purveys fantasy better than Martha. She absolutely fascinates me. I dislike the contributions she makes to the perfectionist angst in this country, and yet I can't stop observing her. Her message is one of the worst that American women could adapt—and yet women adore her. They want to emulate her and be like her. Even I feel the pull sometimes. Who can look at the cover of her magazine in a checkout line and not want to live the kind of life it presents?

I actually had a patient tell me that Martha Stewart was the reason she was seeking therapy. She had seen the Martha Stewart Thanksgiving special on television, and she wanted to create the same Thanksgiving bonanza that she'd seen on the special, so she ordered a whole bunch of stuff from Martha's website. She came to me wondering what was wrong with her that she couldn't make her Thanksgiving table look TV-perfect. She felt like a failure and a slob.

I had to remind her that Martha's world is a fantasy and that real women can't do what Martha does. It's like expecting that you can re-create Disney World in your backyard.

Why is Martha one of the most successful women in American business history? What is the appeal? I think it's because she understands the desire all of us have to bring beauty into our lives. I'll never forget one of the stories I read about her in a book called *Martha Inc.* by Christopher Byron. She was trying to pitch her television show to a broadcasting executive. The pilot episode featured a segment on the perfect way to cut a long-stem rose. The executive asked Martha why she would do such a piece on a show that would be airing in big cities like Detroit, Chicago, and New York. Few of these women have rose gardens, the executive said. Martha's response summed up her amazing comprehension of what fuels American women: "But they want them."

Martha Stewart represents what women want. We want our roses to be perfect, we want our Thanksgiving tables to be perfect, we want our cupcakes to be perfect. Her whole empire is built on that desire. It's fine as eye candy. But when it starts to suck the joy from your life, you've got to reprioritize. If you stay up late baking cupcakes for the school party using cake mix and canned frosting (which is how I do it) but feel guilty for not creating dazzling Martha-cakes, that's a problem. I have nothing against amazing cupcakes. But I have a problem with Martha not showing that it takes several hours to *make* amazing cupcakes.

I'm picking on Martha, but the media is full of examples of household perfection being passed off as everyday expectation. I strongly recommend that you look at the effect the media has on your own image of what you want your house to look like. It's very helpful to separate fantasy from reality.

Make Peace with Your Dust Bunnies

## JOURNAL THE QUESTION: WHY AM I DOING THIS?

Pull out your journal and write about the perfectionist feelings you have about your home. Why do you want a truly perfect house? Is that really how you want to live? Do you really need every surface to be immaculate? Is that the way you want to spend your time? If your visitors judge you by the cleanliness of your kitchen floor, are you spending time with the right people? Is this the best way for you to take care of yourself?

If you're a stay-at-home mother, ask yourself whether you feel that you have to keep the house spotless and gorgeous to justify staying at home. Is guilt fueling your perfectionism? If so, some rethinking and restructuring these thoughts would serve you well.

## PRIORITIZE GOALS

A number of years ago, I learned an important lesson about keeping my perfectionist priorities straight.

I joined a bunko group so that I could get to know more women in my town. (Bunko is a group dice game that's something like Yahtzee.) It's the rage in a lot of suburban towns—women like it because it's fun and is really just an excuse to hang out and chat and drink wine with a bunch of other women, which I'm all in favor of. There were twelve women in this group—eleven stay-at-home moms and me. We took turns meeting in one another's houses.

I remember, month after month, going to play bunko in each different house. I was amazed: These women's homes looked gorgeous. They had furniture in every room. All the furniture matched. Pictures hung on the walls. Each month I became more anxious about having everyone over to my house, which is clean but cluttered and definitely not beautifully decorated. We painted our family room two years ago and still haven't gotten around to rehanging the pictures.

Finally it was my turn. I scrubbed and straightened and baked and vacuumed and spent way more time than I had getting the house ready for the bunko ladies. As I greeted people at the door, one of the women walked into my front hall and said, "I can't believe you have white walls." I was shocked. What kind of person would say something like that? I felt terrible about it all night for two reasons: I was amazed that someone could be so rude but also a bit ashamed that I clearly did not keep up with what were apparently well-known decorating guidelines.

My pride was wounded, but soon I realized how silly it all was. My priorities got all jumbled up by that bunko group. I just don't invest myself that much in how my house looks. I don't pay attention to trendy paint colors, so why should I care if someone comments on my white walls? People are creative in different ways. Some women channel their creativity into their homes. I direct most of mine into my family and my work.

Needless to say I dropped out of the group soon after. No more bunko for me. I'd rather socialize with women who share more of my priorities—which I do now. Every month my three Girls' Night Out buddies and I accomplish an amazing amount of sharing, supporting, giggling, and Chardonnay consumption with no talk of decorating.

My point is that the more you can prioritize, the happier you'll be. What's most important to you? For me the priorities are being a good parent and spouse, being a good friend, and doing work I feel passionate about. Decorating my house is one thing I can let go. I'm not going to spend my weekends looking for the perfect accent pillow for my couch. But I know lots and lots of women who do—which is fine if it's what they enjoy and it's really important to them. But if it's not a top priority, why spend time on it?

It can be helpful to write down your priorities in order of their importance. If having a breathtaking house isn't one of the top five priorities, then spend less time on it and more time on the more important things.

Janet is a great example of someone who benefited tremendously by prioritizing her goals:

*About ten years ago I bought a brand-new house. It was perfect— but I was constantly trying to keep it perfect. If a scuff mark appeared on a wall, I had the paint on hand to fix it. I was constantly touching up the risers on the staircase and cleaning and fixing the little things that happen over time. It consumed me and I was miserable because it's impossible to keep up with. I hired a cleaning person to help me and I spent every weekend being obsessed instead of having fun! But I've learned. Recently I bought a 166-year-old house with so many dings and dents that I can't let them bother me. I have also bought a used car that already has a ding or two so that I don't get obsessed with trying to keep it perfect. I keep the house and the car looking nice, but I can't make them perfect, so I don't get obsessed. I'm much happier now.*

## PRIORITIZE THE "WANT-TO" TASKS

There are a million tasks in every house, from making beds to taking out the garbage. Some have to be done—keeping the kitchen safe, for example. If you're defrosting chicken, you don't want juice dripping down the counter and onto the floor where your toddler can lick it. Bathroom hygiene is also pretty important—it's no fun for anyone when the bathroom smells. Those are some "have-to" tasks.

Then there are the "want-to" tasks. These include things like making beds and putting up curtains that match the sofa.

Perfectionists tend to put the want-to tasks on the have-to list. An important way of releasing yourself from perfectionism's grip is to draw clear lines between what you have to do and what you want to do. You have to take out the trash. You don't have to put the spices in alphabetical order.

That's not to say you shouldn't do the "want-to" tasks. If you have time and they make you happy, go ahead and do them. But make them the first things you'll jettison when you're feeling stressed and overwhelmed, as Sandra does:

*I just picked twenty-five pints of raspberries, and this weekend I made jam and pies. I'm just as capable of buying a pie. I am proud that I can do this, but I'm not above stopping at the farm stand and buying a pie.*

Once you've separated the have-tos from the want-tos, take a closer look at the want-to list. Spend some time putting the items in priority order. What's most important to you? In my house, the number one item on the want-to list is making the beds. I grew up with a very meticulous Russian father, and we didn't leave the room in the morning without making the bed. It's really important to me now that beds always be made—I can't stand walking into my room and seeing my bed unmade. I also don't like having dirty dishes in the sink, so before I go to bed, I usually make sure the sink is empty, although since I've been working on this book I've been more likely to leave them there until the next morning. But vacuuming? I can let that go. Baking from scratch? Forget about it. I do these things when I have time, but if I don't, I know what I should focus on: The have-to tasks and the very top of the want-to list. Over time you'll find yourself letting go, as Betty has:

*I don't cook much, so the kitchen isn't a big problem. I don't obsess about it being clean. However, if I'm defrosting chicken on the counter, even in plastic, and the counter gets wet, even though I know it's condensation and not chicken juice, I still get skeeved out. I wash down that section of the counter with antibacterial spray even though I know rationally that there are no germs there.*

*I'm starting to let the kids' rooms go. I want the sun room downstairs to be neat and picked up, so I let go on the bedrooms. I used to be really obsessive about cleaning up after the kids—all the matchbox cars had to be in the matchbox basket, all the balls in the ball basket. Now, if there is a board game with one missing piece, I tell myself we don't have to throw the game away because there's a piece missing. The game can be played with one less player.*

As you make your lists, try to avoid approval seeking. Separate the tasks you do because they are important to you and your family from the tasks you do to satisfy, impress, or earn approval from others.

If you keep bumping your head against something—say you promise yourself that you're going to spend less time keeping the garage neat, but you keep doing it anyway—try giving yourself written permission to let it go. Write a permission slip, sign it, and hang it somewhere that you'll see it often. Sometimes that kind of deliberation and emphasis can be very helpful.

## BE CAREFUL WITH COMPARISONS

It's human nature: You're happy with what you have until you see that someone else has something better. It's normal to compare, but I urge you to compare with caution. If you're a working mother and you compare your house with that of a woman who doesn't work or whose children are grown, chances are pretty good that your house won't stack up to hers. Comparing your house to the houses of your mother, friends, or sister is an open invitation to dissatisfaction and discontent.

## PAY THE PRICE

If you have a house task that causes loads of stress, consider hiring someone to do it. Spending a small amount of money could significantly increase your quality of life. If housecleaning drives you crazy, maybe you can pay someone to come in for a few hours every other week and do the jobs you hate most, like cleaning the bathroom and scrubbing the floors. Maybe you'll have to make some sacrifices to afford it—I personally would forgo almost anything to avoid cleaning the bathroom. A little help can go a long way and, as Sandra says, may even help preserve your marriage:

*We have a very large yard, and it takes thirty to forty hours over the course of six weeks to rake up all the leaves. Every year it causes ten-*

Be Happy Without Being Perfect

sion because I do more raking than my husband. It causes so much stress between us. I start getting stressed about the leaves in September, before they've even started changing, and it doesn't stop until Thanksgiving. Every hour I'm out there raking and he's inside on the computer working I'm furious because I'm doing more than he is. This year I convinced my husband to hire a landscaper to do the leaves. We don't have that money to spend, but you make certain decisions that are marriage-keepers, and this is one of them.

## REMIND YOURSELF: NOBODY IS KEEPING TRACK

Perfectionists tend to think visitors notice every speck of dust and cluttered table. One of my patients confided that if there were dirty dishes on the counter when friends dropped by unexpectedly, she wouldn't answer the door. The truth is, people don't notice, and if they do notice, they don't care. Visitors see much less than we think. If they do notice the pieces of burnt spaghetti that have cemented themselves to the burner pans on your stove, they probably won't judge you for it—and if they do, then shame on them for being so rude. What kind of friend thinks less of you (and comments on it) if there are cobwebs on your ceilings? You don't need friends like that.

*I only obsess over the house when I'm having company. That's when I'm wiping dust off the baseboard. I tell myself nobody will see the baseboard if I keep the lights dim. I used to get upset when the kids' rooms were messy, but now I say that only the downstairs has to be clean, and the bathrooms. When people come over they have a couple glasses of wine and some good appetizers, and they just don't care if the house isn't perfect.*

*I loosened up after we had a real spur-of-the-moment get-together one time. My house wasn't up to my usual standards, and nobody noticed, nobody cared, nobody complained. They all had fun even though there was dust on the baseboards. Also, I've been to other people's houses and have seen clutter on the counters and dust on the table, and I don't care. So they probably don't care when they see it at my house.*

*—Betty*

As Betty found, people sometimes feel *more* comfortable in your home if it's a little messy. I am much more at ease in other people's homes when they're cluttered but clean. Those kinds of houses look lived in and feel inviting. I hate going into homes where I'm scared to move, especially with my kids.

My husband and I made a decision when we moved into our house that there would be no *possession* in the house that was more important than the *people* in the house. Do I still put coasters out? Sure. But if someone spills something on the carpet, so what? It's a carpet. People are more important than objects. The relationships we have in life are more important than our furniture. Gloria tells this story:

*A friend invited me and my husband over for dinner and she served all store-bought food—frozen lasagna from Costco, salad in a bag, salad dressing from a bottle, and rolls and pie from a supermarket bakery. Everyone had just as good a time as they would have if she'd spent the entire day shopping, chopping, and baking. That was a big wake-up call for me, especially since it was obvious she was having as much fun as everyone else. Enjoying my own dinner party? It had never occurred to me. For some reason I always had the feeling that if I didn't serve a gourmet meal, people would think less of me.*

If you're a perfectionist in your house, look at your self-esteem, how you judge yourself, how you think others judge you. Are you hiding behind your perfect house and using it to mask a problem within the family?

Housework is one of the main things couples fight about. Women say men don't help out. Men say women criticize them when they do. Women say men take forever to do a simple task. Men say women expect too much. And on and on it goes.

The ways in which men and women tackle housework are worlds apart. "Men and women think differently, approach problems differently, emphasize the importance of things differently, and experience the world around us through entirely different filters," says Marianne J. Legato, M.D., author of an absorbing book called *Why Men Never Remember and Women Never Forget.*

For example, because of the way their brains are wired, women respond to stressors (such as an untidy house) much more dramatically than men, Legato says. That's why, five minutes before guests arrive, your husband can calmly watch a football game while you rush around cleaning up. Women's bodies release a hormone that motivates us to make and preserve social connections—which is why it's so important to you (and less important to your husband) that you bring homemade cookies to a party.

Women notice details that men simply don't see, and they remember them better. When there's a heap of dirty laundry sitting on the bedroom floor, women are more likely than men to notice it, be irritated by it, and remember that it's there. It was really helpful for me to learn this because I would get annoyed at my husband for walking past a pile of newspapers or toys. Now I realize that it's not that he's being a deliberate slob—he just doesn't see that stuff. And I understand that I have to say, "Please pick up the glasses on the coffee table and put them in the dishwasher," because those glasses are invisible to him. It's counterproductive to assume that men and women have the same household standards—it's much better to acknowledge the differences and work around them.

This makes sense from an evolutionary standpoint—back when

men were hunting buffalo and women were taking care of the cave, gender differences helped keep people alive. Men were wired to go out and find dinner—they put all their attention into catching and slaying the buffalo, and those who succeeded survived. On the other hand, the women who survived were the ones who were able to remain at home and simultaneously take care of the children, gather nuts and berries, prepare the meals, sweep the cave, and form bonds with the other cave-women. The men who lived longest and passed on their genes were single-task oriented; the women who endured did so because they could multitask.

Today's men and women still have some of the wiring that allowed their ancient ancestors to survive, but in the modern world, those tendencies sometimes make it hard for men and women to coexist peacefully.

Just because women and men approach home chores differently doesn't mean you can't work together. "Simply understanding the differences between us allows us to celebrate those differences instead of bumping up against them," Legato says. "Each sex has something valuable to offer." Studies show that because of the way their brains work, women are better at multitasking and men are better when concentrating on a single task from beginning to end.

I've worked with many couples who have figured out how to work together on house care. Here are some tips from the trenches.

## MAKE A DIVVY LIST

Just because your husband doesn't notice that the house is a mess doesn't mean he doesn't have to help clean. He's still got to pull his weight. I've found that the best way to do this is to make a divvy list. I tell couples to write down a list of what has to get done, then divide it up. To make an effective divvy list, you can each keep a pad and pen at hand for a couple of weeks and write down all of the chores you both do. Then decide who will do what.

There are usually things that bother one and not the other, and tasks that one doesn't mind and the other despises. I hate taking out the garbage, for example, but my husband doesn't mind it. He can't stand doing dishes, but it doesn't bother me. If you divvy up chores in an orderly, consistent way, you each know what you're supposed to do. When there are dishes to be washed I know it's my responsibility. When the garbage is piling up I know it's his.

As you discuss housework with your husband, be sure you're on the same page regarding *when* jobs need to be done—don't assume he thinks about things the same way you do. Before I was married, I shared a house with two male roommates. None of us was particularly neat, and we were all busy. I would let the garbage in the kitchen trash can get to the top and then take it out; my roommates would wait until the trash was spilling out onto the floor. Their tolerance levels were higher than mine, and the same is true with my husband, Dave. So when you divvy up jobs you have to agree on when they should be done. If it's his job to do the dishes, does that mean it's dishwashing time when one dish is in the sink or when you run out of clean pots and pans? You may have to compromise— something that's hard for a perfectionist to do. If you believe in daily vacuuming and he thinks it can be done every two weeks, you've got to come to an agreement or you'll be fighting about it nonstop.

Writing down all of the jobs you both do can be a helpful way for you to see how much the other one does. I sometimes feel that I do everything in my house, but when I sit down and really think about how much my husband does, I usually see that it's more than I realize.

In some couples the husband is more of a house perfectionist than the wife. I've counseled couples like this—often the woman reports that the man criticizes her and complains that the house is a mess. My response is, "OK, buddy, pick up the vacuum."

## BITE YOUR TONGUE

If you're going to divvy housework up between you and your husband, you have to learn to step back and let him do the jobs his way. I know, it's hard. You literally may have to hold your hand over your mouth to stop yourself from redirecting your husband as he folds the towels crookedly. If you want him to help, you've got to find a way to let him do it his way. (Cognitive restructuring is a great tool to use in this situation.) Remind yourself that it's OK for the towels to be a little wrinkled. If you criticize nonstop, he'll get annoyed and frustrated, and you'll end up doing everything yourself.

Keep in mind that your way is not necessarily the best or the only way to do something. Women make dinners so that everything's done at the same time. Men make the chicken and when it's done they start the rice. But either way, the kids get fed. A baby who wears stripes and plaids won't get sick. There are very few things that have only one right way.

## GET HELP IF YOU'RE CROSSING THE LINE

If you find yourself obsessing about your home you may benefit from hands-on cognitive-behavioral therapy. Excessive perfectionism at home can be a sign of trouble elsewhere in your life.

### Should You See a Therapist?

Some problems are too big to cope with alone. If you find that you're really struggling with emotional issues, consider seeing a therapist. I'm biased toward therapy—I am a therapist, after all. But even so, I believe there are times in life when sitting down with an expert can do a lot of good. It forces you to look at your thought patterns and behaviors through another's eyes.

There are a number of different kinds of therapists. Cognitive-behavioral therapists like me look at thoughts and behaviors. We help patients recognize and restructure maladaptive behavior patterns and cognitive distortions. Cognitive-behavioral therapy is very effective for mood disorders such as depression and anxiety and less effective for personality disorders, bipolar disorder, and schizophrenia.

Some patients need medication during therapy, and others do just fine without it.

To find a qualified therapist, ask your primary care physician for a referral. Other places to look are hospital psychology departments and the British Association for Counselling and Psychotherapy (www.bacp.co.uk).

Feel free to interview a therapist over the phone before making an appointment. Even five minutes of conversation can give you a good sense of whether the therapist's personality and approach mesh with yours. People interview me over the phone all the time. I'm a pretty chatty therapist, and that works for some people and turns others off.

Chemistry is crucial. I saw a new patient recently who told me, after the first appointment, that I had given her more insight in fifty minutes than her previous therapist had given her in four years. It's not that I'm a better therapist—it just means we were a great fit. I felt like I really understood her. The opposite happens, too—I'll see a patient and we just won't click. When that happens, I have no problem with the patient choosing a different therapist.

Finally, remember that a well-known therapist is not necessarily the right therapist for you. Someone who has been interviewed on television, quoted in the newspaper, or written a book may not be a great therapist—just because the media thinks she's good doesn't mean she is. Even if a therapist comes highly recommended from a friend, she may not be the right person for you. Personal style plays a huge part in the therapist-patient relationship, and if your styles clash, your therapy may be less effective. Go with your gut on a decision like this.

# CHAPTER 7

# Find Happiness at Work

*M*y job requires me to do a lot of speaking engagements. Sometimes my friends poke fun at me because I get so stressed out
ahead of time, even though I could do these speeches in my sleep. But
I don't want to make mistakes. I want to do them perfectly—I want
to have the answers to everything that might be asked, and I want to
be articulate when I respond to questions. If I don't have an answer
or don't answer articulately enough, I tend to beat myself up about it
afterward.

My company is launching a new review process, called a 360
review. Everyone who works under me is going to be evaluating me.
That's seventy people. I do a good job, but I know I make mistakes,
too. I'm scared to death about what people are going to say about me.
I know they like working with me—well, I'm pretty sure they do.

It's impossible to make everyone happy. I intellectually know
that, but my wanting to do everything perfectly and respond to what
everyone needs when they need it conflicts with reality. I think the
way to do the job is to do what you can, delegate what you can, and
let go of the need to have everyone's approval all the time, which is
not something I'm particularly good at. I'd just as soon have everyone
like me. But that's unrealistic. I know that there will be negative

*comments. I'll be disappointed, but I have to prepare myself because I know they're coming. I think there are some people who are just complainers, and that's going to come through. Maybe in my heart of hearts I think other people feel I'm not doing my job well enough. I think I'm my own harshest critic.*

*I have a pretty demanding job. A lot of times I have to do work at home on the weekends. I also travel a fair amount. I second-guess myself about working so much. My husband's salary is substantially lower than mine. If our salaries and earning capacities were flipped, I probably would have stayed home with my children. But I can't see not working because of the discrepancy in earning capacity. I just wouldn't feel comfortable living on my husband's salary. I think it has something to do with the way I grew up. My parents separated when I was a kid, and I felt their anxiety over money. I always felt that I had to find a way to take care of myself—not in case my husband and I split up, but because he's older than I am, and if anything happens to him, I have to be prepared to take care of myself and my children. I tend to be much more practical about those kinds of things. I feel like there's so much riding on my job performance.*

*—Amy*

The workplace is a minefield for anyone with the tendency to be a perfectionist. At home and in our personal lives we may *feel* like our performance is being judged, but at work, our performance really *is* being judged. The pressure to succeed is quite real, and the ramifications of failure can be substantial.

But that doesn't make perfectionism an effective strategy at work. In fact, it can cause a lot of unnecessary problems. Perfectionism in the workplace sets the stage for job dissatisfaction, procrastination, disagreements with coworkers, lower ratings on performance reviews, and loads of stress that can spill over from work into your home life.

At certain times, having perfectionist tendencies at work makes

Be Happy Without Being Perfect

sense. I want my accountant to be a perfectionist when she's preparing my taxes, and I want the obstetrician who's doing my C-section to be a perfectionist. But there are plenty of times at work when insisting on perfection is a disadvantage rather than an advantage. For example, a writer who wants her work to be perfect may spend so much time checking it over that she can never complete her assignments on time. A supervisor who insists on perfection will be unable to delegate and will end up working eighteen-hour days because she does too many tasks herself.

Aiming to do your job with excellence is healthy; expecting to do it perfectly is unrealistic and sets you up for disappointment, shame, anxiety, depression, and anger. An accountant who double-checks every figure is being thorough; but she's going too far down the perfectionism hole if she freaks out because her husband forgets to write down one expenditure in the checkbook.

We think of paying attention to detail as a positive quality, and many times it is. But often paying attention to detail causes you to lose track of the big picture, as it does for Barbara:

> *I hold an academic position, and I need to publish my work. I don't publish as much as I should because I'm always trying to improve my work. I'm hampered by this constant feeling that it's not as good as it should be, that I should be doing more, that there are things I haven't done.*
>
> *When I review other people's papers, I realize that my work is better than so much of what is published. I wish I could accept my work as being good enough, and just get it out there. But it never meets my standards. Finally, when the work is published, I look at it and I feel satisfied. Only then do I feel it's good enough.*

The fact is, being a perfectionist at work doesn't necessarily mean you're doing a really good job. Say that on Monday your boss gives you three tasks to do by Friday. If you spend Monday, Tuesday, Wednesday, and Thursday doing task number 1 perfectly, you may not have time to do tasks number 2 and 3 on Friday. Then you have to ask for a deadline extension.

It depends on the situation, of course, but in most cases, a boss would rather have all three jobs done adequately (and on time) than one job perfectly done and the other two late. It's hard to let go of details, but at work, it's sometimes the most effective strategy.

In this chapter I'll describe some of the ways perfectionism can sabotage workplace success. I'll also tell you about tools that can help you cut down on perfectionism and feel happier on the job.

## Women at Work

Compared to men, women face some unique challenges at work because of the way we're wired and socialized. For eons, men went off to work and women took care of the children and the home. Their female characteristics—the ability and desire to nurture, empathize, and form bonds with others—helped them succeed for thousands of years. The cavewomen who knew best how to nurture their children passed along their genes. We're wired to take care of others, and that drive is socially enhanced throughout our lives when we see other women caring for children, elderly parents, and other family members.

We are motivated differently than men in the workplace: A recent LLuminari study found that men are fired by a desire for money and power; women, on the other hand, appreciate social interactions—their relationships with people are their motivating force. Working with a supportive team and having time flexibility is far more important for women than men. When a patient of mine received a promotion recently, she chose an extra week of vacation rather than a pay increase. At this point in her life, time is more valuable than money.

Unfortunately, these qualities don't necessarily lead to success in the world of work. Even though millions of women in America work outside the home, most offices, factories, schools, hospitals, and other workplaces continue to operate with rules and traditions that were forged by men.

This adds a layer of challenges for all women, but especially for perfectionist women.

Women in the workplace are expected to perform as well as men, but most are juggling more responsibilities than their male coworkers. Most workplace routines, demands, and schedules clash with the needs of working mothers, as Arlie Russell Hochschild writes in her book *The Second Shift*:

> *The housewife pays a cost by remaining outside the mainstream of social life. The career woman pays a cost by entering a clockwork of careers that permits little time or emotional energy to raise a family. Her career permits so little of these because it was originally designed to suit a traditional man whose wife raised his children.*

A great study done by researchers at Harvard and the University of Arizona found that on average, men worry about three things on a daily basis—money, their job, and their immediate family—while women on average worry about twelve things (money, their job, their immediate family, their extended family, their friends, how their home looks, etc.). It's easier to keep up with three things than twelve.

At work, men do a much better job of pushing aside other areas of concern and zeroing in on their jobs. That's harder for women—and for perfectionist women in particular. Your desire to be a really good mother doesn't stop when you walk into work. Your wish to be thin doesn't stop when you walk into work. If you're a perfectionist at home, unmade beds and dusty furniture weigh heavily on your mind when you're at work. Every area in which you have perfectionist tendencies follows you onto the job. So does the tendency to beat yourself up when you don't do what you "should" at work. If someone brings in donuts and you eat three, you think about it all day. If your child cries when you drop her off at daycare, you think about it all morning. All of the things you're juggling come into work with you.

# Working Mothers

I gave a stress-management lecture recently at a Fortune 500 company and the women told me there was a war going on between the women with kids and the women without kids. The mothers leave work promptly at 5 p.m., but the nonmothers were expected to stay later. This caused a lot of friction—the women without children resented the women who left on time. The women who left on time felt guilty doing less work than their childless coworkers. But if you have to pick your kids up from day-care by 6 p.m. you have no choice. You've got to leave.

Sometimes, working mothers realize that the best strategy is to put the brakes on their careers while their children are small. This can feel excruciating to perfectionists, as it does for Denise:

*After my daughter was born, I decided to work four days a week instead of five. The people I work with were* not *happy about it. To succeed in my line of work you really have to be on-call all the time. But I put my stake in the ground. As a result, I am no longer a central part of my organization, as I had been. I feel like I'm on the bench. As a type A, it's hard to be on the periphery. I don't spend much time with senior management, so my work isn't noticed. It's hard, because I'm competitive. I have to check my pride at the door and think about what I have, not what I'm giving up. When I see someone else ascending in the company, I think that should be me. I have to talk myself off that ledge. If I got back into the mosh pit, though, my lifestyle would suffer.*

Women go to work, but they don't leave behind their caretaking duties. When my elderly mother developed health problems, I kept my cell phone on at work so she could call me anytime. Now I leave it on for my kids. I make home-related calls at work—you can't call the pediatrician or the electrician at night. Like most working mothers, I don't stop thinking about all the stuff going on in my life just because I'm at work.

If you're a perfectionist at home and at work, it's impossible to be the employee you want to be and the mother you want to be. Or if you are, you pay a price. I have a patient who works so much she uses two nannies. She barely sees her three kids on weekdays, but her weekends are devoted entirely to her children, from morning till night. I asked her when she had time for herself, and she said never. She's maintaining in her own mind that she's a very good mom and a very good employee, but she's lost herself. She's depressed and anxious. There's nothing in her life but her job and her children. There's nothing that nourishes her soul.

## We Asked Women . . .

### How has perfectionism affected you at work?

*I feel like I have to do more when I see that others aren't doing their share. My partners and I are supposed to take turns doing a daily 7 a.m. teleconference. For a while they were dropping the ball, so I ended up doing them all. Looking back now I see that it was nutty for me to do that.*

*—Jessica*

*I was pretty intolerant of the people working around me because I felt they were not working to the level that I was. I took some time off to figure out how I could be happy in my work. I decided to start my own business, and I've been happy ever since. I have no employees—I can be a perfectionist all by myself. I have been in situations where I couldn't take on work because I couldn't do it all by myself. People ask me why I don't hire someone to help out, but I'm not happy having someone working for me and not working up to my standards. It's self-imposed.*

*—Carol*

*I am a photographer, and I print my own photos. One of the aspects of printing photos is that inevitably there is dust on the negative that shows up as little white dots on the print. You can get rid of them by inking them out. This was a real source of anxiety for me when I first started because I didn't know how far to go. If there were three big white globs, I knew I had to take care of them. But the more I looked, the more I'd find. I'd spend an hour finding these spots that just weren't noticeable. I really felt stupid because I would see them, and I knew other people wouldn't, yet I felt compelled to go on.*

*—Patricia*

*I notice myself wasting time at work rewriting a list of to-do's or a note to myself because it's not neat enough or has a scribble on it. It's ridiculous, but I'm just not satisfied, or I can't see past the messiness or disorganization to the actual things I need to get done until my lists are written cleanly and beautifully.*

*—Stephanie*

## Tools You Can Use

How can you reign in your perfectionist tendencies at work? Here are my suggestions.

### RETRAIN YOUR BRAIN

The workplace offers fertile ground for all kinds of distorted thinking: All-or-nothing thinking, black-and-white thinking, using mental filters, catastrophizing, using "should" statements, and approval seeking. Many of these crop up frequently among working women. Cognitive distortions like these lodge themselves into your mind and become automatic thoughts that feel as comfortable as a pair of worn-in slippers. The secret to reducing perfectionism and stress at work is to identify these auto-thoughts, challenge them, and replace them with more realistic ones.

Spend a week or two writing down all of your auto-thoughts at work. Then, use the cognitive restructuring instructions in Chapter 2 to challenge them. Do they make sense? Are they realistic? Are they perfectionistic? Are they necessary? Do they add to the quality of the work you do? Do they reduce your work satisfaction?

Once you've identified and challenged your thoughts, keep the useful, sensible ones and restructure the cognitive distortions to make them more realistic. Write down your restructured thoughts and look at them every day— it will take some time for the new, constructive auto-thoughts to replace the old, unhelpful ones.

Some examples of auto-thoughts at work:
- The only way to do the job right is my way.
- I can never get everything done.
- I can't start a new project unless everything on my desk is finished.
- Everyone else is doing a better job than I am.
- I should be able to do my job without having to work late or take work home.
- I'm no good at this.
- I blame my boss (or coworkers) for my problems at work.
- If my boss criticizes my work, I'm a failure.
- I can't leave this job because there are no other jobs out there that are right for me.
- My coworkers are a bunch of fools.
- My boss is aware of everything I do.
- It's all my fault that the team didn't reach its goal.
- If I had a more talented boss my job would be better, my life would be better, and I would be happier.
- If I take time off for personal reasons I won't get a promotion.

## LOOK AT YOUR "UNCONSCIOUS INJUNCTIONS"

Many of us work with assumptions that hold us back. Challenge the "rules" that you labor under, and if they are distorted, use cognitive restructuring to change them.

Some examples of unconscious injunctions:
- I have to get to work before everyone else.
- I shouldn't ask for help.
- I cannot fail. Ever.
- I shouldn't make mistakes.
- I must get perfect reviews.
- I must do my job perfectly in order to get promoted.

So many women hold the unconscious injunction of having to get a perfect performance review. Margaret tells a typical story:

> *My goal has always been to be evaluated as an "outstanding performer" for my annual review at work. I have somehow managed to achieve this annually with the exception of the first year of my professional career. I got the "excellent" instead of "outstanding" rating on my first-ever annual performance review. I bawled my eyes out in the women's washroom for an hour after receiving my review. As a kid I grew up under the unspoken standard of "B is a failing grade" and anything other than an equivalent grade is perceived as failing.*

## EXAMINE WHETHER FEAR OF SUCCESS HOLDS YOU BACK

Perfectionists are most comfortable when they've mastered their domain—if you know how to do your job very well and you can control your work environment to a high degree, you feel relatively content. This feeling of contentment can inhibit you from seeking or accepting promotions, however—being elevated from a comfortable job that you can do in your sleep to a new position that requires a whole new level of mastery can provoke lots of anxiety. Sometimes it makes the most sense to stay in a more comfortable job while your children are small so you can kind of coast through work—that's what I did. I didn't switch jobs until I had completed my family and my younger daughter was a toddler.

Accepting a higher-level job can cause social apprehension if you must leave a team of supportive peers behind—or worse, become their boss. If you feel insecure about your abilities, you may worry that a promotion will put flaws and imperfections—real or imagined—on display in an embarrassing way. You may even fear that people will "see through you" if you rise to a higher job level.

If you're afraid of progressing because of distorted judgments and expectations, you need to look at that. Understanding what thoughts stand behind your behaviors, and whether they're distorted in any way, makes it easier for you to pick the best career-related choices. I'm not saying you have to force yourself to leave a comfortable job so you can scramble up an anxiety-provoking career ladder. Having a comfy job that fits like an old sweater may be the best thing for you at this point in your life. But I do think it's important to have a reality-based awareness of what motivates you so that the work you choose to do is a real choice and not just an anxiety-based default.

## BASE YOUR EXPECTATIONS ON YOUR EMPLOYER'S

Perfectionists are very detail-oriented, and we are often our own worst critics. We check things over and over, and never quite feel like our work is good enough. But not every project has to be done perfectly.

If you're not sure what needs A-plus effort and what can be done just adequately, think carefully about what your employer wants. If you feel comfortable doing so, work with your boss to set expectations. There's no point wasting time doing something perfectly if your boss is happy with "good enough." What satisfies you as a perfectionist may be far more than what your employer actually needs. When you're doing a project, ask yourself: What are my employer's expectations on this? You don't have to get an A-plus on every task.

*I've finally accepted that my best can be imperfect—I've learned that as I got older. For instance, if I'm writing a brochure or news release, and I don't know what to write, I can give myself permission to do a shitty first draft. If it's still not as perfect as I want it to be, but it's the best I can do, I'm OK sharing it with my client at that time. I work with deadlines, so I have to be realistic. But it still bothers me if I'm not completely happy with the work. I feel guilty and disappointed when I don't meet my own expectations, but I try to let that go. I see details my clients don't notice, and if they're happy, that's what matters; it's OK if I'm not 100 percent satisfied with my own work.*

—Carol

## TREAD LIGHTLY IF YOU'RE THE BOSS

Perfectionism can really get in the way if you're an employer or manager. Not only do you subject yourself to your attention to detail and drive to do things perfectly, but you inflict it on your employees, too. Perfectionists find it excruciating to delegate tasks because they feel that nobody can do a task as well as they can. "I recently found myself copying a big report at work because I didn't like the way my secretary lined up the edge of the document," says Gloria, a senior manager. "She was having a cup of coffee while I was sweating over the output key." Unless you have perfectionists working for you, nobody can live up to your standards.

If this describes you, you have to take a step back. First of all, you've got to delegate, or you'll be working eighty-hour weeks, as Nancy has discovered: "I like to be in control, but there are some areas where I know to let go. I am a manager, and I am able to let people do things their own way. Otherwise if I try to tell them to do it a different way or redo things myself, I would never get any of my own work done."

Be Happy Without Being Perfect

When you give someone a task, be very clear about the minimum standards of acceptance. Be aware that it's fair to expect their work to be acceptable, but not to assume it will be superlative. When the work is handed in and it's not as good as you wanted, ask yourself: Does it meet the minimum standards of acceptance? If not, what's the best tack—to redo it yourself or to give it back to the employee with suggestions on how to make it good enough? Although it's tempting to just do it yourself, that may insult your employees. Better to let them fix it, so they can learn and take pride in it.

Remind yourself that working for a perfectionist is not easy. You have a choice—be more flexible in your standards and judgments, or expect high turnover among your staffers. If you want to avoid spending huge chunks of time looking for new employees to replace the ones who quit or are fired because of your perfectionism, take a good look at how you view your workers and whether your expectations are realistic.

As a perfectionist boss, you have to have a mantra: "How good does it need to be?" When the work needs to be perfect, then insist on it being done perfectly. If good enough is good enough, then settle for it. Demanding that everyone do everything perfectly all the time will frustrate you and everyone else.

A manager who has nobody else at her level to bounce ideas around with may struggle to figure out how perfectly a job has to be done. An employee can talk things over with her colleagues, but when you're the boss you don't always have that option. In this situation, I recommend a team approach. Sit down with your employees and ask for their input about how well they think the job has to be done. Tell them, "I know I have high expectations and I know they're unrealistic sometimes, so let's work as a team to find something we all feel comfortable with." The team approach will elicit more buy-in from your employees. Plus, it will give you valuable perspective—if everyone agrees that 80 percent is good enough on a job that you think should be 100 percent, it may be time for you to reevaluate your expectations. (It may also mean you have a team full of slackers, but that's a whole different issue.) If your employees see that you're trying to be less exacting about some things, they'll be more likely to crank up their efforts for the projects or tasks that really do require perfect work.

## SCHEDULE CALMNESS

If at all possible, plan your schedule so that you can start and end your day on a peaceful note. Avoid scheduling any meetings for the first and last hours of the day. In the morning, use the time to plan the day's tasks. At the end of the day, use the time for doing low-stress tasks such as returning phone calls and e-mails, cleaning up the day's loose ends. That way you have fewer things hanging over you when you're at home.

Cultivate calmness wherever possible. Be organized (but not over-organized). Keep your desk neat—studies show employers and coworkers think less of sloppy workers—but not too neat, because then you look neurotic and not busy enough.

When you feel stressed at work, take a moment to do a mini relaxation (see Chapter 2). A mini takes only a moment, and you can do one while you're in a meeting, on the phone, listening to a ranting customer, or waiting for a fax to arrive. Mini relaxations calm and refresh you in the time it takes to count to twenty.

## REWARD GOOD BEHAVIOR

As any child-development expert can tell you, positive reinforcement works better than negative reinforcement—rewards are more effective than punishment. If you're trying to change your behavior, stop procrastinating, meet deadlines, or get moving on a project that's weighing heavily on your mind, think of something special you can give yourself when you succeed. When I wrote my dissertation, I gave myself five M&Ms for each page. Instead of beating myself up for imperfections in what I was writing, I rewarded myself for my accomplishments. The goal is not to be hard on yourself when you are engaging in perfectionist

Be Happy Without Being Perfect

behavior, and to reward yourself when you're not. The outside world isn't going to give you the acknowledgment you need, so you have to give it to yourself.

## DO COMPARE YOURSELF TO OTHERS

I know, you thought I was going to tell you not to compare yourself to your coworkers. But if you're a perfectionist, comparisons can offer good perspective. It's easy to sit at your workstation in your own little world thinking that everyone around you is doing as good a job as you are—or better. But you know what? They probably aren't—and you can learn from them. Look around. Do your coworkers arrive at work later than you? Do they take longer lunch breaks? Do they occasionally skip meetings? Do they hand in work that isn't 100 percent perfect? Do they send out e-mails with occasional typos? If they do, and they don't get fired, maybe you can let up a bit and slack off sometimes, too. Balance what you are doing with what others are doing. You're probably far harder on yourself than others are on themselves.

It depends on the job, of course, but some employers are OK with you arriving late once in a while, leaving early, or taking a long lunch—provided you're getting your work done. In other words, do the job, not the time. If your employer is flexible about time, it's probably fine to spend a few minutes at work doing your online holiday shopping or having a phone meeting with your child's teacher if you're all caught up on your work.

Ground yourself in reality when comparing yourself to others. Perfectionists are famous for making very uneven comparisons. For example, a perfectionist who's in sales may compare her numbers with those of the department manager, rather than her peers. Or a working mother may feel that she's not working hard enough when she compares herself to a single twentysomething who is free to stay at work until 9 p.m. every day. If you make comparisons between yourself and others, be sure you're being fair to yourself.

# PONDER YOUR RUMINATION HABITS

Women tend to have excellent communication skills, in part because we are good at inferring meanings, reading body language, and listening thoughtfully. The downside of this is that we have a terrible habit of ruminating on observations and criticisms and taking from them much more than the speaker intended. We analyze everything we hear, and if we have perfectionist tendencies, we tend to interpret remarks in the worst possible way. We view everything through the prism of our own insecurities, as Anna describes:

> *When a fault of mine is exposed, or when actual, implied, or potential criticism is raised, my "perfectness" is threatened, and I am unhappy. Today was a day off from my job. A colleague called to tell me that something I worked on yesterday sent a client into a tizzy. She said the client freaked and called my supervisor and sent e-mails complaining about the state of the project (but not necessarily about me). My morning had been going really well, but this news ruined it. I was in tears with a good friend at lunch as I told her the story. Because I assumed that I was being faulted for this client's freak-out, I could not be happy—though I feel better, having spoken it out with a trusted and respected friend.*

This is a bigger problem if you work with men, because men don't pay as much attention to communication—they have less of a filter between their brains and their mouths. Look at how boys speak to each other— they talk trash and trade insults and let criticisms roll right off their backs. The same is true with many men. They can say harsh things even when they don't really mean them.

If someone makes an offhand comment that upsets you—for example, if your boss said, "You look tired today!"—don't presume the worst. Make a list of all of the remark's possible meanings, and challenge

Be Happy Without Being Perfect

the auto-thought belief that the speaker had the most offensive meaning in mind. The more you can defuse a comment, the better able you'll be to let it go and move on to other, more productive thoughts.

Perfectionist women are famous for using the cognitive distortion known as "mental filter." Someone says five good things and one bad thing, and what do we do? We filter out the good and focus on the bad. Or when we receive a compliment on a task well done, we disqualify it by belittling the quality of the work. When that happens, challenge your thoughts and try to restructure them in a more realistic, beneficial way.

Here's a good exercise to do. Write down a list of the strengths you bring to your job. After you've listed everything you can think of, take some time to study the list and meditate on your strengths. Give yourself permission to be proud of what you do well, to think about how good it feels when you accomplish something. Refer back to the list when you're feeling negative about yourself or when a destructive auto-thought is going through your head. Use it as evidence against cognitive distortions that dog you.

## CHALLENGE YOUR PEOPLE-PLEASING HABITS

Perfectionists are notorious people-pleasers at work. We want everyone at work to like us, from the top manager to the guy who empties the trash. Women tend to be people-pleasers—many of us were raised that way.

Unfortunately, people-pleasing requires a huge amount of time and energy, and it can trigger anxiety and depression. People-pleasing ultimately ends in failure because it is impossible to please everyone.

Of course, some people-pleasing is necessary at work—if you don't please your boss, you'll be out of a job. And to some extent, giving coworkers and employers what they need paves the way for success and congeniality. But trying too hard to please everyone, to want everyone to like you, is not a healthy behavior, as clinical psychologist Harriet B. Braiker, Ph.D., describes in her wonderfully helpful book, *The Disease to*

*Please*: "The dilemma you face is that in staying so finely tuned to the real and perceived needs of others, you often turn a deaf ear to your own inner voice that may be trying to protect you from overextending yourself and from operating against your own self-interests."

How can people-pleasers change their ways? Developing awareness of your own people-pleasing patterns is the best place to start. Using the list of behaviors below, identify your own people-pleasing habits. Write them down in your journal, and spend some time reflecting on how you can change your behavior. Start small, by speaking up at a meeting or saying no to a small favor. Express some of your emotions rather than holding them in. Put your needs first sometimes. It will feel uncomfortable in the beginning, but over time the discomfort will subside.

## Some of the Most Common People-Pleasing Behaviors

- Putting others' needs before yours.
- Keeping your opinion to yourself because you think it will upset others.
- Saying yes to every request.
- Feeling guilty when you say no.
- Feeling selfish when you do something for yourself.
- Suppressing emotions because you fear that if you express them, you'll upset others.
- Feeling that you have no control over your life.
- Avoiding confrontation.
- Appearing perennially happy even when you're not.
- Going out of your way to appease others.
- Feeling crushed by criticism or disapproval.

Cognitive distortions lurk behind most people-pleasing impulses. A commonly held automatic thought among people-pleasers is "Doing something for myself is selfish." If you can identify your automatic

Be Happy Without Being Perfect

people-pleasing thoughts, challenge them, and restructure them to make them more accurate and constructive, you'll go a long way toward reversing your people-pleasing habits.

## DEVISE A STRATEGY FOR WORKING WITH SLACKERS

Did I say slackers? I meant people who are not perfectionists. It can be hard for perfectionists to work with nonperfectionists. If you find this applies to you, ask yourself whether you are setting unrealistically high expectations for your coworkers by requiring perfect work from them. Don't make the mistake of using all-or-nothing thinking and regarding anyone who's not a perfectionist like you as a completely useless slacker. There is middle ground.

But let's face it: Every workplace has slackers. If you need something from a slacker, figure out a strategy of how to get it. Can you work around them somehow? Can you fudge the deadlines and build in extra time to accommodate their lateness? Try to figure all this out ahead of time, not in the heat of the moment.

You might want to keep your boss in the loop, so when the slacker messes up your boss knows about it. But think very carefully about complaining about the slacker to your boss. Many employers hate to discipline or fire people. It's terribly uncomfortable and training new employees is expensive and time-consuming. As someone who hires and fires (only when I absolutely *have* to), I live in fear of losing employees. If I can't find a replacement quickly, I have a gap that has to be filled (often by me). Be careful about complaining to your boss, because the slacker probably won't be fired, and your relationship will worsen if/when the slacker finds out you've tattled.

Whenever possible, look for common ground and a way to compromise. If you think the project needs 100 percent effort and the slacker thinks it needs only 25, maybe you can both settle agreeably on 50 or 60.

## REEXAMINE "GREENER PASTURES" THINKING

"Greener pastures" thinking is a cognitive distortion that allows you to believe you would be much, much happier if you could leave your job and do something else (staying at home with your children, going back to school, working a better job, and so on). As the saying goes, the grass always seems greener in the other pasture—but once you jump the fence, you find that the grass isn't quite as green as it appeared.

What all this means is if you spend your day hating your job and dreaming about how perfect your life would be if you could quit and be a stay-at-home mom (or whatever), you're doing yourself a disservice. Sure, you might prefer to stay home. But don't think of it in black-and-white terms. The work world isn't all bad and the home world all good (and vice versa). If you're a stay-at-home mom, you won't have to cope with the stress of daycare, commuting, dealing with an unreasonable boss, and so on. But you won't be on easy street. At home you'll face a whole new set of challenges—feeling bored, having less money, missing your friends. If you idealize the road not taken, not only will you feel less happy with the choice you've made, but you set yourself up for disappointment if you eventually change course. Happiness comes from inside you, not from your external environment.

## STOP YOURSELF FROM BEING THE "MOM" AT WORK

Women bring a different approach to work than do men. Women lean more toward working in teams, and they tend to care for and support their coworkers in an almost familylike way that engenders commitment, cooperation, and intimacy. There are definite advantages to this approach, because they can give women a sense of belonging. But this "familial" attitude toward the workplace can backfire.

Ilene Philipson, Ph.D., a sociologist and clinical psychologist, worked with groups of women at the University of California, Berkeley, Center for Working Families. Philipson, author of the book *Married to*

Be Happy Without Being Perfect

*the Job: Why We Live to Work and What We Can Do About It*, describes the phenomenon of "bringing the second shift to work." The women she portrays think of their workplace as a home away from home, and in doing so, they take on a motherlike role at work:

> *Based on clinical case studies of women who have come to psy-chotherapy with work-related problems, I have discovered that women refuse to leave commitment, sharing, cooperation, material and emotional obligation, personal loyalty, and a willingness to sacrifice for others at home. They transport these qualities to the workplace. Surprisingly, they also bring with them aspects of the second shift: They routinely bake and cook for coworkers, buy food and candy for them, run personal errands for their supervisors, and vacuum the office and clean the bathrooms secretly after work.*

Women who adopt the role of work-mother not only add to their workload, but they threaten their ability to advance, notes Philipson. They are "taken for granted, as most maternal figures are. Their care is seen as unconditional, offered perhaps too freely. The fact that they seem so eager to please makes them vulnerable to exploitation . . . In today's workplace, to be too identified with a traditional female role is tantamount to not being taken seriously, diminishing one's chances for advancement and achievement in a work world defined in opposition to familism."

Take a look at yourself. Are you taking on the chores of a work-mother? Are you constantly organizing parties, planning potlucks, passing around birthday cards, and cleaning out the office refrigerator? As Philipson notes, does your self-esteem, sense of belonging, identity, and purpose seem to revolve around work? If the answer to any of these questions is yes, your relationship with your job may merit further reflection.

## WEAR WHAT'S EASY

Shopping for, cleaning, folding, and ironing work clothes takes a huge amount of time, especially if your perfectionism keeps you ironing until every last wrinkle is banished. Make dressing for work as easy on yourself as possible. Buy clothes that don't require a trip to the drycleaner or a stint on the ironing board. Choose darker colors, so stains don't show. Select styles that stay in fashion indefinitely—don't dress like a slob, but don't go for the spinster look, either. Most women can't go wrong with black pants, a black blazer, and a rainbow of shells that give the outfit a different look on different days. Jazz up your look with colorful scarves, bold jewelry, or a cool purse or belt. Pick skirts and slacks with a little give, so you won't beat yourself up when you gain a pound or two and your waistline feels tight. Wear sensible, easy-to-care-for clothes. You'll save yourself time, money, effort, and opportunities for self-criticism.

## WATCH OUT IF YOU WORK FROM HOME

Whether you're self-employed or telecommute for a company, working at home can be a difficult situation for perfectionists. When you work from home, there's no escaping the job. It's easy to work at night, on the weekends, and in the middle of the night when you can't sleep because you're obsessing about that one tiny detail you may have forgotten.

If you work at home, it's important to set firm boundaries between your home life and your work life. Create physical boundaries by locating your workspace in a room with a door (if possible) so that at the end of the day you can physically walk away from your work and not return until the next workday. Create time boundaries by setting a strict work schedule and sticking to it. If you work on a computer, you can even set electronic barriers by having a home e-mail address and a work e-mail address that you use only for work-related messages. That way you won't be coming across work-related notes when you're checking to see if any of your friends have been in touch.

# TAME YOUR TO-DO LIST

How often does this happen to you: You start to write down everything that needs doing. Before you know it, there are thirty items on the list. Frustrated, you realize you can't possibly get them all done. You feel defeated before you even finish writing the list. You end up spending more time panicking about what you have to do than actually doing it.

You can circumvent this frustration by changing the way you write your to-do list. Here's what I recommend:

- Make three lists: One of what *must* get done today (list A), one of what you would *like* to do (list B), and one of what has to be done eventually, but not immediately (list C). Already your to-do list feels less intimidating, because the only one that really matters is list A. Set out to accomplish your list A tasks and then move on to list B and list C. This can be hard for a perfectionist, because we think *everything* needs immediate attention and deserves list A status. If you aren't sure what belongs on list A, look at it through your employer's eyes: What would he put on list A? What would he relegate to list B or list C?
- As tasks present themselves during the day, triage them onto one of your lists. When something that needs doing pops up during the workday, it's tempting to take care of it right away. Resist that temptation—if it's not a list A task, set it aside and do it later.
- Check to see if the tasks on your lists really are your responsibility. Are you doing someone else's work, perhaps because her work doesn't live up to your expectations? Can you embrace more reasonable expectations and delegate some of the work that doesn't have to be 100 percent perfect?
- Be realistic when you're scheduling your day. Don't underestimate how much time a job will take—if it's a three-hour job, don't wedge it into a two-hour slot. Not only will the job not get done, but you'll feel frustrated because you'll feel like you've failed. If possible, slot a

Find Happiness at Work

three-hour job into a four-hour time period. Then if unexpected interruptions occur, you'll still have a chance of finishing the job on schedule. And if you finish early, you'll feel great.

- Set realistic goals that are based on what you *can* do, not what you *should* do. Tasks on a can-do list can be accomplished. A should-do list never ends and leaves you feeling overwhelmed and discouraged.

- Compartmentalize your day. Grouping similar jobs saves time because you don't have to keep switching gears. For example, instead of checking e-mail throughout the day, look at it only during the first and last hours of your day. Try to do all of your personal tasks at once (first thing in the morning, if possible)— call the doctor, e-mail your son's teacher, schedule a massage. Then you can put them aside and focus on work.

- Compartmentalizing your week can help, too. My cowriter tries to schedule all interviews, appointments, meetings, and doctor visits on Tuesdays, Wednesdays, and Thursdays so she has large chunks of uninterrupted writing time on Mondays and Fridays.

- Finally, try compartmentalizing your work life and home life. It doesn't work for everyone, but women such as Betty feel it is the best way to work effectively and enjoy life outside of their jobs:

*I'm pretty good at sectioning off my work life from my home life, but it's harder to keep the home life out of the work world. You've got the phone calls and the routine doctor's appointments, scheduling pick-ups for hockey games, and all that. Up until a few years ago, I'd lose sleep over big work projects. Lately, though, I've been able to compartmentalize and put it in perspective. It's a job, and I want to do it well, but I don't want to come home thinking about it. I want to leave it in the office and when I get home focus on getting the home-work done and hearing about preschool. It's focusing on what's really*

Be Happy Without Being Perfect

*important. I had to learn how to shut it off. It came over time. It's a*
*matter of getting my attitude in the right place.*

## DON'T LET YOUR FEARS OF A JOB LOSS CHOKE YOU

Losing your job is a real threat in today's workplace, and it's especially worrisome if your finances are tight.

Part of what bothers perfectionists most about potential layoffs is the lack of control. It's disturbing to know that at any time, despite your performance, you could be laid off because of events that are outside your control, such as your company's merger with another company. When this anxiety flares up, think of it this way: Although you don't always have the power to control life events, you do have the power to control how you react to them. You can't control whether you are laid off, but you can control your response to a layoff. You can decide right now—don't wait for a layoff to occur—that if you lose your job, you will make the best of the situation, consider it an opportunity for positive change, and refuse to let it ruin your life. Make up your mind that although a layoff might cause financial and career-related difficulties, you firmly believe that you will find ways to wring some benefits from it (even if you have no idea right now what the benefits might be). If you focus on what you can control—your reaction—you can reduce the anxiety produced by events like this.

That said, if there are layoff rumors in the air, take steps now to put yourself in the best light possible. Working mothers feel especially threatened by the thought of layoffs because of their family obligations—you may worry that if a layoff is planned, the fact that you left early one day last week to take your daughter to the orthodontist will put you at the top of the layoff list.

If you're worried about losing your job, be up-front with your employer. If you're going to be an hour late, tell her that you'll work through your lunch hour or take work home. Show her that you are dedicated to your work and not taking your job for granted. If you're blithe or sneaky, your boss won't think of you as a serious team player. There are ways of doing what you need to do without looking bad to your employer.

*I used to be such a perfectionist at work. That was fine when I worked in marketing—there was never a typo in my copy, never a photo mistake. At one point I owned my own business and was handling all of the marketing in three states for a major company. My perfectionism served me well in that job. I was rewarded for my attention to detail.*

*Eventually my perfectionism got in my way. I took on a job that required give-and-take with people. I couldn't play the politics. I finally began to understand how limiting myself to "perfect" was holding me back. Everyone used to joke and call me "Miss Perfect." That wasn't what I wanted written on my tombstone.*

*I'm retired now. Recently the opportunity fell into my lap to housesit in France. It required me to live in a foreign country—really live there, not just be a tourist. I had to shop, have holes in the roof fixed, put gas in the car, deal with a broken water heater, all with my imperfect French. I can speak tourist French, but that wasn't what I needed to get someone to fix a hole in a tile roof during a wind storm. It was a humbling experience in many ways. I decided to just let myself go and try to speak the language even though I'm not very good at it. Believe me, the French people correct you when you make a mistake.*

*It was a wonderful experience, because it's helped me let go of my personal perfectionism. I have finally learned to say good enough is OK, things don't have to be perfect. I don't have to be perfect. There's no such thing as a perfect world.*

—Linda

CHAPTER 8

# Find Joy in Relationships

*I don't think I recognized that I was a perfectionist until I got married and I began to see myself in my husband's eyes. He started telling me constantly that the bed didn't need to be made perfectly as soon as I got up, that store-bought desserts are acceptable, and that every social obligation did not have to be returned within a certain number of days. But the problems started not so much with his pointed observations about my behavior, but when I began to turn my expectations of perfection onto him. Dating was pretty easy, then I got caught up with the frenzy of planning a wedding, but when we moved into the same apartment it started getting intense. I began to get annoyed when he left a bath mat on the floor, when he left the table and didn't wipe up the crumbs, and even by how loud he was with his friends when watching a game on television.*

*But my issues with him as a housemate pale in comparison to my current issues with him as a father. I am embarrassed to say this since I hate it in myself, but I know that I am constantly criticizing him even though deep down I know he is a great husband and father. I work part-time and only have to travel twice a year for meetings. Before I go I type up these dissertation-length pages of*

*instructions, reminders, and suggestions. I call every day to talk to*
*the kids but also to check in to make sure that he is doing everything*
*right—i.e., my way. When I get home, I look right past the fact that*
*the kids are happy, healthy, fed, and that they made it to all or at*
*least most of their activities. I focus on the sloppily made beds, the*
*pile of laundry, the pizza boxes in the garage, and his unshaved face.*
*And I don't keep it to myself; he knows what I am thinking either*
*directly or indirectly.*

*So we fight a lot, always with the same theme. He feels that he*
*is doing a good job and all he hears from me is what he didn't do or*
*how he could do things better. I am afraid that he is going to leave*
*me for a more easygoing woman, one who appreciates the fact that*
*he is a good wage-earner, that he would never cheat, that he doesn't*
*drink or mistreat any of us.*

*Why can't I see all the good he does, and how good he really is?*
*Why do I have to nitpick at him all the time?*

*—Gloria*

Having fulfilling relationships of all kinds is important to women. We
rely on our partner, friends, families, and coworkers for friendship,
emotional support, and advice. We are, even more than men, wired to be
social creatures. When faced with stress, men tend to go it alone, says
Marianne J. Legato, M.D., author of the book *Why Men Never Remember
and Women Never Forget*. "By contrast, women respond to stress by reaching out to other people, especially other women. They bond, they talk
about their issues, and they recruit help. This response may not only help
them to cope with the immediate threat, but protect them against the
ravages of stress in general."

Women are biologically designed to seek social support. When a
woman feels isolated, her blood levels of the hormone oxytocin rise.
"This not only calms her, but it prompts her to get help, in the form of
bonding with others, especially other women," Legato says. If you've
nursed a baby, you know the power of oxytocin firsthand: It is one of the

hormones that is released during and after childbirth and is credited with helping to form the bond between women and their babies.

Unfortunately, unrealistic expectations can sabotage a woman's chances of having a happy marriage and gratifying friendships. Because of the way perfectionists view the world, they often struggle to form and maintain relationships of all kinds. For example, perfectionists tend to:

- Have unrealistically high expectations of others and feel that others have unrealistically high expectations of them.
- Believe that others are constantly judging them, criticizing them, and feeling dissatisfied with them.
- Feel hypersensitive to criticism from others.
- Be reluctant to form relationships with others for fear of being rejected or looking foolish.
- Form shallow relationships because they are unwilling to open up to others and risk exposing their imperfections.
- Engage in approval-seeking behaviors in an attempt to make others like them and feel disappointed when others fail to live up to expectations.
- Criticize others, sometimes without even realizing it.

Most women's closest relationship is with a husband or partner, so it's the relationship most affected by her perfectionism. In this chapter, I'll discuss some of the roadblocks that perfectionism can bring into a marriage, along with some great strategies that will help perfectionists turn down the heat a bit. Then I'll offer some explanations about why perfectionists sometimes struggle in their relationships with friends and family, along with advice on how to improve those relationships.

## Bedtime Stories

In my years counseling perfectionist women and their husbands, I have seen one very detrimental cognitive distortion come up over and over:

The belief that if you find your Mr. Right, you'll have a wonderful, near-perfect relationship filled with blissful happiness, great sex, and no fighting beyond an occasional spat about toilet seats or toothpaste caps. You'll understand each other and you'll both be able to meet all of each other's emotional needs. In this distorted fantasy, once you fall in love, your hard work is done. The tough part is finding the ideal man, not keeping him.

I wish this were true, but it's not. The truth is, marriage is really hard. And there's no such thing as a perfect marriage.

I can't criticize my patients for thinking this way because for many years, I did. When I was a child, my parents had more than their share of arguments; they were both European immigrants who shared their "opinions" freely. I remember thinking, when I heard them fighting, that when I got married, true love would protect me from arguments like theirs. The reasoning was simple: If I found someone I *really* loved—my own Mr. Right—then marriage would be clear sailing. Waking up to this person every day of my life would be a joy, we would never argue as my parents had, we would always look at each other with stars in our eyes, and we would function as a seamlessly matched team. You know—the live-happily-ever-after myth that we read about so often as little girls.

I continued to believe this as a young adult even though my experience was showing me the opposite. I spent so much energy in my twenties searching for the man of my dreams—but I could never find him among the mere mortals I dated. One day my roommate, who was engaged, mentioned that she had to work really hard on her relationship with her fiancé. This bewildering comment floored me. I wondered why my roommate would find it so hard to sustain a relationship. I decided that it must have been because she chose Mr. Wrong instead of Mr. Right.

Eventually I wised up and realized that even great marriages require work—many days, you have to make some kind of effort to keep the bond between you strong. I realized that no matter how much you *love* someone, you don't always *like* them. The two of you are not going to

Be Happy Without Being Perfect

get along all the time—you can disagree, argue, feel disappointment, and even feel flat-out disgusted with someone and still love them. Why? Because no spouse is perfect, no relationship is perfect, and no marriage is perfect. And if you harbor the expectation that your significant other *should* be perfect, you're headed for trouble. Take it from Ruth:

*I guess I still have remnants of the "Cinderella" syndrome. I'm waiting for the total Prince Charming to come and sweep me off my feet, keep me swept off my feet, and fulfill all the other romantic notions I have about the way love affairs and marriages should be. I have been married four times. Number four comes the closest to my ideal, yet I still wonder. Will there be a next one because I foolishly still desire my total dream man? Will I ever be able to let go of that illusion? I am still working on this issue.*

## Feelings Change

The first six to twelve weeks of a relationship can be wonderful—that's the getting-to-know-you unconditional love time. He thinks you're perfect, you think he's perfect, and in your imagination you will marry him and have a perfect life. But after that, cracks begin to show. He talks too much about politics. You want to get serious too quickly. He spends too much time with his immature friends. You complain too much about work. And on it goes. A lot of relationships don't make it past this point. Those that do last transition into a more reality-based connection, but whether they realize it or not, many people continue to expect near-perfection from their partners.

My roommate was right: Marriage can be really difficult sometimes. Even a great marriage can go through huge storms—not because the couple is poorly matched (although that's sometimes the reason) but because a successful marriage truly does require work on many, if not most, days. There are times when you're in a really bad place, all your thoughts and feelings are about what *you're* going through, and the last thing on your mind is your husband's emotions (or vice versa). There are times when the two of you feel as close as you were when you first fell in love, and there will be times when you'll ask yourself if you married the wrong person. Having fluctuations like these is normal. Being disappointed by them—and feeling that they shouldn't happen—only compounds the problem.

It's a lot easier to put in the work a marriage requires if you accept some level of imperfection. Acknowledging imperfection and compromise—recognizing that love does not solve every problem—is the first step toward building a deeper, more satisfying relationship. The irony is that if you can let go of the myth of the perfect marriage, your marriage will probably become less imperfect.

## Highs and Lows

When you slide into a low part of your marriage, the first thing to do is acknowledge it. Then consider what action you should take. Should you schedule more time together in the form of date nights, increased sexual encounters, a vacation, or a few long walks? Or should you just be patient and know that something in your life—a new baby, a family illness, a career bump—has gotten in the way, and things will return to normal on their own when the disruption calms down?

Sometimes doing nothing is the answer. It's OK to have space sometimes. All relationships fluctuate in intensity. People are relieved to hear that, because they think a happy marriage is a *Cosby Show* marriage, where husband and wife like each other every minute. That's fantasy. You don't always have to like your spouse to maintain being in love with him. That can be hard for perfectionists, because they think they should feel happy all the time.

People change over time, and hopefully as a couple you'll change in comparable directions. If you have less and less in common, do you have to get divorced? Not necessarily. You can still love someone who is different. You can each pursue interests you like—you don't have to do everything together.

For example, men and women tend to handle obstacles differently: Women like to ruminate, and men like to listen to the problem, come up with a solution, and go back to their newspaper or baseball game. Occasionally when I have a particularly vexing or complicated problem, I like to discuss it at length and examine all possible solutions. Over and over. My husband usually supports me during these times, but occasionally, I need my female friends to step in—they're the ones I can turn to when I need to be listened to, when I have a crisis that I need to talk about and analyze from all angles. It doesn't weaken the bond between me and my husband when I talk to my friends instead of him. Just the opposite—it strengthens our relationship. Expecting that your partner will be the sole source of your happiness is a recipe for disaster.

You can't meet all your partner's needs, and you can't be mad at him for not meeting all of yours. Many people, male and female, expect that if someone loves you they'll know exactly what you need, they'll be able to meet all your needs, and they'll have the capacity to make you happy all the time. That's simply not possible. Compare it to wearing socks on a cold day: You have to wear socks when it's cold because they keep your feet warm. But wearing socks alone certainly won't keep you warm—you also need to wear shoes, pants, a coat, and so on. Having a loving partner is an integral ingredient for happiness for many (not all) women, but it doesn't mean it's the only thing that *can* make you happy or that you need nothing else *to* make you happy. The best husband in the world couldn't give you all the happiness you need.

The perfect husband doesn't exist—and even if he did, you'd still have other problems. A great guy can't make your boss more reasonable or your father less sick or your thighs thinner. He can be your soulmate and a great father to your children, but he can't be your everything.

## Dangerous Perfection

Are you a born perfectionist—or are you trying to be perfect in order to satisfy your partner? Are you afraid of what will happen to you if you let your partner down?

Perfectionism in a relationship can sometimes be a red flag for abuse. It's common in abusive relationships for the man to expect his wife to be perfect and to hurt her if she fails to meet his expectations. Abusive men often want to be in control of their partners; when they perceive that they are losing control, they may become violent.

Women with low self-esteem—a symptom of perfectionism—are more likely to be drawn to abusive men than are women with a strong sense of self.

If your perfectionism is linked to domestic violence, you can get help. A doctor can treat your injuries, document the abuse, and refer you to local programs for abused women. Or contact Women's Aid (www.womensaid.org.uk).

## Not a Clue

You may sometimes feel that your husband is clueless when it comes to giving you what you need. Before you get all annoyed at him, ask yourself: Have I told him what I need, or am I expecting him to read my mind? If, like many perfectionists, you feel that he should just *know* what you need without your telling him, you're wrong. You need to speak up and let your husband know what you want.

A patient of mine who was experiencing difficult medical problems felt terribly frustrated that her husband wasn't doing a good job of helping her to deal with it emotionally. I suggested that he might not *know* how to help her, so maybe she could come up with a list of twenty things he could do to help her cope. She did, and it solved a lot of the misunderstandings between them because when she needed comforting, he didn't have to try to read her mind to figure out what would help—he could just look at the list.

There is no man or woman who can satisfy all his or her partner's needs. That's why it's so important to acknowledge what needs your partner can and can't fulfill. Then you can decide whether to end the marriage or change your expectations and stop getting mad at him for not meeting them all.

## In His Place

Perfectionism can ravage a marriage. Put yourself in his place. Imagine how he feels trying to make love to you when you're feeling anxious about having gained five pounds. Imagine how he feels when you insist on having a spotless kitchen and he knows how upset you'll be if he messes it up. When you were dating, he may have found it cute that you insisted on making the bed with hospital corners, weighed yourself every day, or taped Martha Stewart's shows to watch each night before bed. Some of your perfectionist personality quirks may have attracted him to you. But after a while, it gets annoying living with a perfectionist. Unless he is a perfectionist, too, he just doesn't get why you can't leave the house until the kitchen is clean or why you iron the jeans you wear around the house.

If you project your perfectionism onto your husband, he may feel he can't do anything right. It sends a very destructive mixed message: "I love you as long as you meet my standards. My love is conditional." That's not a good place to be, as the following patient stories show:

- One of my patients told me her husband did nothing to help around the house. When I asked him about it, he told me that early in their marriage he had taken on the task of doing the laundry, but she would stand over him while he was sorting and tell him he was doing it wrong, and then, after he folded it, she would refold it her way. He decided to give up on the laundry.

- A stay-at-home mother complained that when her husband got home from work at night, he'd read the paper or watch television and not talk with her. When I asked him for his side of the story, he said that whenever he talked about his job, his wife would criticize him for the choices he'd make at work. It drove him crazy because he knew more about his business than she did, and he knew he was doing a good job. Yet she constantly passed judgment on him. He gave up talking to her about work because it was too frustrating.
- A patient who travels a lot for business counts on her husband to take care of their children while she's gone. Her husband became very angry with her when she came home from a five-day trip. He felt he had handled everything well—he had cooked meals, gotten the kids to school on time, and made sure their homework was done. When his wife came home, the first thing she noticed was that he hadn't opened all the mail or stacked up the week's newspapers. He was livid that she had ignored all the hard work he did and focused instead on what she considered to be an imperfection. What he wanted to hear was, "What a great job you've done!" but her comments suggested that she considered him incompetent. That's a case where a perfectionist wife was applying truly unrealistic expectations, much to her husband's frustration.

I don't mean to suggest that you should never criticize your husband. If it's winter and he's letting your toddler play outside without a coat, hat, and gloves, he clearly needs a reminder about appropriate winter wear. That's fine. But if you get on his case because he allowed your child to play outside in mismatched mittens, you're going too far.

It's hard to be married to a perfectionist. "There are times when my husband tells me that all I do is criticize him, and it breaks my heart because I love him so much and don't want to hurt him," one of my patients told me. As you work to restructure your perfectionist thinking, remember that your husband will be one of the first people to benefit from it.

# Communication Style

Perfectionism makes things worse because perfectionists think their way of communicating is the "right" way and their spouse's way of communicating is the "wrong" way. Neither way is right or wrong—they are just different.

Accepting and understanding men's and women's differing communication styles makes it easier to interpret each other's messages and explain yourself more clearly. "Once people realize that their partners have different conversational styles, they are inclined to accept differences without blaming themselves, their partners, or their relationships," says Deborah Tannen, Ph.D., author of the eye-opening book *You Just Don't Understand*.

# Nagging

Nagging is one of the most common complaints from the husbands of perfectionist wives. I hear about it all the time when I counsel couples. She nags, he shuts her out, she gets mad that he's not listening to her and nags more, he shuts her out more . . . and on it goes.

Nagging demonstrates a fundamental difference between the ways men and women look at the world. Because status plays a major role in most men's relations, men bristle at being directed because it makes them feel like they are in a lower-status position, according to Tannen. Women, on the other hand, tend to use conversation as a way to reach consensus; because of this tendency, women are more open to direction from others. Tannen writes: "A woman will be inclined to repeat a request that doesn't get a response because she is convinced that her husband would do what she asks if he only understood that she really wants him to do it. But a man who wants to avoid feeling that he is following orders may instinctively wait before doing what she asked, in order to imagine that he is doing it of his own free will. Nagging is the result, because each time she repeats the request, he again puts off fulfilling it."

# We Asked Women . . .

## How has perfectionism affected your relationship with your spouse?

*My husband and I are so preoccupied with our careers, the kids, the house, and going to the gym that I don't see him very much. I just don't have the marriage I thought I would. It's not a perfect marriage, and that disappoints me.*

—Denise

*My husband gets really irritated when it takes me forever to decide on something. He usually buys the first thing he sees—and I usually don't like the first thing that he sees. It causes fighting and conflict.*

—Barbara

*My husband and I go to counseling once in a while just because I believe that if you go to a doctor once a year for your body, why not do the same for your mind?*

—Susan

*My husband brings in the money, and I do everything else because it's so frustrating trying to get him to do what I want. I try to ask him only to do things I can't do by myself. This weekend, all he had to do was to take out one air conditioner that I couldn't lift. All day Saturday it didn't get done; then he started doing it at ten at night. After several furious exchanges, he stopped. He did it the next day. Very frustrating.*

—Sandra

*My need for perfection often spills over to my husband. I have to remind myself that we have different styles. He is not able to juggle more than one project at a time, nor does he like to plan. We are repairing the walkway to our house. I want my husband to come up with a plan on how he intends to complete the project before he starts it. I know that it will take a number of weekends, but he thinks he can just jump right in and do it in one weekend.*

—Rebecca

*Sometimes my husband breathes too loudly while he's sleeping, and I tell him. He would never say something like that to me. If I could figure out how not to be bothered by things like that I could probably be happier.*

—Helen

*I'm pretty particular about how I like things done—for example, setting the table. The fork belongs on the left. If my husband sets the table and puts the fork in the wrong place, I have to catch myself and not change what he's done. In the long run, what does it matter if the fork is not on the left? Part of me feels obsessive/compulsive about it, but that's not it. I just want things to be done the way they should be done.*

—Cheryl

## We Asked Women . . .

### How does perfectionism affect you as a single woman?

*As a thirty-eight-year-old woman who has never been married and is not currently in a relationship, I find that it is the issue that is in the forefront of my mind in virtually all social situations, particularly when I am seeing people I haven't seen in a long time. I feel that I have failed somehow—that I have missed the magic formula that everyone else seems to understand and has figured out. I feel less valuable as a single person.*

—Martha

*I have very high standards. I know that refusing to settle may mean I'll end up alone, but I'm OK with that. I've had an excellent example in my parents. That's the kind of relationship I'm looking for—a relationship from another generation.*

—Mary

*My perfectionism definitely gets in the way with men. No man ever seems good enough for me or for my mother and brother. I know when I* really *like someone because I can look beyond his imperfections and not care that he has a hairy back or crooked teeth.*

—Anna

## Tools You Can Use

Being a perfectionist doesn't have to hold you back from having satisfying relationships with others. The techniques in this chapter can help you build a rich, fulfilling social network.

### RETRAIN YOUR BRAIN

There's an old Hebrew saying that perfectly sums up the meaning of cognitive distortions: "We do not see the world as it is. We see the world as we are." I mention this because I think it applies especially well to relationships. Often we don't see other people as they are, but as we are—especially if we are perfectionists and we expect others to live up to the standards we set for ourselves. Without even realizing it, our own cognitive distortions can give others motives, emotions, and intentions that they don't have. Cognitive distortions can blow others' comments or reactions out of proportion and can affect how we treat the people we love.

Cognitive restructuring can help you do a better job of seeing other people as they are. It allows you to remove a filter that stands between you and others' words and actions so that you can see them more clearly for what they are.

Be Happy Without Being Perfect

One of the most common distortions that crops up in relationships is mind reading. It happens all the time: A friend or loved one is irritable, moody, or short-tempered. If you fall into the trap of mind reading—as most of us perfectionists do—you blame yourself and assume it's your fault. Doing so opens you up to a lot of unnecessary unhappiness.

When you mind read, you usually presume that you are the cause of the other person's bad mood. You hold yourself responsible whether or not there is evidence that you have anything to do with it. Sometimes you even get angry at the person for being angry at you—but you don't really even *know* if the person is angry at you! You might even change your behavior based on what you've concluded from your mind reading, even though it may be completely false.

The problem with mind reading is that it's impossible to know what another person—even your spouse or closest friend—is thinking. A friend may be upset about something that happened at work, but you take it personally because you're assuming she's annoyed that you were fifteen minutes late when you met for lunch.

Instead of trying to read your partner's mind, ask what's up. Say something like, "I'm picking up that you seem irritated. Have I contributed to it? And if so, is there anything I can do to help you feel better?" If you did play a role in his annoyance, you can talk about it and try to straighten things out. If you have nothing to do with it, give him space. It's easier to cope with someone else's bad mood if you understand it and know that you haven't contributed to it.

A number of other cognitive distortions plague relationships as well. Take a look at them to see if any ring a bell with you. If so, use the instructions in Chapter 3 to change your unhelpful thinking patterns.

**Distortion:** Overgeneralization

**Example:** Your husband forgets and launders your favorite hand-wash-only bra by machine; you explode and tell him he messes up every job he ever does around the house.

**Tell yourself:** "At least he's trying—lots of husbands don't even know where the washing machine is. Better to let him do laundry and mess up once in a while than to hound him so much that he gives up on it. I can always buy a new bra."

**Distortion:** Mental filter

**Example:** When your mother visits she compliments your outfit, the house, and the dinner you cooked, but all you can think about is the fact that she pointed out the stain on your toddler's shirt.

**Tell yourself:** "Isn't it amazing that Mom was 75 percent positive!"

**Distortion:** Disqualifying the positive

**Example:** A friend thanks you profusely for volunteering to run the school bake sale; you belittle the comment by telling yourself that it's just a little fundraiser and nothing compared to the Monte Carlo night that she runs every year.

**Tell yourself:** "It was nice of her to take the time to thank me—since she runs so many fundraisers, she knows how much work they can be."

**Distortion:** Mind reading

**Example:** Your partner, who's usually very sociable after dinner, says he wants to be alone; you assume it's because he's annoyed with you.

**Tell yourself:** "I'll ask him if we're OK, and if he says yes, I'll assume he's upset about something that has nothing to do with me. I can't assume that I'm the only person he gets annoyed with."

**Distortion:** Fortune-telling

**Example:** You are grumpy on the phone with your sister because you know she's going to forget your birthday again this year.

**Tell yourself:** "Hey, at least she remembers Christmas. I think I should lower my expectations of her because I just keep getting disappointed, and I don't want to feel that way. That's just how she is."

**Distortion:** Jumping to conclusions

**Example:** Your husband doesn't bring you flowers on Valentine's Day and you

Be Happy Without Being Perfect

react by thinking that he doesn't care enough about you to spring for a bouquet of roses.

**Tell yourself:** "Look at all the money we saved on overpriced roses!" Or, "It's really important to me that he gives me flowers for Valentine's Day, so I'm going to sit down with him and tell him this and then remind him of it next year."

**Distortion:** Magnification

**Example:** Two couples you know go out to dinner together without you, and you decide that they didn't invite you because they don't like you anymore and no longer want to be friends with you.

**Tell yourself:** "It's hard being left out, but sometimes people prefer a smaller party because it's easier to talk. Maybe they had something private to discuss."

**Distortion:** "Should" statements

**Example:** You tell yourself that happily married people should never disagree or argue—if you're truly in love, you should be happy all the time.

**Tell yourself:** "I must be dreaming. All couples argue—it's good for a relationship to get small disagreements and resentments onto the table before they become huge problems."

**Distortion:** Labeling

**Example:** When your best friend forgets to ask you about a doctor's appointment you told her you had been dreading, you label her as being uncaring and selfish.

**Tell yourself:** "I'm disappointed that she forgot, but maybe she doesn't understand its importance. Or maybe it slipped her mind because she's so busy. It doesn't mean she doesn't care."

**Distortion:** Approval seeking

**Example:** You offer to do unnecessary favors for your neighbor because you want her to like you and approve of you.

**Tell yourself:** "Do I really want to be friends with someone who takes advantage of me? If she doesn't like me for who I am, then we shouldn't be friends."

**Distortion:** Woe is me

**Example:** When your family leaves the dinner table without offering to help clean up, you play the martyr and grumble to yourself as you do the job yourself rather than calling them back into the kitchen and asking them to pitch in.

**Tell yourself:** "I have to speak up and ask for help. Better yet, I should convene a family meeting and assign everyone clean-up chores. If I don't speak up, I own it."

**Distortion:** Comparison

**Example:** You compare the attention a friend gives you to the attention she gives another friend and feel inferior.

**Tell yourself:** "That other friend must be having a crisis, and my friend is helping her through it. That's really good of her. When the crisis passes, we can spend time together."

## LEARN TO CONVERSE, NOT FIGHT

Disagreements are inevitable in every relationship, so it's a good idea to develop good communication strategies that help you solve conflicts by talking rather than fighting. Here are some tactics that work with friends, family members, your spouse, or anyone else you might tussle with:

- **Stick to the crime at hand.** If you're arguing about leaving the cap off the toothpaste, don't suddenly throw in a complaint about always having to be the one who takes the dog to the vet. Avoid "kitchen sinking"—throwing in everything but the kitchen sink.
- **Speak with "I" statements rather than "you" statements.** Instead of saying, "You are inconsiderate," say, "I get upset when you criticize me."

- **Avoid using angry language.** Using name-calling, negative labeling, and accusations of incompetence and stupidity only add fuel to the fire.
- **Think before you speak.** Ask yourself: Is what I'm about to say too harsh? Would I want someone to say it to me? Even though it might feel satisfying to say it now, will it harm our relationship in the long-term? Will it hurt the other person?
- **If you're wrong, admit it.** This isn't easy for a perfectionist, but it helps the relationship when you own up to your mistakes and apologize. Admitting you've made a mistake doesn't make you a failure—instead, it suggests a mature and thoughtful commitment to the other person.
- **Choose your battles.** Sometimes it's better just to let things go.
- **Say something funny.** After my husband and I argue, we attribute percentages of blame. He might say, "I'll take 78 percent of the blame." Or if I've been unreasonable, I'll say, "I'll take 84 percent of the blame." It's a gentle way to break up the tension and transition out of the argument.
- **Try not to hold on to resentment.** Joan Borysenko, Ph. D., a psychologist, author, and one of my earliest mentors, says that resentment is like holding a hot coal in your hand—you pick it up to throw at someone else, but you get burned. Try to solve conflicts rather than burn with resentment.
- **Do a mini.** Mini relaxations can help calm you down so you can talk rather than rant. You can do a mini before, during, or after a conflict without the other person even knowing.

## AVOID "MY WAY OR THE HIGHWAY" THINKING

Many an argument has started when a perfectionist insists her approach is right and everyone else's is wrong. Yes, there are times when your way is the best and only way, but usually there are a couple of equally good ways to do something. Keep this in mind if you've just had a baby—I have seen so many cases where a new father tries to care for the baby but backs off because of his wife's criticism. If it's a safety issue, go ahead and correct him, but otherwise, try to give a wide berth. There's no one best way to change a diaper or burp a baby. This is something that Nancy struggles with all the time:

*I have a hard time letting go and letting my husband do things his own way. When I get it in my head that things need to be done a certain way, I become blind to the fact that there may be more than one right way, or that doing it differently is not going to cause irreparable damage to my kids. Recently my husband has been staying home with the kids while I work outside of the home full-time. He's got his way of making lunches, dressing the kids, scheduling naps, and I can't force him to do everything my way. I ask for a detailed list of what happens during the day and sometimes end up criticizing him for things that I would have done differently. I wish I could be less controlling in this area.*

## UNDERSTAND WHERE HE'S COMING FROM

When it's your husband's turn to cook dinner, he makes the same thing all the time—grilled chicken breasts, baked potatoes, and salad. You're annoyed that he cooks same food all the time. But he feels like he's doing a fabulous job because he's making dinner. Why is there such a disconnect?

It's important to understand where your husband is coming from culturally. Most of the men who are now in their forties and fifties grew up with fathers who did nothing around the house—they never changed a diaper, didn't know how to use the vacuum, and aside from an occasional stack of Sunday morning pancakes, they didn't cook. All they had to do was bring home a paycheck. Today, a husband and father's role is so much different than it was fifty years ago. You have to have some empathy for that.

The men of our generation feel proud of themselves because they're

Be Happy Without Being Perfect

doing so much more work around the house than their fathers. They feel like they're being such good sports—and yet their perfectionist wives are constantly criticizing them.

Obviously there are slobs and jerks out there. But I'm talking about the men who truly are trying to contribute. When their perfectionist wives apply completely unrealistic standards, it's no wonder they become angry and withdrawn. They feel like a hot ticket because they're helping out, and we cut them down by noticing only the shortcomings. Like everyone else, they want compliments. When there's no positive reinforcement, they stop contributing, and resentment and anger start to build.

Many perfectionists know they're being unfair, but they find it so hard to stop themselves. If that's how you feel, I'm happy to tell you that there are some techniques that will help you a lot.

## TAKE TIME TO FEEL GRATITUDE

When you're so busy criticizing your imperfect husband, it's easy to forget how much you love him. Try to step outside yourself and cultivate feelings of gratitude, as Kimberly does:

*I try to keep perspective and be grateful. My husband and I had significant marital issues years ago, so I think about how good I feel about where we are and where we're progressing to. Even in the lowest of my lows, it doesn't take much to remind me that no matter how bad it is, it's good. My bads aren't really that bad. When I keep things in perspective and remember to feel grateful, I'm happy with my life.*

## START WITH BABY STEPS

It's unrealistic to think that a perfectionist wife can change her ways overnight. You can't. But you can take baby steps. Start with the things that don't show. I've done that—in my world, sheets are folded perfectly when they're taken out of the dryer. In my husband's world, there's no reason not to just roll them up and stuff them in the linen closet. This drives me crazy, but you know what? Rolled-up sheets work just as well on the bed as folded sheets. Letting go of perfectly folded sheets is an example of a baby step.

Think about where you can give the most leeway. Pick what's least painful to you. Go back to the quiz in the beginning of this book and look for the areas in which your perfectionist scores are lowest, and start your baby steps there. For me, it's house stuff—how laundry is folded, for example. For someone else, it might be the way dinner is cooked. There will be some places where you can't give. Sit down with him and say, "I know I'm being a little irrational here, but I absolutely can't stand having crumbs on the kitchen counter." If he sees you trying in other areas, he's more likely to be OK about the crumbs.

Inform your husband that you're trying to be less of a perfectionist. Tell him that you need his support—ask him to compliment you when you let something go, and to praise you when he sees you trying.

## DO REALITY CHECKS

During the holiday season, you're running around buying dozens of gifts for family, friends, teachers, coworkers, and neighbors. Seeing how frantic you are, your husband asks, "Why don't you just cut some people off your list and give fewer presents?" You want to laugh—isn't it just like a man to have no concept of the importance of gift-giving. But then you think, what if he's right? Is he being totally haphazard, or are you being a perfectionist? Is it normal to make a gingerbread house for the mailman?

These are hard questions because we tend to feel that the way we do things is the right way. But perfectionism clouds your view. Look for ways to part the clouds. Ask friends who are neither perfectionists nor slackers what they would do. Go back to the quiz at the beginning of this book and review your areas of most marked perfectionism—if your husband is complaining about an area in which you're an off-the-chart perfectionist, he may have a valid point.

Be Happy Without Being Perfect

When you and your husband hit points like these, talk about it. Look for compromise zones. Work together to get to a place where you can both be comfortable. It takes effort, but in the end you both benefit.

## TAKE TURNS

Perfectionists sometimes have trouble compromising because if both parties offer concessions, nobody gets what they want. Say you're going out to dinner. If you want Italian and he wants Indian, settling on Mexican because it's a compromise doesn't make sense (unless you both like Mexican). Instead, try taking turns—you pick the restaurant this week, he picks it next week. Or you pick the restaurants and he decides where to get takeout. If you like ethnic food and he's a meat and potatoes guy, go out for Thai food when you're eating out with friends, and stick to steak places when you're with him. If you love someone, his needs should count as much as yours. Figure out what's important to each of you and work around it.

## DON'T BE A PEOPLE-PLEASER

In a healthy relationship, both people give and take. They care about each other, communicate openly, compromise (or take turns), reciprocate each other's affectionate gestures, and share fairly equally in the benefits of the bond. In a people-pleasing relationship, the connection is far more one-sided.

In the book *The Disease to Please,* Harriet B. Braiker, Ph.D., paints a very clear picture of what people-pleasing looks like:

# The Ten Commandments of People-Pleasing

1. I *should always* do what others want, expect, or need from me.
2. I *should* take care of everyone around me whether they ask for help or not.

3. I *should always* listen to everyone's problems and try my best to solve them.
4. I *should always* be nice and never hurt anyone's feelings.
5. I *should always* put other people first, before me.
6. I *should never* say no to anyone who needs or requests something of me.
7. I *should never* disappoint anyone or let others down in any way.
8. I *should always* be happy and upbeat and never show any negative feelings to others.
9. I *should always* try to please other people and make them happy.
10. I *should* try *never* to burden others with my own needs or problems.

This list may make you chuckle—who would really do all those things? The truth is, many people do. Look at the list again and replace "other people" with "my husband" or "my mother" or "my best friend," and you may discover that you're more of a husband-pleaser or mother-pleaser or best friend–pleaser than you realized. If so, try to be more aware of your people-pleasing behavior—acknowledging it is the first step toward altering it. Use cognitive restructuring to modify your thoughts and behaviors, and try to understand why you feel the need to please people.

Braiker suggests going through the list and rewriting it, replacing each statement with a personalized corrective thought—for example, replace "I should always do what my mother wants, expects, or needs" with "I know that I don't always have to do what my mother wants, needs, or expects from me. I can choose to give when and if I want to do so."

## The Power of Friendship

For women, the power of friendship cannot be overstated. Social support is not a luxury—studies show that it is important for good mental and physical health. Compared with people who lack social support, people who have a network of caring friends and family are more likely to exercise, feel less stressed, sleep better, feel less moody, get regular medical checkups, and live longer. Spending time with people we love lowers blood pressure, boosts immunity, promotes healing, reduces feelings of depression and anxiety, and builds self-esteem. Having a solid group of friends and supportive family members heightens positive feelings during good times and helps you cope better when crisis strikes.

Despite all the proven benefits of social support, Americans are actually becoming more isolated. Researchers at the University of Arizona and Duke University conducted a survey on social support in 1985 and then again twenty years later. They made some startling discoveries about how social networks changed in two decades:

- The number of people saying they have no one with whom they can discuss important matters nearly tripled.
- The average American now has two close friends, compared with three in 1985.
- Compared with 1985, 50 percent more people now say they have nobody to confide in besides their spouses.

"There really is less of a safety net of close friends and confidants," says Lynn Smith-Lovin, a Duke University sociologist who co-conducted the study.

When women fall in love they sometimes let go of their friends. They depend on their husbands and expect them to meet all their needs. This is such a mistake. No matter how great your husband is, you're still going to need your friends.

That's not to say your relationships with friends won't change as your lives change. I've noticed this in my own life. When I was single, it was more fun to hang out with single friends. When I got married, we had lots to talk about with other couples. When we had children, we had more in common with other parents. This is true of most people. But although it's human nature to want to spend time with people who have a lot in common with you, it is really important to maintain friendships with other women no matter what your marital status and whether you're a parent. Marriages can end, children grow up—but friendships can be forever, provided you nurture them.

Women in our modern society are isolated, and that's not how women are meant to live. In older societies, women looked out for each other. Their mothers, sisters, aunts, and in-laws lived nearby, and they knew their neighbors. A hundred years ago, newlyweds lived close to (or in) their parents' houses. It was like the movie *My Big Fat Greek Wedding*. When a woman had a baby, all of the women in her family would swoop in and take care of her and the baby and get supper on the table for Dad and other children. If she needed someone to watch her kids, she could send them over to her neighbor's house or her sister's house for a few hours. Years later, when Grandma got older and developed health problems, her daughters and daughters-in-law and granddaughters would care for her.

That's not happening anymore. In the space of just one or two generations, many women have lost their female support systems. In the 1950s and '60s, a woman who gave birth stayed in the hospital for a week. Female friends and family kept the household going. That's not happening now. After giving birth, your mom or your mother-in-law may help out for a few days, but most women find that after a very short time they're on their own.

## Perfect Friends

Perfectionism can take a toll on your friendships, as Brenda describes:

*My friends would tell you I'm a good but difficult friend, because of my expectations. Birthdays are a very big deal to me—they always have been. When I was a kid, my mother would make a huge fuss for me on my birthday—a big cake, the whole nine yards. You're not supposed to want to have a birthday party over thirty, but I think birthdays should be celebrated. When I was thirty-two, nobody*

*remembered my birthday. Not a soul. From that day on I have let
everyone know it's my birthday. I throw parties for myself, but they're
really parties for my friends because I spend all my time making sure
all of my guests are happy.*

Perfectionists give their friends a lot, and expect a lot in return. This can
set them up for disappointment, as it sometimes does for me. I like to
bake birthday cakes for my friends who live nearby. I usually bake about
twenty cakes a year for my friends' birthdays and their kids' birthdays. It's
something I choose to do and enjoy doing—I love baking with my kids.
But I have to remind myself not to feel forgotten when my friends don't
bake a cake for me. (It's probably just as well, or I'd have to eat twenty
birthday cakes!) If I choose to do something for my friends that goes
above and beyond the call of friendship, it's not fair to expect them to do
the same for me. It's hard sometimes—when my birthday rolls around
and nobody bakes me a cake, am I disappointed? Sometimes, yes, I feel a
little let down. But then I remind myself why I do it—it's something that
I like to do. It makes me feel good. I don't do it so that others will do it
for me. Everybody has to set her own standards. If there's something you
want to do for your friends, you have to own it and do it because it's what
you like, not so that it will be reciprocated.

That's not to say you shouldn't expect anything from your friends. If
they are true friends, they'll be there for you when you need them. My
friends may not always bake me birthday cakes, but if there's a crisis,
they're with me every step of the way.

Perfectionists must be careful not to jump to conclusions about
their friends. If you don't hear from someone for a while, don't jump
to the conclusion that she's mad at you and doesn't want to talk to you.
She's probably busy and stressed out, and her silence has nothing to do
with you. One of my patients told me she was upset because her best
friend never invited her to her house. I suggested that she speak honestly
and ask her friend why. The friend said she had stopped inviting people
over because she was ashamed of how run-down her house was.

Try to keep your friendships balanced. If you try to do too much for or with your friends, it may drive them away and make them feel guilty and uncomfortable. If, like some perfectionists, you give your friends lavish gifts that they can't reciprocate, it can make the friendship feel uneven. People don't like to be in uneven relationships.

There are ways to even out such friendships, however. Joan, one of the women we interviewed, has a wealthy friend who offers her the free use of her oceanfront vacation home for two weeks each summer. Joan, who is not wealthy, can't even begin to pay her friend back, but she balances the friendship in other ways, like knitting her a lovely cardigan sweater and baking her favorite homemade cookies.

## Friendship Challenges

It can be hard to be a good friend—I almost think it's easier to be a good mother or wife because the rules are clearer about parenting and partnerships. But being a good friend requires sensitivity and judgment. When something goes wrong in a friend's life, you don't want to be intrusive, but you don't want to be distant. You want to share thoughts and advice, but you don't want to offend. Friendship is delicate—there's always the potential for it to be severed. You're stuck with your relatives, but friends can be lost. Expectations among friends can vary, as Helen knows:

> I know it's a lot to expect, but I want each one to be as best a friend to me as I am to them. But that leads to disappointment. It would make my life better if I could spread out beyond close friends. I get a little jealous when one of my close friends is friends with someone else. That's something I work on, though.

A friend of mine grew up with a family tradition of sending two or three greeting cards for every holiday or birthday. It never occurred to me to send her three cards on her birthday, but one day she blew up at me and told me she'd been upset with me for years because I sent her only one birthday card each year. It really floored me because I'd been impressed with myself just for remembering to send one card—forget about sending three.

Perfectionists often project onto their friends their own standards of how to raise children, keep house, or succeed in a career. That gets friendships into trouble. You can love your friends despite the fact that they have completely different feelings about politics or potty training.

We sometimes outgrow friendships, and that's OK. You may feel that once you're someone's friend you've got to remain friends forever. You don't have to—although you'll probably end up sending each other holiday cards for the rest of your life. But people change, and life experiences change. If you find that you're always calling someone who never calls you, it might be time to let go of the friendship. If you'd rather not, then discuss it openly and honestly with your friend. Ask her why she doesn't call you—write an e-mail if you'd rather not do it in person. Maybe she's facing a problem you don't know about. Either way, try not to hold on to anger and resentment.

It's good to have different kinds of friends. My husband refers to our closest friends as "foxhole friends"—because if crisis strikes, we can call them at 2 a.m. and they'll be at our house as soon as possible, no questions asked. Other friends are a ton of fun to be with—we call them our party friends, because they're always the life of the party—but they're not necessarily the ones we would call in a crisis. You can't expect all your friends to be foxhole friends *and* party friends. Some of my quiet friends would never be the life of the party, but oh, man, were they there for me when my mother died. You have to understand the capabilities of your various friends. It's not necessarily that they don't want to be there for you, but they may not be capable of it. Some people don't know how to help in a crisis—they can't handle the idea of illness or death, for example.

Like ice cream, friends come in all different kinds of wonderful flavors.

Women are genetically programmed to take care of other people, including other women. That worked out well in our grandmothers' day. But now we are following our genetic drive to take care of others, but nobody is taking care of us. That is a massive change. If nobody's taking care of you, you have to do it yourself—something that rarely happens since self-care tends to fall to the bottom of most women's to-do lists. Family, work, housework, and community responsibilities all come first and seem to take up so much time that there's no time left for you. And there's no cluster of female friends, relatives, and neighbors who stand ready to step in when you need them. You can change that by making friendship a priority.

Good friends give us the space to explore our thoughts, feelings, and challenges. "I talk to my best friend three or four times a week," says Debra. "We solve all the problems in our worlds on the phone. She is a huge part of my life."

Friends give us perspective, support, and love that is different than what we receive from spouses or families. "I was going through a really tough time over the past few years," remembers Kathleen. "My best friend sent me an e-mail that said, 'I just want you to see in yourself what everyone else already knows and loves.' That comment will be forever engraved in my memory, and was the turning point in my decision to look at myself more positively."

If you have no ready-made support system of friends and relatives—perhaps you've recently moved to a new town—spend time creating one. It's not easy, particularly if you're a busy working mother. But you can do it. Susan Ahern and Dr. Kent G. Bailey, authors of the book *Family by Choice: Creating Family in a World of Strangers,* offer this advice: "Many of us in today's society must choose new family structures in order to survive. If blood families are not nearby, geographically or emotionally, we can re-create supportive families." How? By looking for kindred spirits in your neighborhood, church, or workplace and carving out time to nurture friendships with them.

If you're a working mother, build relationships with women with whom you can exchange support. Look for areas of potential reciprocity. Don't limit yourself to women your own age—having friends of all ages nourishes your soul. Forming a bond with an older neighbor can benefit both of you: She can watch your kids while you run to the supermarket, and you can save her a trip and pick up the milk, eggs, and bread on her grocery list. We need these support networks for practical and emotional reasons.

## SPEAK UP

Many women find it hard to ask for help—they don't want to be thought of as taking advantage of their friends, neighbors, and family. Most women don't mind being there for you if you're there for them. I saw this in action recently. I overheard two mothers at my daughters' school the other day complaining the hassles of having to pick their kids up at school and drive them to after-school activities. When they realized both of their children attended the same chess class, they immediately agreed to work together, with one driving the kids to chess and one picking them up.

Opening up to friends can be difficult for perfectionists, but I urge you to try because it can bring friendship to a new, very satisfying level, as Laura discovered:

> I have millions of friends, but I know a lot more about them than they know about me. I grew up believing that you just don't tell other people your problems. I never remember my mother and her friends sitting around sharing their problems. If you failed, you didn't talk about it—you just worked harder. But I've learned that doesn't always work. A few years ago I was experiencing a very difficult emotional issue, and I didn't tell any of my friends at work about it. Finally someone asked me what was wrong and I broke down and explained everything. Soon everyone knew, and I felt a lot better.

Finding time for friends isn't always easy, but if you make friendship a priority, you discover ways to spend time with them even if you're very busy. I take hour-long walks every weekend, and I always try to find a friend who will walk with me. I'm taking the walk anyway, so I might as well kill two birds with one stone and make it a date with a friend, too. There are lots of ways to piggyback friend-time onto other obligations— if you're going to a parent meeting at school, go with a friend and use the time in the car to catch up. If you're going to be home all afternoon with your kids, call another mom and have her bring her kids over so you can have tea while the children play. If you're creative, you can find lots of ways to have more women in your life. It will bring you so much joy, as it does for Sarah:

> *I've started selling cosmetics in people's homes, and I'm having a ball. It gets me hanging out with other women. My feminine side has been neglected for so long—as an engineer, I've been surrounded by men most of my career. It's so great to spend time with women.*

## Family Expectations

This is such a loaded topic—I can barely scratch the surface. Family expectations are huge, compelling forces that push perfectionists around like leaves on a windy day.

Siblings compete with each other. Some parents model perfectionist behavior; others model the complete opposite. Families label us as "the good one" or "the smart one." Even grandparents, aunts, and uncles get involved, giving opinions and making judgments.

Family expectations can set off all of your perfectionism alarms. They are influenced by events from your childhood, guilt, insecurity, and fear of rejection. They tend to reach a boiling point during the holidays, with gift-giving, decorating, cooking, and all kinds of attempts at memory-making. When we're with our parents and siblings, we all tend to fall into old roles that may be way out of date—a grown woman can still be referred to as "the messy one" simply because she threw food around as a toddler. If you grew up with a perfectionist label, you may feel you have to continue to play that role in front of your parents.

Even if you left home at eighteen and have had years of therapy, you're still a kid when you're with your family of origin.

Perfectionists like routine, so it can be tough for us when things change. The world can feel crooked, for example, when your parents focus on their own lives rather than doting on yours or when one parent dies and the surviving parent remarries. Having your parents suddenly become unpredictable can really shake up your world.

You can't change your family, but you can change the way you think about them and interact with them. Take a step back and ask yourself what bothers you about your family. Why do you feel irritable, sad, angry, or impatient with them? Spend a few pages (a few hundred pages?) in your journal writing about your relationship with your parents and siblings. Think about the expectations that they have for you and you have for them.

Make a list of your three most pressing concerns. Using cognitive-restructuring techniques, ask yourself where these concerns come from, whether they are causing you stress, and how you can either solve them, avoid them, or restructure them in a way that causes you less anxiety. Experiment with the other relationship-building techniques in this chapter, too—they can work effectively for everyone, even your mother.

As you think about your family-based feelings of perfectionism, consider the advice of Christel Nani, a medical intuitive and author of the book *Sacred Choices: Thinking Outside the Tribe to Heal Your Spirit*. Nani believes that the unexamined "tribal beliefs" passed on to us by our families can prevent us from leading fulfilling, happy lives. She advises people to scrutinize our tribal beliefs and "rewrite" the ones that don't work for us. It's a kind of cognitive restructuring that can be very helpful in terms of uncovering the assumptions that influence our behavior.

In her book, Nani lists some of the unexamined tribal beliefs that people commonly hold about their families:

# Unexamined Tribal Beliefs About Family

1. Blood is thicker than water (so stand by your family no matter what they do or say).
2. If your own mother doesn't love you, no one will.
3. Holidays should be spent with your family.
4. Give in to keep the peace in the family.
5. Good daughters/sons take care of their parents no matter what.
6. Nonblood relatives or friends will never be as dependable as your "real" family.
7. It's selfish to be happy when your family isn't.
8. Keep the family secrets at all costs.
9. When the chips are down, your family is the only place you can turn to or trust.
10. Taking care of yourself before your family is selfish.
11. Families stick together and take care of each other, no matter what.
12. You can't have an easy life if your family doesn't.
13. What's cooked at home is eaten at home.
14. Honor your mother and father no matter what.
15. You owe it to your parents to take care of them in their old age.
16. A good son or daughter should drop everything in his or her life to take care of an ailing parent.
17. Family loyalty is more important than taking care of yourself.
18. If your mother gave you up for adoption, you are not lovable, and no one else will ever love you.

Unfortunately, there is no such thing as a perfect family—although it can be therapeutic just to acknowledge that fact. Parents change over time. Siblings do, too—their needs and their ability to love you and support you fluctuate. It's easy to forget this, but you have to work to maintain family relationships just as you have to work at marriage and friendship. That said, you also have a right to be happy, and if your family's expectations block the way, you have a right to push them aside.

Be Happy Without Being Perfect

*After two years of therapy I realized that so many of the choices I had made in life were for my family. They had very high but unspoken expectations of what kind of person I should be. When I finished college I wanted to move far away from them. I thought at the time that I just wanted to have an adventure, but I see now that I was desperate to get away from them and their expectations. I'm forty-four now, and I have finally learned to do what I want to do, not what they want me to do. It's still hard, especially because my mother is elderly and I feel sometimes like I'm a bully, saying no to her when she asks me to do something for her that I think is unreasonable. But I have a right to be true to myself.*

*—Theresa*

CHAPTER 9

# Enjoy Imperfect Parenting

*I*n general I'm a pretty easygoing person, but when it comes to my kids, I am way more of a perfectionist than I ever would have expected. It started during my pregnancy, when I became very fastidious about nutrition and having the right amount of various nutrients every day. Once when my husband and I were on vacation I realized as we were getting ready to go to bed that I was one cup of milk short for the day. The hotel kitchen was closed, so I sent him out to buy milk from a convenience store.

I wanted to deliver naturally, without an epidural, and I did. It was really important to me to be in control of my son's birth. After three hours of pushing, the delivery stalled and the midwife called the doctor, who used suction to pull my son out. I felt so happy and relieved to have the pushing over with—and needless to say, I was overjoyed that my son was healthy—but to this day I think of the suction as marring an otherwise beautiful delivery with an "unnatural" intervention.

Looking back at my days as a new mother, I realize I must have had postpartum depression. All the other mothers that I had befriended during my childbirth preparation classes were out socializing and attending postnatal exercise classes a few weeks after delivery, but I couldn't get out of bed before noon. I was so angry at myself for not being a more together mother. My son reacted to many of the foods I ate while I was nursing, and I had to cut out one food after another. I was losing weight too quickly, not getting the nutrients he and I needed, and I was exhausted because he was waking up four or five times a night to nurse and cry. Plus, I'd gone back to work when my son was two months old—I didn't want to take the full three months of my maternity leave because I thought it would suggest to my employer that I wasn't serious about my career. I quit nursing after four months because it was just too much—a decision I still regret.

During my children's toddler and preschool years I got a little less neurotic, except for milestones—if a child who was the same age as mine walked or talked or learned to read before mine, I felt what I call "failure pangs." I wouldn't get all upset, but I'd silently tell myself that my child wasn't as advanced as the other child due to some failure of mine—because I worked and the kids went to daycare, or I wasn't reading to them enough, or I wasn't taking them to toddler tumbling classes at the Y or whatever.

I read all these books about how kids should start to learn to play the violin and speak a foreign language and bat as a switch-hitter when they are very young and their minds are information sponges, but I didn't have the time or energy to take them to all kinds of classes. I felt guilty that I was letting a window of intellectual and artistic opportunity shut, dooming my children to a lifetime of ordinariness.

Now that they are in school, we're butting heads about schoolwork. My younger child works hard, but my older one feels that average is good enough—he's actually said that to me in those very words, and his teacher told me he has been doing just enough work to get by. We had a long conversation about that, but as I was saying, "You have to work to your full potential," I was thinking, "No son of mine *is going to be average.*"

Be Happy Without Being Perfect

*After that, I started paying much closer attention to his school-work and homework. That was a disaster until I realized that I was carping on him for every mistake he made. Now, instead of looking at his homework when it's finished and criticizing him for not meeting my expectations, we sit down together before he starts his work to define what the expectations should be. I'm trying to focus on the quality of his effort, rather than the finished product. But I'm still not sure what to do about the mistakes. If he works really hard on a composition, I praise him for it, but I also circle the spelling errors. He asks me why I always have to find something wrong in his work. What am I supposed to do, let seven misspelled words go by uncorrected?*

*—Catherine*

Perfectionism is a moving target for parents. As Catherine points out in the story above, it's often hard to know the difference between reasonable conscientiousness and unreasonable caution. It's an incredibly fine line. If your infant's babysitter shows up with a cold and you send her home because you don't want your baby to get sick, are you being rationally sensible or irrationally overanxious? What if you forbid your fourteen-year-old to get her nose pierced? Or you don't let your eleven-year-old watch PG-13 movies that every other kid in the neighborhood watches? Or your twenty-one-year-old son wants to share his bedroom with a new girlfriend he brings home from college for the weekend? Would you tell Catherine to correct her son's spelling mistakes or praise him for his effort and let the spelling go?

I didn't need to take my own perfectionism quiz to know that I have some tendencies in that direction, so when our first daughter was born I was determined not to be a perfectionism role model. As soon as she could understand language, every time I made any kind of mistake I pointed it out. "Look Sarah, Mommy spilled some milk. Oh, well." "Gosh, Sarah, I missed that turn, now I need to turn around." "Shoot, I burnt the cookies. No biggy, I will just make some more." Since I trained as a child psychologist, I thought that modeling such acceptance of mistakes would enable both of my daughters to accept mistakes in a healthy way. So you can imagine my horror when I went for my very first parent-teacher conference with Sarah's kindergarten teacher. The first thing the teacher asked was whether my husband and I were perfectionists! She asked that question, she said, because she had been noticing perfectionist behavior in Sarah. Proof (in my mind, at least) that some of these tendencies are indeed genetic.

It's not easy to see where the perfectionist parenting line falls, but if you cross it on a regular basis, there is a potential to harm your child. I hate sounding like an alarmist—God knows perfectionists feel guilty enough already. But if you are subjecting your children to perfectionist parenting, you would serve yourself and your children well by trying to change that behavior. I can help you with that, but first, let me tell you what's at stake.

## Anxious Children

Research shows that the children of perfectionist parents have an elevated risk of general anxiety, social anxiety (having trouble interacting with others), depression, eating disorders, anger, body-image issues, low self-esteem, and adolescent rebellion. They may develop a fear of making mistakes, a fear of being judged harshly by others, self-doubt, and a reluctance to speak or read in front of others. In other words, children of perfectionists run the risk of becoming perfectionists and suffering many of the same consequences faced by adult perfectionists.

Troubles often start to show when a child is in school. Children who grow up believing they're not living up to expectations may experience low self-esteem. They may spend so much time on school projects that they can't get their work done on time. Or they may stop trying to succeed because they feel that no matter what, they'll never do well enough to satisfy their parents.

# Early Start

Researchers at Smith College have found evidence of perfectionism-related anxiety in children as early as third grade. In one study, psychologist Patricia DiBartolo asked third, fourth, and fifth graders to perform computer tasks. She found that even before beginning the tasks, the perfectionist kids predicted they would do less well than the nonperfectionist kids, suggesting a link between perfectionism and low self-esteem. She also found that the perfectionist kids showed much more anxiety and dissatisfaction with their performance on the computer tasks even when they performed just as well as their nonperfectionist peers. "Perfectionist kids get caught in a vicious cycle," DiBartolo says. "When approaching a task or project, they feel less able to succeed, get anxious, and then evaluate their performance more negatively than their nonperfectionistic peers."

Perfectionist parenting is particularly damaging to daughters, who tend to model their behavior after that of their mother. Whether she does it consciously or unconsciously, a mother influences her daughter's body image, eating habits, dieting behaviors, physical activity, and feelings of self-esteem. A perfectionist mother who is never satisfied with her appearance or performance, puts herself down, never admits mistakes, makes critical comments about herself or others, is afraid of failing, or who is preoccupied with weight loss teaches these thoughts and behaviors to her daughter, putting her at an elevated risk of developing eating disorders.

One of the things I fear most for my children, especially since I have two daughters, is eating disorders. I worked on an inpatient unit at Children's Hospital in Boston during my training and remain spooked by the hospitalized anorexic girls. It is so crucial as a parent to model acceptance of physical flaws and body size, rather than complaining about our extra pounds in their presence.

I touched on this topic while giving a talk in Michigan. A woman stood up and asked the audience, "How many of you can say that you are truly good role models about your body image to your children? How often have you said in their presence that you look fat in a certain outfit? Or that you need to lose weight?" And pretty much all of the women in the audience admitted that they had indeed made such comments, over and over, while their children listened. Obviously we would all be healthier if we shed our extra pounds. But focusing on health, rather than weight or appearance, is the way to go.

## Parenting Potholes

Perfectionism can start to play a part in parental behavior and emotion even before a child is conceived. Many of the infertility patients I've counseled have described the inability to get pregnant easily as one of the greatest failures of their lives, even though infertility is usually caused by factors that are beyond a woman's control. Perfectionist women have told me of the anger and disappointment that infertility has brought them because, unlike so many other challenges in their lives, it can't be fixed through hard work and perfectionist effort.

Perfectionism blooms during pregnancy and delivery, as Catherine's story at the beginning of this chapter shows. Perfectionist women want to do everything "right" in order to have a perfect pregnancy and delivery, and a perfectly healthy child. As in most other parts of life, a woman can do everything right while pregnant and still experience discomfort and medical complications. Premature babies and babies with significant problems and defects can be born to the healthiest, most conscientious of mothers; many of the factors that contribute to these difficulties are beyond a mother's control.

I'm not saying pregnant women have *no* control over their baby's fate—quite the opposite is true. Eating nutritious food, taking prenatal vitamins, avoiding cigarette smoke and other environmental toxins, gaining the recommended amount of weight, and following other prenatal recommendations can slash your risk of giving birth to a baby with health problems. But even if you follow every recommendation to the smallest detail, you don't have complete control. That can be frustrating and frightening to a perfectionist.

Perfectionism can continue to emerge after your baby is born and during her infancy, toddlerhood, and childhood. If you're a working mother, you may fire sitter after sitter because no childcare provider meets your expectations. If you quit your job to stay home with your baby, you may feel that you have to be the world's most perfect mother.

Expecting nothing less than perfection can tear you apart, as it does with Dorothy:

> *My children are a constant reminder of my shortcomings and fail-ures. I want to wake up every day and do my best, but perfectionism gets in the way, and if I have so much as a five-minute fall from grace I beat myself up over it for weeks. I knock myself out to try harder with them and for them. It's horrible. I always remind myself that even though I make mistakes I'm still a good mother—I don't lock them in a closet or abuse them. But the tiniest infraction bothers me enough that when they go to bed at night, I cry for everything I didn't do right. I don't see motherhood as a learning process and a growing opportunity. I see it as something I should do perfectly or I'll mess them up for life. I've never wanted to do anything more per-fectly than being a mommy.*

The teen years, with their random emotional outbursts and unpredictable behaviors, test perfectionist parents even further. And young adulthood requires perfectionists to do something they're terrible at: letting go.

Perfectionist mothers set high goals for themselves and their fami-lies. Sandra, one of the women we interviewed, says she wants to be a "first-class" mom:

> *I have very specific ideas about being a first-class mom. I want to be at home in the afternoon when they get home from school. I want to be the one to supervise homework. I want to be the one who's there*

when they're practicing their instruments. I want to show them how to ride a bike and shoot a basketball, to talk them through problems. I want to be there to play games with them, to read with them, to run around the yard with them. My kids don't watch TV. My kids eat extremely healthy food—homemade bread, homemade cookies, homemade ice cream—I don't want them eating all the preservatives and chemicals in commercially made foods. I'm not perfect, I yell at my kids all the time. But I want to be the one yelling at them. There's nobody else who can be a better parent to them than me.

I see a lot of kids who are under pressure, so I try not to go overboard. But I do expect certain things from them. If my son wants to sign up for karate, then he goes to karate—if you sign up, you do it. Homework is done ahead of time, not the night before. You arrive on time for things. People know that about our family— we aren't late. You don't say you're going to do something and not do it. I try not to put any pressure on them, but I do expect them to follow family rules and use their God-given talents to the best of their ability. They have been given good genes, and I expect them to use what they have.

A lot of my friends are soft with their kids and let them get away with stuff I would never allow. If Jimmy is tired, he doesn't have to go to baseball. If he has a lot of homework, he doesn't have to go to practice. Well you know what? If you sign up for something, the team expects you to be there. You can't just bail. What's the matter with these parents? The same with school lunches—my kids tell me what the other kids take to school and I can't believe the crappy lunches that people pack. These are smart parents—people who are college-educated—and they're sending junk to school.

Perfectionist parents may expect top academic achievements and superlative athletic performance. Unfortunately, the underside of these expectations is disappointment: We are disappointed when children are not attractive enough, not popular enough, not smart enough. When we send the message, "I want you to be the best," our children may instead hear the message, "You are not good enough."

## What Kind of Parent Are You?

Diana Baumrind, Ph.D., a renowned research psychologist at the University of California, Berkeley, has defined three main parenting styles. What kind are you? Here's a nutshell summary:

- The **permissive parent** gives a child great freedom in regulating his own activities. "She makes few demands for household responsibility and orderly behavior. She presents herself to the child as a resource for him to use as he wishes, not as an ideal for him to emulate, nor as an active agent responsible for shaping or altering his ongoing or future behavior. She allows the child to regulate his own activities as much as possible, avoids the exercise of control, and does not encourage him to obey externally defined standards." The permissive parent rarely resorts to punishment.
- The **authoritarian parent** wants to be in control. She "attempts to shape, control, and evaluate the behavior and attitudes of the child in accordance with a set standard of conduct, usually an absolute standard. . . . She values obedience as a virtue and favors punitive, forceful measures to curb self-will. . . . She believes in keeping the child in his place, in restricting his autonomy, and in assigning household responsibilities in order to inculcate respect for work. She regards the preservation of order and traditional structure as a highly valued end in itself. She does not encourage verbal give and take, believing that the child should accept her word for what is right."

- The **authoritative parent** attempts to direct her child's activities, but not excessively. "She encourages verbal give and take, shares with the child the reasoning behind her policy, and solicits his objections when he refuses to conform. . . . She exerts firm control at points of parent-child divergence, but does not hem the child in with restrictions. She enforces her own perspective as an adult, but recognizes the child's individual interests and special ways. The authoritative parent affirms the child's present qualities, but also sets standards for future conduct. She uses reason, power, . . . and reinforcement to achieve her objectives, and does not base her decisions on group consensus or the individual child's desires."

Although most child-development experts agree that the third kind of parenting—authoritative—is best, perfectionist parents tend to fall into the first two categories because of their tendency to indulge in black-and-white thinking. They tend to be either too lenient or too strict. Understanding what other approaches there are, and how your parenting methods compare, can be a helpful way of determining whether your techniques are on target.

## Perfect Little People

Perfectionists are not awful people who want to raise damaged children. Quite the opposite—the vast majority of us are extremely loving, caring, and engaged parents who want the absolute best for our kids. Unfortunately, that's part of the problem. Because we want our children to be happy and successful, we try to form them into perfect people. We pressure them to excel in school and sports, we sign them up for all kinds of classes and lessons, we hire tutors or send them to wildly expensive private schools. We don't want to stress them out, but we do want them to succeed. Barbara sees this kind of behavior all the time in her town:

*We live in a suburban area where there are all these psycho parents who put so much pressure on their kids. They push their kids and start to worry in first grade about whether their kids will get into Harvard. They are so consumed with their kids being brilliant. My thirteen-year-old and I talk about it—he says his friends really feel pressured to succeed.*

Some perfectionist parents criticize their kids for everything. Others go to the opposite extreme, praising everything they do. This can backfire, because it can create kids who are spoiled, self-centered, and poorly prepared for the inevitable rejections, failures, challenges, and hardships of real life. It can also contribute to depression later in their lives.

I'm so glad to tell you that there are changes you can start to make in your life immediately that will prevent your children (and the world!) from feeling the negative effects of perfectionist parenting.

## One Expectation at a Time

Perfectionism is not a piano that falls off a rooftop one day and crushes your children. It's more like water torture—day after day, year after year, drip, drip, drip, perfectionist parenting wears away at them. A comment here, a judgment there, an unfulfilled expectation somewhere else—it all adds up. It's insidious. But it's also recognizable. If you see any of the following signposts in your life, it's time to slow down and examine how much perfectionism there is in your parenting.

## SIGNPOST #1: YOUR SELF-ESTEEM IS CLOSELY LINKED TO YOUR CHILD'S

One of the women we interviewed told us that she'd recently helped her fifth grader do a school project about the Aztecs. When he brought the project home, her first question was: "What grade did we get?" When you think of your child's achievements as your achievements and his failures as your failures, flashing lights should go off in your head. Those are clear signs of perfectionist parenting.

Some of us want our kids to be perfect because we feel that if they fail, we fail. If they can't get along well with other kids, if they drop the baseball and the other team wins the playoff game, if they bring home a poor report card, if they are diagnosed with a learning disability, if they abuse drugs or alcohol, if they don't get into an ivy league college, it brings us down, too.

A perfectionist parent may press a child to succeed in an area in which the parent failed. The classic examples of this are the homely mother pushing her daughter to win a beauty pageant or a klutzy father expecting his son to be a star athlete. It takes a lot of self-control not to project your own ego, wants, and needs on your child. I have had several patients who have adopted a child and also have a biological child, and they all say the same thing—that it's much easier to parent an adopted child because you don't project your own stuff onto the kid, such as being athletic or artistic. It's like having a blank canvas—you can't paint the kid so you let the kid paint himself. You don't push your own desires or talents on him.

## SIGNPOST #2: YOU CRITICIZE A LOT

Perfectionist parents are very critical of themselves and their children and are unable to tolerate mistakes of any kind, including genuine accidents. If your child spills his milk and you call him clumsy, you can cause a lot of emotional damage.

## SIGNPOST #3: YOU WITHHOLD APPROVAL

Parents should love their children unconditionally. It's incredibly harmful when a child feels that her parent's love is tied to her performance or appearance.

Be Happy Without Being Perfect

# SIGNPOST #4: YOU ALWAYS PUT YOUR CHILD FIRST

The myth of the perfect mother is that your children's needs *always* come before yours. Obviously there are times when your child needs something and you immediately drop what you're doing to help him, but there are other times when your child has to get in line and wait his turn. In no family should the needs of the children always come before the needs of the adults.

I see this happening with a lot of perfectionist patients. Their adult relationships are always second to the children. Women squelch their own needs for eighteen years or more because they want to be a perfect mother, and in their minds, a perfect mother always puts her children first. Not that you wouldn't work three jobs to put a roof over your kids' head and food on the table—that's not what I'm talking about. I'm talking about women who make a date to go out to dinner with friends and cancel at the last minute because their kids don't want them to leave. If the child has a 102-degree fever, fine. But if you feel that you have to give in to every one of your child's demands to meet the expectations of so-called perfect motherhood, you need to reevaluate your priorities.

It's so important to take care of yourself—and to let your children see that you deserve self-care. I've heard parents of kindergartners say that they've never left their child with a babysitter. What message does that send a kid? Aren't they egocentric enough without their parents making them the complete and total center of their world? When babies are born, they're an ego in a diaper—seven and a half pounds of pure need. It's their parents' job to teach them that everyone's feelings count, not just theirs.

It's so much fun to indulge kids. I do it myself—I love doing stuff for my daughters, buying things for them and taking them special places. But I balance that with what I do for myself, my husband, family, friends, and the community. Our job as moms is to raise our children to be happy, successful, and productive members of society, not the king or queen of the world.

The best kind of mother is one who balances her needs and the needs of her family, who is able to set limits for kids, who is a healthy role model for her kids, and who takes as well as gives.

## SIGNPOST #5: YOU EXPECT PERFECTION OF YOURSELF

If you have unrealistically high expectations for yourself and try never to let your children see you make a mistake, you're telling them that perfection is the only option for you and for them. If you make a mistake, acknowledge it and, if the situation warrants, apologize. But don't hide it from your children and lead them to believe that you are perfect.

## SIGNPOST #6: YOU EXPECT MOTHERHOOD TO MAKE YOU EXQUISITELY HAPPY

Parenting is hard work. Sure, it can be satisfying, but it can also be incredibly frustrating. If you go into parenthood expecting it to be an always-joyful, always-rewarding experience—and if you criticize yourself as being a not-good-enough parent because of the frustration and impatience you sometimes feel—you're living in a fantasy world. This is particularly common among women who had trouble getting pregnant.

In his book *Stumbling on Happiness,* Daniel Gilbert explains that people believe some things about happiness that simply aren't true. The joy of money, for example—research shows that wealth does not necessarily bring happiness. The joy of children is another. "Every human culture tells its members that having children will make them happy," he writes. "When people are asked to identify their sources of joy, they do just what I do: They point to their kids. Yet if we measure the actual satisfaction of people who have children, a very different story emerges." One study asked women to rank the daily activities that made them happy. Taking care of children ranked lower than eating, exercising, shopping, napping, and watching television. "Indeed, looking after the kids appears to be only slightly more pleasant than doing housework," Gilbert says.

Be Happy Without Being Perfect

Of course you love your children, but don't expect yourself to like them all the time. It's normal to have days when you feel like sending them off to boarding school. If you expect that being a mother will fulfill you completely, or that your failure to enjoy every minute of motherhood means you're a terrible parent, you're likely to be disappointed, angry, and stressed. Try to let go of this myth.

## SIGNPOST #7: YOU FEEL THAT IF YOUR CHILD IS UNHAPPY, YOU'RE A BAD PARENT

*From the outside, everything looks fine—the kids have bows in their hair, and people see them looking perfect sitting in their wagon. I would never admit that I'm tired, exhausted. I'm afraid that if I admit I'm tired, people will think I can't do this job. If the kids cry in the night and I am worn out the next day, I feel like a failure. Other people's kids sleep through the night, so mine should too.*

*—Laura*

Perfectionist parenting can twist your ideas about setting limits for children. Some perfectionists feel that if they have to say no to a child, discipline a child, or limit the child in any way, it's proof that they're bad parents. In an effort to feel like good parents, they let the children run the family—they set no limits at all. This is confusing and upsetting to children. They thrive on having limits and boundaries clearly defined.

Perfectionist parents often feel that if a child experiences any negative emotion—if she cries with anger or feels sad or scared, for example—it means they haven't done a good enough job as parents. That's simply not true. It's good for a child to experience sadness, jealousy, anger, and other difficult feelings so she can learn how to handle them. If you in your perfectionist parent zeal try to raise a child who never knows anything but happiness, you set her up for a difficult adulthood. It does way more harm than good. Having unlimited freedom can provoke tremendous anxiety in children.

Saying no does not make you a bad parent. One of my patients told me that the first time her son was ever told no was when he was in high school and failed to make the varsity football team. He threw a tantrum that would have done a two-year-old proud. Kids have to learn from an early age that failure happens to everyone. You deal with it and move on.

Asking a child to do things she dislikes doesn't make you a bad parent, either. It makes you a better parent, and it helps build a better child. Establish reasonable rules based on your child's age, and stick to them. Even a two-year-old can learn to put toys away. Kids can clean their rooms, empty the dishwasher, walk the dog, take care of the yard. It teaches them responsibility. Remember, though, when you ask a child to do a job, keep your perfectionism in check when you're inspecting the work. Don't pounce on your seven-year-old if she puts the forks in the part of the drawer reserved for spoons. Show her where the forks belong and praise her for her effort.

## SIGNPOST #8: YOU BLAME YOURSELF FOR YOUR CHILD'S PROBLEMS

Having a child with any kind of a difficult challenge—from asthma to a learning disorder to a drug problem—can be heartbreaking for a parent. You want the ideal child—smart, healthy, popular, well-behaved. If you're a perfectionist parent, you're likely to take your child's difficulties, failures, and poor behaviors personally. You're likely to blame yourself for anything that goes wrong in your child's life.

Self-blame solves nothing, so don't waste your energy on it. No matter how good a parent you are, so many things are out of your control.

One of the women we interviewed had just discovered that her son had attention deficit/hyperactivity disorder (ADHD). She was devastated, and she blamed herself. But it wasn't her fault. Things just happen, no matter how well we parent. Her challenge is to get beyond the self-blame and move on to helping her child. How she handles the ADHD diagnosis will influence how her son handles it. She can pull her hair out over it, or she can be grateful he was diagnosed and can now be placed into a learning environment that meets his needs. The better able she is to use her energy helping him rather than blaming herself for not being a perfect mother with a perfect son, the more likely it will be that he will succeed in school despite his condition and go on to find a career that suits his personality and his strengths. Having an imperfect child does not make you a bad parent. It just makes you a parent.

## Tribal Beliefs on Mothering

In her book *Sacred Choices: Thinking Outside the Tribe to Heal Your Spirit,* medical intuitive Christel Nani lists some of the motherhood myths that many of us swallow without question. She urges women to think consciously about these ingrained beliefs:

1.  My children's needs always come first.
2.  A good woman takes care of her husband and family before herself.
3.  A good mother is responsible for her children's happiness.
4.  A good mother does everything for her children.
5.  If children are not happy or successful, the mother has failed.
6.  A good mother can motivate her children to change.
7.  You are only as happy in life as your least-happy child (said by Charlie Gibson on *Good Morning America*, quoting his wife).
8.  A good mother is always patient.
9.  A good mother stays at home with her children.

*Printed with permission from Christel Nani, R.N., medical intuitive, author of* Sacred Choices

# Clashing Parenting Styles

One of the greatest struggles you face as a perfectionist parent is disagreeing with your husband about how best to raise your children. You have your way of parenting, and you think it's best. Your husband has his way, and he thinks it's best. If he's not a perfectionist, you may feel that his standards are unacceptably lower than yours. You love each other and the children, but you keep clashing with your parenting styles. Nicole describes the situation in her home:

> I should start by noting that my husband is a terrific husband and father, yet I seem to have insanely high standards for him, particularly as a parent. When the kids were babies, I wanted him to do things exactly as I would have done them, and would get quite irate if he deviated. This came out in particular around mealtimes and naps, because I was very big on adhering to the schedule, and he was not. So, for example, one day he brought our two-year-old son home from a day at the beach with friends. Alex was obviously happy and healthy and had had fun. But I grilled my poor husband about when Alex had eaten and what he ate and how well he slept. And when it transpired that Alex hadn't napped at all, I got very critical. I remember this because my sister was there as well and she still gives me a hard time about it years later.

So many of the perfectionist women I talk with expect their husbands to be parenting perfectionists, too. When their husbands fail to live up to their expectations, they push them away. Fed up, the husbands back off in their relationship with their wives and children. It's a no-win situation in which everyone suffers.

The most important lesson you can learn is that there's almost always more than one right way to do something as a parent. Don't force your husband to parent your way. Remember that women *mother* differently than men *father*. Mothers play more quietly—they're more likely to engage in gentle play. Men roll around and get physical with kids. Research shows it's good for children to experience both kinds of play. You don't want your husband to mother the kids—that's your job. So let him do his job. You may *think* your instincts are better than his, but you can't *know* that.

Talk with your husband about your parenting styles. Work together on areas where your methods differ. Try to let go. Set up some basic family rules, and then, unless your children are in danger, try to let your husband do things his way. As Susan discovered, a perfectionist mom can learn a few things from a nonperfectionist dad:

> *I travel a lot for business. Once I was in the back of a taxi going to see a client, and my daughter called and told me she needed to get some Japanese food for the school travel fair. Before I knew it I was on the phone ordering $60 worth of sushi for a bunch of sixth graders. My husband, who was home with the kids, just wanted to make Ramen noodles, but I thought sushi would be more authentic. Looking back now, I realize I should have just gone with the Ramen noodles.*

Keep this crucial piece of advice in mind: Never disagree with your husband over parenting styles in front of the children. Try never to let your children hear you undercutting or contradicting your husband's choices—doing so can lower children's respect for their father (and perhaps for you). When you hit a parenting roadblock, pull him aside and have a private conversation. This helps prevent anger, name-calling, and disrespect as added fuel to the fire.

To put things in perspective, rent the movie *Mrs. Doubtfire* some night. Sally Field plays a totally anal, alphabetize-the-spice-rack kind of perfectionist mom. Robin Williams plays the wild, nutty dad. It would be hard to find two more different parenting styles. Their marriage falls apart—but once they stop trying to change each other and acknowledge that they each bring different but worthwhile parenting skills to the table, things work out.

## How does perfectionism affect your ability as a parent?

*I have a lot of friends who are really whipped up into a frenzy about their kids getting into college. I'm trying not to do that, but I know I could get wrapped up in it if I let myself. My son is more interested in being safe and comfortable and enjoying things than achieving. He just doesn't want to work that hard. It bothers me—I wish he would aim higher. But I'm being quiet about it to preserve our relationship.*

—Susan

*When I was a kid, I didn't get good training in the basics of mathematics, and it held me back. My kids aren't doing well in math, and I'm trying to show them that it really matters. I hired a tutor, but they resent it. I don't need them to get A's, but I can't accept C's and D's.*

—Amy

*I'm very hard on my kids—particularly my five-year-old daughter—when it comes to public conduct. I have this constant fear that they are going to act out and not live up to the level of etiquette that exists in my head. I'm constantly watching them for infractions and worrying that they are out of line—which, admittedly, they are at times, but I really think I go overboard on this and jump the gun too fast if I spot a pending "situation." If I could relax more and let them be kids—annoying kids—more in terms of yelling and bickering, I think we'd all be happier.*

—Nicole

*My son's grades aren't fabulous, and I'm trying to instill better work habits and push him to be the best he can be. But I'm also trying to show him that I don't expect him to be the best all the time and get an A on every test. I don't like when I see him not trying his hardest, or rushing through his work, or goofing around. But I also don't want him to feel that I expect perfection. It's difficult to know where the line is that separates the two.*

*—Betty*

*I have a hard time rooting in a positive fashion for my daughter when she plays soccer. She is not in love with the sport and consequently doesn't give it her all. This frustrates me to no end on the sidelines and I have a tendency to be short and critical with her on the topic of soccer. She has so many other wonderful qualities though, so I hope not to get hung up on this one!*

*—Joyce*

*I try to be a "perfect" parent, or as perfect as I can be in a given situation. So when I see myself making a mistake, I feel almost paralyzed. I know I'm reacting the "wrong" way and I get frustrated with myself. Then I end up either creating a worse situation, or blowing up. It's totally irrational.*

*—Diane*

## Tools You Can Use

Don't worry—just because you're a perfectionist doesn't mean your child is destined to follow in your very perfect footsteps. The mind/body tools described in the next few pages will help you lighten the burden that perfectionism places on you and your kids.

## RETRAIN YOUR BRAIN

Cognitive distortions twist the way perfectionist parents see themselves and their children. What auto-thoughts spring into your mind when you're dealing with your children? What kinds of distorted thinking impact the way you make parenting decisions and choices?

The most common cognitive distortion among perfectionist parents is black-and-white thinking. If you've ever thought, "It's my way or the highway," you know what I'm talking about. Black-and-white thinking leads you to believe that unless a task is done to your high standards, it's done inadequately. Black-and-white thinking tells you that your daughter's birthday party has to be a pageantlike celebration with a homemade cake in the shape of a ballet slipper, twenty-two of your daughter's closest friends, pony rides, arts and crafts projects, and party bags filled with clever handmade doodads—and if it's not, it will be a terrible party. With black-and-white thinking, there are only two ways to do things: your way and the wrong way.

Personalization is another cognitive distortion that plagues perfectionist parenting. You take responsibility for things that are not your fault or that you have no control over. A classic example of this is the parent who blames herself for her child's negative behavior. "If I had been a better parent, my child wouldn't have failed out of college." Personalization is so destructive because, as parents, we want to make everything right for our children, and it's so easy to blame ourselves when anything at all goes wrong.

Here are some other common cognitive distortions that crop up among perfectionist parents:

**Distortion:** Overgeneralization

**Example:** Your son makes a couple of mistakes at a piano recital; you conclude that he has no musical talent and you're wasting your money on piano lessons.

**Tell yourself:** "How brave of him to be willing to perform! I am proud of him for trying and for spending so much time practicing and taking lessons. Sure, he made a couple of mistakes, but the other kids probably did, too, and I didn't even notice."

**Distortion:** Mental filter

**Example:** The classic perfectionist parent reaction to a report card that has all A's and one B: "Why did you get a B?"

**Tell yourself:** "If I criticize the B, she may feel that my love for her is tied to her grades. I should celebrate her A's rather than pointing out her B's. Besides—B is still a good grade."

---

**Distortion:** Magnification

**Example:** Your teenager does poorly in a science class, and you tell yourself that her chances of ever becoming a doctor are over.

**Tell yourself:** "Failing one class won't end a career. And maybe she doesn't want to be a doctor—maybe I'm pushing her in a direction that's not right for her." (By the way, I got a D in my freshman biology class in college. Despite that D, I was still accepted to graduate school!)

**Distortion:** "Should" statements

**Example:** You're the mother of a six-year-old, and you see that one of your child's classmates can read better than your child. You decide that your child "should" be able to read as well, and there must be something wrong with her if she can't.

**Tell yourself:** "Eventually, all the children in the class will know how to read. The pace of learning does not determine how good a reader a child is. By the end of first grade, my child will probably be reading as well as her classmate."

---

**Distortion:** Labeling

**Example:** Telling your child that he's dumb or lazy when his homework is messy.

**Tell yourself:** "It is never OK to call him names. I should apologize and then sit down with him and work together on how he can make his homework look neater."

---

**Distortion:** Approval seeking

**Example:** You can't stand it when your children disapprove of your decisions, so you allow them to run the show. You want to be their close friend rather than their mean parent. You want them to like you.

**Tell yourself:** "I have to make the decisions that are best for my kids, whether they like it or not. The healthiest kids have parents who set clear limits and boundaries."

---

**Distortion:** Self-righteousness

**Example:** When your child is working on a school project, you give her some advice. You feel annoyed when she doesn't follow it.

**Tell yourself:** "Isn't it great that she is an independent thinker who is willing to go out on a limb and do things unconventionally?"

---

**Distortion:** Fallacy of fairness

**Example:** Your child develops a learning disability, and you take it as a huge unfairness personally directed at you.

**Tell yourself:** "It's normal to feel disappointed and sad about challenges that face my child in the future. But this is not about me, it's about her. I need to spend my energy figuring out how I can help her succeed rather than ruminating over how unfair this is. Lots of kids have bigger problems than mine."

---

**Distortion:** Comparison

**Example:** Your friend's husband takes his kids camping; you decide that your husband is a lazy lout and a poor father because he never takes your kids camping.

**Tell yourself:** "If it's that important to me that the kids go camping, I'll take them myself. And maybe if I plan the trip, my husband will want to come along."

---

Cognitive restructuring works with children, too. If your child expresses a perfectionist auto-thought, help him restructure that thought in a way

Be Happy Without Being Perfect

that is less damaging to him. For example, say your son tells you he's upset because he missed a free throw and, as a result, his basketball team lost a game. "I should have gotten the ball in the hoop!" he tells you. Help him identify the thought behind that statement—that he feels he "should" make every shot, or that he feels he "should" be good at all sports and never make a mistake. Ask him to analyze why he thinks that and where the thought came from. Perhaps he feels that you or your husband have been pushing him too much, or maybe a respected coach lost his temper and gave your son a hard time. Talk with him about the difference between *wanting* to succeed and *expecting* to succeed. Help him restructure his thinking from "I should always get the ball in the hoop," to "I should try my best to get the ball in the hoop, but even LeBron James misses sometimes. It's OK to miss a shot as long as I'm giving it my all."

## PRACTICE EMPATHY

An empathetic parent can give a child a comforting feeling of security. Empathy is the ability to see something from another person's perspective even if you don't agree with that perspective. When you show empathy, you validate your children's feelings. You tell them that it's OK to have those feelings, that they are legitimate and not shameful.

## SHOW YOUR KIDS THAT IT'S OK TO MAKE MISTAKES

You may feel that allowing your children to see you fail hurts them, but in reality, the opposite is true. Modeling self-accepting behavior teaches your children to accept themselves. Point out your mistakes and explain how you handle them. If you calmly set out to rectify the situation, you teach your child a much more helpful lesson than you do if you ignore it, hide it, flip out from it, become angry over it, or overcriticize yourself for it. If your children never see you fail, they'll assume that they should never fail, either.

## RECOGNIZE YOUR CHILDREN'S STRENGTHS AND ACCEPT THEIR WEAKNESSES

It's so tempting to push your children into doing what you love rather than what they love. You know the type—a music-loving dad who pushes his son to play the violin even though he'd rather play on the hockey team; a mom who loves to write nags her daughter to work on the school paper even though she'd rather join the maths team. You have to recognize that your kids have strengths and weaknesses. Let them develop in their own way, guided by their own needs, interests, and strengths.

## HELP YOUR CHILDREN ACCEPT THEIR WEAKNESSES

I often tell my daughters that they can't be good at everything—some things will come easily, and others will be really hard. That's OK. All children have weak spots. Help them to accept those weaknesses as a normal part of life rather than an embarrassing failure. Help them understand the difference between goals and expectations—having perfection as a goal is way more constructive than having it as an expectation. Point out the things you're not good at.

I'm awful at geography, and I let my daughters know that. If I hide my weaknesses, my daughters may think I don't have any, and that they can't, either. I want my girls to see that I don't know everything and can't do everything, so that when they observe weaknesses in themselves, they will figure that it's normal. Last year when Sarah was studying state capitals, I asked her to quiz me. Let me just say that my geographical disability was in full force. (OK, I knew only fifteen of the fifty capitals.) My family teased me about it mercilessly, although they've now moved on to making fun of me because I recently asked my husband why it wasn't possible to take a train from Dublin to London. As I said, we all have strengths and weaknesses!

Be Happy Without Being Perfect

## HELP YOUR CHILDREN SET REALISTIC EXPECTATIONS

Just like perfectionist adults, perfectionist children become angry at themselves when their performance doesn't meet their expectations. You can help by working with your child to set realistic, achievable goals. Nothing illustrates this better than paint-by-number sets. These things are marketed for children, but they are impossible even for adults to do well. Kids can't paint those little tiny numbered spaces. But they think they can—and should—because they look at the cover of the box and see a perfectly painted picture. Then they look at their own blotchy work and feel tremendously disappointed. They feel like they've failed.

When your children set out to do something, help them set realistic expectations. If your child is applying for college, for example, work with her to get a realistic handle on what types of colleges she can probably get into. If she runs a solid C average, Oxford is unlikely to accept her. That's not to say she shouldn't shoot for the stars—but she shouldn't expect to be accepted and condemn herself when a rejection arrives.

You can do this with children of all ages. One of the women we spoke with, Theresa, has discovered the importance of setting realistic expectations before family vacations. When her children were in pre-school, she and her husband took them to Disney World. The kids were crazy with excitement, but once they got to Disney, they cried with disappointment. Where was Mickey Mouse? (They had expected him to greet them at the front gate.) Why couldn't they go upstairs in the castle? And why was there a fifty-five-minute wait at the flying Dumbo ride? "It was supposed to be a perfect dream-come-true vacation, but instead, it was a nightmare," Theresa said. "Disney World was nothing like they expected. It was hot. They were exhausted. One of them had a meltdown in the Hall of Presidents, which we ducked into just to cool off."

Theresa learned (the hard way) how important it is to work with kids to set realistic expectations. Next time she takes the kids to Disney World (if there is a next time), she will prepare her children beforehand by discussing the difficult parts of the trip. Then her kids won't feel like their perfect vacation is ruined when they discover a two-hour wait for the Pirates of the Caribbean ride. They'll know what to expect.

## FOCUS ON THE POSITIVE

It is human nature to focus on the negative, but it can really chop away at your child's self-esteem. It's not always an easy thing to focus on the positive. I've observed friends and relatives seeing a child's report card for the first time and zeroing in on the lowest grade, rather than the highest. And once Sarah began to bring home graded tests and reports from school, I realized how easy that was to do. You want to say, "How could you have misspelled that word? We practiced it over and over and you had it down cold!" But that is exactly the wrong message to give a kid. If your child gets a 75 percent on a test that he worked hard studying for, it means that he knew 75 percent of the material. Focus on that, rather than on the 25 percent he didn't know.

## MODEL "GOOD ENOUGH" BEHAVIOR

Kids imitate adults. If you do everything perfectly, it makes sense that your children may try to do everything perfectly, too. Help your children learn that sometimes good enough is good enough. Once in a while, let them see you putting towels away without folding them perfectly. Keep using a mug even though it's chipped. If you make a mistake on a grocery list, let them see you crossing it out rather than rewriting the whole list. And let them do things "just good enough" once in a while. Let your child mess up the kitchen making pancakes with Dad. Let it go when your children wrap a birthday gift for another child and get the paper all crumpled. Show them that not everything has to be perfect.

Be Happy Without Being Perfect

# PRACTICE "THOUGHT-STOPPING" WITH YOUR CHILDREN

As I mentioned in Chapter 3, thought-stopping is a wonderful mind/body tool that allows you to stop the negative automatic thoughts that run through your mind. For parents, it's a great way to stop your judgmental, critical thoughts from turning into sharp comments that can hurt your child. When you find yourself thinking an automatic negative thought about your child's performance or behavior, visualize a big red-and-white stop sign. Immediately come to a mental standstill. Take a deep breath. Ask yourself about the thought—where did it come from? Why are you thinking of it? How would it hurt your child if you expressed it to her? Then make a deliberate, mindful choice to reframe the thought and, if necessary, adjust your behavior. Remember these four steps: Stop, breathe, reflect, and choose.

## DO "A MINI"

Mini relaxations are a perfect way to take a quick, refreshing break from a stressful situation. You can do a mini anytime—when you're having a tussle with your teen over his homework, when your daughter is begging to stay up late, when you and your husband are locking horns about whether to punish your kids for spilling juice in the back of the car. There are several ways to do a mini—see page 75 for details. One of the quickest ways is to inhale deeply; as you inhale, count very slowly from one to four, and as you exhale, count very slowly from four to one. Repeat several times.

## NURTURE YOURSELF

Taking care of yourself is essential—and it's something that perfectionist parents often neglect to do. How can you take time for yourself when you're so busy being a perfect mom? Self-nurturing is not selfish. It is self-care, and in addition to helping reduce your stress levels, it actually helps you be a better parent. Aim for thirty minutes of self-nurture a day. Here are some excellent ways to take care of yourself:

- See a movie (kid movies don't count).
- Have coffee with a friend.
- Take a long walk with your sister.
- Escape with a good book and a cup of hot cocoa.
- Go out to dinner with friends.
- Take a long bike ride.
- Play tennis.
- Treat yourself to a one-hour session with a personal trainer.
- Take a yoga class.
- Eat a piece of really rich, dark, heavenly chocolate.
- Ask your husband to check the homework.
- Order pizza instead of cooking.
- Go for a run.
- Cuddle up on the couch and listen to music.
- Lie in a hammock and listen to an audiobook.
- Draw, sketch, or paint (it doesn't have to look perfect).
- Play the piano.
- Ask your husband for a massage.
- Pour a glass of wine or brew a cup of tea and watch *Casablanca*.

## REMEMBER HOW YOU WERE PARENTED

Were your parents perfectionists? Was perfectionism part of your family culture, woven into your family's religious, social, or ethnic traditions? If so, how did you feel always trying to live up to their standards, being criticized for the slightest mistake, being praised only when you did everything well? Remind yourself of those feelings and ask yourself if that's how you want your child to feel.

Try practicing what I call "mindful parenting." So many of us make

Be Happy Without Being Perfect

seat-of-the-pants parenting choices. Often those choices are fine, but if you are a perfectionist, your first instinct may be too harsh. Be mindful as you interact with your children. Be mindful of what you say to them, how you react to them, what you expect of them. Think ahead about future reactions—for example, on report card day, think about your potential responses before your children come home from school. Use cognitive restructuring to prepare yourself to react supportively but firmly, rather than critically and hurtfully.

Mindful parenting can help you move away from detrimental patterns you learned from your own parents when you were a child. It allows you to examine your parenting style and choose parenting techniques based on conscious thought rather than gut reaction. You don't have to raise your kids the way you were raised.

## JOURNAL ABOUT YOUR PARENTING SKILLS

Use your journal as a tool to examine and improve your interactions with your children. On the left side of a page, describe an event that occurred between you and your child, including your reaction and any comments you made. Then, on the right side of the page, write down how you would like to have responded. Ask yourself: How could I have better handled the situation? What did I say to my child that I regret? How will I handle similar situations in the future?

You can use your journal to explore the feelings you have about your children. Write about your worries, fears, expectations, disappointments, frustrations—getting your feelings down on paper can help you understand them better. When you understand yourself and your motivations, you can experience greater mindfulness—which always leads to better parenting.

## GET HELP IF YOUR CHILD NEEDS IT

In rare cases, children with perfectionist expectations and behaviors need professional help. If your child is really struggling, consider making an appointment with a child psychologist or other counselor. Your pediatrician or school counselor should be able to refer you to a qualified professional.

If your child is a perfectionist, watch for signs of depression, anxiety, panic, disordered eating, obsession with appearance, and substance abuse. Talk with your doctor if your child behaves in an obsessive, compulsive, or ritualistic way.

Of course, as a perfectionist you may bristle even at the *thought* of taking your child to a shrink. Restructure that thought right out of your head. If your child needs professional help, don't let your reluctance to appear imperfect, or your fear of being judged a bad parent, keep you from getting your child needed help. It's not about you, it's about your child.

*I think that I get so caught up in things being done the "right way"—whatever that is—that I sometimes don't see how ridiculous I am being. There is a certain look my kids give me when I have gone over my perfectionist edge, almost fright, or even horror, and when I see that look it forces me to take a deep breath and examine the sanity of my actions. And to be honest, during these occasions, even I can see how irrational I am. Being able to laugh at myself feels so good, and it relieves the kids, too. Who wants a mom who goes berserk if they leave a wet towel on the floor? When I catch myself during these moments, I add humor and sarcasm and we have fun with it. If only the neighbors knew about the wet towel slap fests, or the time that I stuffed dirty socks that I found on the kitchen counter up my shirt to give myself a really big bust . . .*

*—Gloria*

# CHAPTER 10

# Stop Agonizing Over Decisions

*I recently decided to leave my job as a human resources manager at a large airline. I just didn't want to deal with it any more—the travel, the layoffs, the negativity—so I quit and started selling real estate instead.*

*I'm still questioning whether that was the right decision. I put a lot of pressure on myself to do well and to be successful, and so far, I'm not doing well. I joined a real estate company and was led to believe that I would be successful from the beginning, but it's not happening. Other people in the office are selling two or three properties a month, but I'm not selling anything. The business is out there; I just have to find it.*

*I'm worried that maybe the timing for this career change wasn't quite right. I just had my second child and we're building a new house. But there would always be a reason not to do it. The timing is never really right for a career change.*

*I keep thinking that this decision has ruined my family's future. It's churning over and over in my mind. I went to the doctor last week and my blood pressure was up. If the new job doesn't kick in within the next two or three months, I'm going to have to give up on real estate and go back to human resources. I dread that because it will require lots of travel. HR is very negative—you're dealing with people who are upset with management, or with managers who want to fire someone, or you have to do layoffs. But I may have no choice. I have to start generating some income.*

*I tend to go over decisions a lot. I agonize over them. I look at everything a hundred different ways. I'm OK with smaller decisions— it's the big, life-changing decisions that are hard.*

*—Jennifer*

We make hundreds of decisions every day. Some are minor—what to cook for dinner, which shoes to wear, whether to watch TV or read the paper. Some are major—whether to have a child, change jobs, get married, get divorced. Everyone struggles to some extent with decision making, but perfectionists can find it particularly hard because they want to find perfect solutions. Often, making a decision means leaping into the great unknown or picking from among several less-than-perfect choices. Perfectionists don't like doing either of those things.

Whenever there's a choice, there's an opportunity for failure. Perfectionists want to do things the *right* way. We don't want to make a mistake. Because of black-and-white thinking, it can be paralyzing to have to choose between two options of equal value—either good or bad— because one really is not any better than the other. You want to pick the best, but when there is no clear best you're stuck, anxiously trying to make a decision that you won't regret.

Having to choose can cause tremendous anxiety. Small decisions can sometimes cause more anxiety than big ones because there are so many of them. Perfectionists tend to think there's one right way or one best way to do something, and they feel enormous pressure to choose the right or best from among all of the many wrong options. A perfectionist's natural insecurity makes matters worse, because it produces the self-doubt and second-guessing that makes decision making even harder. A perfectionist can struggle under the weight of even the least important decisions, as Patricia explains:

*At the gym I couldn't decide whether to do twenty sit-ups or forty sit-ups. Too many would hurt my back, and too few wouldn't strengthen my stomach. I agonized over that one for the longest time—that's a piece of perfectionism for you.*

If you grew up in a household with parents who made all the decisions, and then married a man who makes all the decisions, it's not too late. There are plenty of women who have woken up at age forty or fifty or sixty and realized they can make their own decisions. You have to *want* to get better at decision making, as Patricia did:

*A few years ago, I decided to get better at making decisions and worry about them less. I realized I was fussing over small decisions, and I thought, this is really silly. I am missing things because I'm sitting around agonizing about a decision. Identifying that was key. Once I realized what a problem it was for me, I set a goal to start making crisper decisions. I just started doing it, one decision at a time. If you do it a lot with the small decisions, the bigger ones are easier.*

Oddly enough, some perfectionists actually find it easy to make decisions. Here's why: because they have a very rigid way of looking at things, and all of their decisions are made in a way that supports their rigid worldview. They make decisions without careful thought because that's just the way they do it. There's no decision about where to buy clothes because they always shop at John Lewis. There's no decision about what to make for dinner because they always serve spaghetti and meatballs on Thursday. Grandpa went to Oxford and Daddy went to Oxford, so Johnny should go to Oxford, too. No question about it.

Decision making is easier for these people, but that doesn't mean they are happier. When rigid perfectionists let down their guards and start opening up to other options, it can be very hard at first. But after they get the hang of it, they tend to feel much better as they escape from the rigid rules they impose on themselves.

# A Decision-Making Paradox

Barry Schwartz, a professor of social theory and social action at Swarthmore College, has written a fascinating book about decision making called *The Paradox of Choice: Why More Is Less*. In it he makes a case for the idea that having too many choices can contribute to bad decision making, anxiety, stress, dissatisfaction, and even clinical depression. Some choice is good, he notes, but that doesn't necessarily mean that more is better. He believes that as Americans' freedom of choice expands, we are feeling less and less satisfied.

Schwartz recounts a trip to his neighborhood supermarket. The store, which was not particularly large, offered 85 different varieties and brands of crackers, 285 types of cookies (including 21 kinds of chocolate chip cookies), 85 flavors and brands of juices, 230 kinds of soup (including 29 types of chicken noodle), 175 salad dressings, 275 varieties of cereal, and 22 types of frozen waffles. "If you were a truly careful shopper," he writes, "you could spend the better part of a day just to select a box of crackers, as you worried about price, flavor, freshness, fat, sodium, and calories. But who has the time to do this?"

Because of all these choices, Americans spend more time shopping than members of any other society, Schwartz says. We go to shopping centers about once a week. There are more shopping centers in America than high schools. Not only must we make choices about thousands and thousands of products, but we must pick which phone company to use, what health insurance to buy, and how to invest our retirement money. We have more choices than ever before regarding our work, our love lives, and our religions. With plastic surgery, we can even decide how we want to look, Schwartz says.

The Internet makes decision making even harder because it gives perfectionists unlimited research potential. No matter how much you read about something on the Internet—whether it be a medical procedure or the best snow tires—there's always more information available.

Be Happy Without Being Perfect

It's hard for a perfectionist to stop researching without feeling that she's leaving an important part of the decision-making process unfinished.

## Maximizers and Satisficers

Making all these decisions is tough for anyone. But it's even more excruciating for perfectionists. Schwartz calls them "maximizers" because they seek and accept only the best. Maximizers "spend a great deal of time and effort on the search, reading labels, checking out consumer magazines, and trying new products. Worse, after making a selection, they are nagged by the options they haven't had time to investigate. In the end, they are likely to get less satisfaction out of the exquisite choices they make. . . . When reality requires maximizers to compromise—to end a search and decide on something—apprehension about what might have been takes over."

The opposite of maximizers are satisficers, Schwartz says, using a term that was initially introduced by the psychologist Herbert Simon in the 1950s. Satisficers are the people who can "settle for something that is good enough and not worry about the possibility that there might be something better. A satisficer has criteria and standards. She searches until she finds an item that meets those standards, and at that point, she stops."

Being a maximizer can make you miserable, especially in a world that offers an overwhelming number of choices. Schwartz has found that, compared with satisficers, maximizers take longer to make decisions, spend more time thinking about hypothetical alternatives, feel less positive about their decisions, and are more likely to regret their choices. Maximizers are more likely than satisficers to be dissatisfied with life, unhappy, pessimistic, depressed, and anxious. Not only do maximizers tend to feel regret after making decisions, but they can experience regret before making a decision. "You imagine how you'll feel if you discover that there was a better option available. And that leap of imagination may be all it takes to plunge you into a mire of uncertainty—even misery—over every looming decision," Schwartz says.

The good news: Maximizers can learn to be more like satisficers. I'll tell you more about that later in the chapter.

## Anatomy of a Decision

I counsel a lot of women who have trouble getting pregnant. Once an infertile woman does conceive, she is completely overjoyed. Her prayers have been answered! She's having a baby (or two or three)! Unfortunately, if these women are over age thirty-five, as most are, they soon face one of the toughest decisions of their lives: whether to have an amniocentesis.

Amniocentesis is an extremely reliable test that can detect Down syndrome and other chromosomal abnormalities. During the test, a doctor inserts a hollow needle through the woman's abdomen and into her uterus and removes a small sample of the amniotic fluid that surrounds the baby. The cells in the fluid are analyzed and tested for various defects.

No abnormalities are detected in more than 95 percent of women who have amniocentesis. However, sometimes the test finds that the fetus has a problem of some kind, and the parents must decide whether to end the pregnancy or continue it and deliver a child with a chromosonal abnormality.

Unfortunately, amniocentesis is not without risk. The test causes approximately 1 in 200 women or fewer to miscarry. It's a small but real risk.

However, there is also a small but real risk of delivering a baby with a birth defect. The risk goes up with the mother's age. For example, Down syndrome rates are 1 in 1,250 for a woman at age twenty-five, 1 in 1,000 at age thirty, 1 in 400 at age thirty-five, and 1 in 100 at age forty, according to the March of Dimes (an American foundation to improve the health of babies).

One of my patients, Jean, recently sat crying in my office, paralyzed over whether to have an amniocentesis. Jean and her husband spent six years and tens of thousands of dollars trying to become pregnant. On the one hand, if Jean were to have an amniocentesis and suffer a miscarriage, she would not only lose her baby, but perhaps her only chance to have a biological child. On the other hand, if she didn't have an amniocentesis, she may give birth to a baby with a very serious disability. Jean is forty-two; women her age have more than a 1 percent chance of delivering a baby with Down syndrome.

Talk about a life-or-death decision.

Jean and her husband examined the decision from all angles. They were desperate for a baby, but they didn't feel that they could parent a severely disabled child. No matter how many times they went over it, they still couldn't decide.

I offered them several suggestions. I asked them to think about what they would regret most—having a miscarriage or a disabled child. I told them to visualize what their lives would be like if either of those events occurred, and to think about which would be worse for them. Finally, I told them to listen to what their inner wisdom was telling them—in other words, to pay attention to their gut feelings.

Jean and her husband decided to have an amniocentesis. They used numbers to make their decision: Jean's risk of having a baby with Down syndrome was statistically higher than her chance of having a miscarriage, so they went with the amniocentesis. Luckily, the test did no harm to the baby and the results were normal. Their baby is due in a couple of months.

## The Pain of Regret

Regret for past decisions can haunt you. Melinda, a patient with ovarian cancer, felt crushing regret for having an abortion while in college. She came from a very religious family, and she felt that cancer was her punishment for having an abortion. I explained that the abortion had nothing to do with her cancer, but it made no difference to her—she couldn't escape her regret.

Melinda told me she was going to see a nun who did pastoral counseling. I was not crazy about this idea, because I thought for sure the nun would reinforce my patient's feelings of guilt and regret. Melinda insisted on it, though, and she made an appointment to speak with the nun.

The next visit, Melinda told me what had happened. She had told the nun about the abortion, and the nun was incredibly supportive. She told Melinda something that has stayed with me ever since: Melinda made the best decision for herself *at the time.*

There may be decisions you made in the past that you now regret, but in almost all circumstances they were the best decisions you could have made based on your knowledge, maturity, resources, support, and other factors in place at that time. The problem with regret is that we revisit old decisions and look at them with new eyes—Melinda looked at the abortion she had when she was nineteen and viewed it within her thirty-eight-year-old perfectionist frame of reference. But when she made the choice to have the abortion, she wasn't a woman with thirty-eight years of perspective on life. She was a scared teenager. She did what she thought was best at the time.

We have to forgive and empathize with our younger selves. I'm seeing a patient now who's in her seventies, and she still regrets her choice to get married at age seventeen. In hindsight, she sees that the boy she married was no good. She married him just to get out of the house, to get away from an abusive father. Looking back with the wisdom of a seventy-year-old she can see that she had other options—but the only option she saw when she was seventeen was marrying the first person who came along.

Judging your past does you no good. Regret gets you nowhere. Instead, try to remember past decisions with empathy and compassion.

## We Asked Women . . .

### How does perfectionist thinking affect your ability to make a decision?

*I can't make any decisions. I drive my husband crazy. Every house we've lived in there's been a huge fight and lack of decision on house color. My husband paints a side and gets so mad when I don't like it and change my mind. Once he threw a ladder in the woods and refused to paint for me again. When it all calms down, he says something noncommittal, like, "Let's just finish in this color, and if you don't like it I'll change it in the fall." Then I'm happy because I have an out if it doesn't seem perfect—but I never end up changing the house color in the fall.*

*—Dorothy*

*My decisions take a while and I put a lot of effort into them. This weekend, I wanted to buy a new vacuum cleaner. I read* Consumer Reports *first, and then I went online to do research. I thought I knew what I wanted, but when I went looking I couldn't figure out which models in the store matched the ones reviewed in* Consumer Reports. *I ended up not buying anything.*

*—Helen*

*I am a woman of action. I don't mull over any decisions, large or small.*

*—Ruth*

*I struggle with second guessing the decisions I've made. Today, my daughter is sick. Should I have left her at daycare, or should I have stayed home with her? I second guess the big decisions, too. Should I have become a lawyer or a teacher? Should we be a stay-at-home family*

*or a working family, a big-house family or small-house family? I admire people who can say what's done is done and move on from there.*
*—Kimberly*

*I would say that almost every big decision in my life has caused me undue stress. I don't trust myself, though by now I should have learned that once I make a decision, it's usually a very good one.*
*—Angela*

## Tools You Can Use

If you struggle to make decisions, techniques can come to the rescue. The following are some cognitive tools and strategies that will ease your decision-making processes.

### RETRAIN YOUR BRAIN

Cognitive distortions can stand in the way of sensible decision making. Because they are illogical, cognitive distortions alter your ability to look clearly at a set of choices and pick the best one. Cognitive restructuring can be very useful in decision making because it allows you to view your options with clearer eyes.

As you work on your decision-making capabilities, remember to identify the thought, challenge the thought, and then restructure the thought.

One of the most common distortions that impede decision making is black-and-white thinking. This kind of thinking tells you that one option is right and the others are wrong. Sometimes that's the case, but more often we're called upon to pick from among several equally valid choices—that's why decision making is so hard.

Here are some of the other common cognitive distortions that interfere with decision making:

**Distortion:** Overgeneralization

**Example:** You tell yourself that you "never" make good decisions and you "always" regret your choices.

**Tell yourself:** "I doubt that every decision I make is poor. If that were true, I'd be in jail. All of us make decisions we regret and occasional poor choices, but most of my decisions are good."

---

**Distortion:** Mental filter

**Example:** While deciding whether to accept a job offer, you dwell on only the negatives of your current position and the positives of the new job. Mental filtering prevents you from seeing that both jobs have pros and cons.

**Tell yourself:** "It's highly unlikely that the new job is perfect. And when I think about it, I realize there are some good things about my current job. I'll make my decision after thinking honestly about this and writing a pro-con list."

---

**Distortion:** Jumping to conclusions

**Example:** A friend tells you she likes the new camera she bought, so you buy the same one without taking the time to determine whether it's the right camera for you.

**Tell yourself:** "What's right for other people is not necessarily right for me—we may have very different needs and expectations."

---

**Distortion:** Minimalization

**Example:** When making a decision, you rely heavily on others' opinions and ignore or discount your own gut feeling.

**Tell yourself:** "Nobody else can look out for my best interest better than I can. Other people may not fully understand the choice I have to make. Or their advice may be colored with feelings of competition, jealousy, or their own personal feelings. I have to go with my gut and make the decision that is best for me."

---

**Distortion:** "Should" statements

**Example:** When a friend invites you to a Friday night birthday bash, you can't decide whether to go because you and your kids usually have dinner with Grandma on Friday nights and you feel that you should not break that family tradition.

**Tell yourself:** "Sometimes shaking things up is good. New traditions are sometimes born when older traditions are changed. We'll have brunch with Grandma on Sunday—we'll still see her, just at a different time."

**Distortion:** Labeling

**Example:** When trying to choose a doctor for an important medical procedure, you rule out all physicians with foreign-sounding names because you don't want to have to deal with a doctor who has an accent.

**Tell yourself:** "I am letting bias and discriminatory thinking influence my decision. Having an accent doesn't equal incompetence. Some of the most brilliant doctors and scientists in the United States come from other countries and have accents."

**Distortion:** Approval seeking

**Example:** When eating at a restaurant with a healthy-eating friend, you order a salad even though you're dying for a steak.

**Tell yourself:** "This is silly. I should eat what I want. All I had for lunch was a cup of nonfat yogurt, and I'm starving. Who knows, maybe my friend had a huge lunch and is still full. Or maybe she only eats healthfully when she's with me. Maybe if I order a steak she'll be relieved and order one, too."

**Distortion:** Reductionism

**Example:** It rains every day on your vacation, and you blame yourself for choosing that week even though you had no way of knowing it would rain.

**Tell yourself:** "Yes, it's a bummer when there's rain on vacation. But it happens. Instead of blaming myself, I'll spend my energy on finding some good rainy-day activities. I may even find a fascinating museum or lovely

Be Happy Without Being Perfect

art gallery that I would have missed if I spent the whole week on the beach."

**Distortion:** Comparison

**Example:** You decide which car to buy based on what kind of car your neighbor drives.

**Tell yourself:** "The kind of car I drive should depend on my needs, not my neighbor's."

## LEARN FROM SATISFICERS

*My problem is I have so many ideas that I have trouble choosing. Since my decisions have to be perfect decisions, it's very hard to know which path to go down.*

—*Melissa*

Maximizers search for perfection. They can learn a lot from satisficers, who tend to settle for "good enough." Satisficers understand the difference between a good decision and a perfect decision. They are willing to take risks and make mistakes. And they don't let themselves be consumed by regrets if a decision turns out poorly. As Barry Schwartz notes in *The Paradox of Choice,* satisficers usually feel better about the decisions they make. "The trick is to learn to *embrace* and *appreciate* satisficing, to cultivate it in more and more aspects of life," Schwartz writes. "Becoming a conscious, intentional satisficer makes comparison with how other people are doing less important. It makes regret less likely. In the complex, choice-saturated world we live in, it makes peace of mind possible."

## RELAX

Perfectionists can spend half an hour deciding which jeans to wear. You get stuck in a cycle of indecision and anxiety. The more anxious you are, the harder it is to make a decision—and the longer it takes you to make a decision, the more anxious you get.

You don't think clearly when you're anxious because anxiety puts you into fight-or-flight mode. Your entire body is responding to a perceived threat by preparing you to fight or run away. The problem is, your body is prepared for battle when what you really need is to decide which shoes to buy or how to have your hair cut or whom to marry or what job to take. To make a good decision, it really helps to be in a calm place.

When a decision is causing you anxiety, do some of the relaxation exercises described in Chapter 4. As you calm down and gain control, you'll be able to think more clearly. Relaxation can stop the what-ifs racing through your mind and allow you the peace you need to make a smart decision. So many times my patients have told me that in the middle of a relaxation exercise, the solution to a problem just pops into their minds.

## START WITH BABY STEPS

As you work to strengthen your decision-making muscles, start small. When you feel comfortable, move up to bigger decisions. One of my patients followed this strategy. She had grown up in an extremely structured home with inflexible parents, and at a young age had married an older man who made all of the couple's decisions. They ate out all the time, and I urged her to begin the process of becoming an effective decision maker by stepping forward and voicing her opinion about what restaurant they would go to. It took her three weeks to get up the courage to tell her husband one night that she wanted to go out for French instead of Italian. He said sure—luckily he was good about her asserting more control. It was interesting to watch her over the next few years as she moved from baby steps to much larger decisions. Over time she became an equal decision-making partner.

## VISUALIZE LIVING WITH YOUR DECISION

We usually think of visualization as a good way to relax—and it is. But it's also an excellent decision-making tool, because it allows you to "see" the repercussions of the choices you face. After using one of the relax-

Be Happy Without Being Perfect

ation techniques in Chapter 4 to calm your mind, visualize how each of your alternatives would feel. Visualize yourself living with your decision—take time to really see, feel, and hear it.

Visualization helped my patient Jean decide whether to have an amniocentesis. She spent some quiet, relaxed time picturing herself as the mother of a child with Down syndrome. Then she visualized herself having a miscarriage and not being able to conceive again. Both scenes upset her, but by visualizing them in a thorough, thoughtful way, she was better able to make her decision.

## TRY IT ON

This strategy works well with my six-year-old daughter Katie. She loves Webkinz, a kind of virtual stuffed pet. Recently, after Katie bravely faced a blood test at the pediatrician's office, I told her I'd treat her to a Webkinz critter. At the toy store she narrowed her selection down to two but couldn't decide on one. She did eenie-meenie (an excellent decision-making tool), but when she realized which one her eenie-meenie landed on, her face fell. That wasn't the one she wanted, but she didn't recognize that until she really thought about owning it.

If you can't decide between decision A and decision B, try to visualize making decision A. See how it feels. See what your gut tells you. If it feels good, it's probably the right decision. If it doesn't, then your answer is probably decision B. If neither feels particularly good, then think about which one feels worse. Which would you regret more?

You can also try to imagine that decision A has been taken away from you. How do you feel being left with decision B? If you lose one of the choices and you're happy about it, bingo—that's what you want to do. This is a technique I recommend for women who are facing a medical decision, such as choosing between mastectomy or lumpectomy for breast cancer. I tell them to imagine the doctor telling them that they absolutely cannot do a lumpectomy, and to see how they feel—relieved? distressed? Those feelings can help shape their decision.

## DEFINE ALL OF YOUR OPTIONS

If neither decision A or decision B feels right, maybe there are options you haven't considered. Do a relaxation exercise to calm your mind, and then think about whether you've overlooked decision C and decision D.

## USE A "WHAT IF" TREE TO UNDERSTAND WHAT YOU FEAR

This helps you root out fears that may be hiding behind your decision-making roadblocks. It's a kind of decision tree. A patient of mine used this strategy to decide whether to look for a new job. Using one what-if after the other, she followed her thoughts down the line to her real fear: that if she left her job she'd lose her security and end up on the street. Without realizing it, she was equating "get a new job" with the chance of ending up in a homeless shelter. Once she uncovered this fear, she was able to face it, realize how irrational it was, and do the cognitive restructuring necessary to put it in perspective.

## PUT IT IN WRITING

I'm a huge believer in using journaling to make decisions. Journaling helps dislodge you when you're stuck between choices. Here are some journaling strategies worth trying:

- Use journaling to clarify your goals. What do you want? What is most important to you?
- Clearly define the problem by writing about it.
- Write a pro and con list, keeping in mind the short-term as well as the long-term.
- Describe the decision and how you feel about it. Sometimes just putting it in writing allows the answer to pop out at you.

Be Happy Without Being Perfect

- After you visualize making a choice, write about it as if you've already made the choice and see how it feels. If you're thinking of ending a relationship, for example, visualize being single and write about how it feels. Write about the good things your decision will bring, as well as the bad things. Journaling can help you "try out" your various options in a safe, realistic way.
- Use journaling to review recent decisions you've made. What did you do well? What did you do poorly? If you uncover your decision-making strengths and weaknesses, you'll be better able to use those strengths to your advantage and avoid the weaknesses.
- Write about the information you've gathered as you've done your homework about the decision, including hard data as well as the opinions of others.
- Write about why this decision is so hard for you. Will someone you love disapprove of it? Is it hard because you're choosing between what you want and what someone else wants? If so, are you doing yourself a disservice by giving so much credence to another person's opinion?

The beauty of journaling is that you can go back to it. If in the future you find yourself regretting your decision, you can go back and see, in black and white, the thought process you used to make the decision you made. Reviewing what you've written can help reinforce the belief that you made the decision that was right for you at the time. Or if you realize you made the wrong decision, examining your thought process can help you learn how to make better choices in the future.

## BREAK BIG DECISIONS INTO SMALLER DECISIONS

Gigi, one of the women we interviewed, is an attorney, but she's not sure she chose the right career path. She thinks she might prefer teaching music, but making such an enormous change feels impossible to her. The idea of quitting her job and going back to school overwhelms her.

Gigi would do well to break her huge career decision into a series of smaller decisions. Abandoning her career as an attorney to become a teacher is a major life change—but taking an education class at night is a small decision. Having lunch with an acquaintance who teaches is a smaller decision. Calling the school and asking for a catalog is an even smaller decision. Carving a tremendous choice into a group of smaller, doable choices makes the decision easier.

## BE ANALYTICAL

There are many ways to use statistics, probability, cost/benefit analysis, and other quantifiable approaches to make decisions. Corporations and other large organizations use them all the time to make tactical choices and strategic plans. These decision-making tools can be pretty involved, so I won't go into them here. But if you'd like to learn more, an organization called Mind Tools (www.mindtools.com) is a good place to start.

## GET HELP DEALING WITH ANXIETY

Sometimes, decision making can cause so much anxiety that it literally immobilizes you. If that's happening to you—if anxiety is interfering with your ability to enjoy life and do your everyday activities—you would probably benefit from professional help. Anxiety is a normal reaction to stress, but when it is excessive it can be disabling. Anxiety disorders can be successfully treated with therapy and/or medication. To learn more, go to the National Association for Mental Health's website (www.mind.org.uk). It has lots of accurate, helpful information about anxiety disorders, along with information about how to locate mental health services providers in your community.

## GO WITH YOUR GUT

Ultimately, decision making comes down to going with your gut. I believe this even though I'm a scientist who relies on hard data. Sometimes after you examine all available data you still don't know what to do.

Be Happy Without Being Perfect

# Learning to Say No

"No" is one of the hardest words for perfectionists to say. Perfectionists are people-pleasers. We take care of people. We want people to like us and approve of us and appreciate us. We want to be seen as good folks, and we don't like to disappoint people. Saying no feels selfish— but it's not. It's an act of self-care and self-nurturance, as Melissa knows all too well: "My son's school was having an assembly, and at the last minute the music teacher couldn't be there to run the sound system. They called me and asked me to manage the music and introduce people and sing some songs with the kids. I should have said no. I had to load CDs into a machine that I'd never worked with before. I was getting really anxious about getting the music right, plus singing songs and introducing all the people. Afterward, nobody said thank you—nobody said anything. I thought, God, what was that for? I bent over backward and didn't get noticed. I wish I'd said no."

The truth is, we have a right to say no. We do not owe the world 24/7 assistance. Our personal value is not determined by how many bake sales we run.

When your neighbor asks you to take care of her cats for three weeks, you can say no in four ways:

1. Just say no, which is really tough to do.
2. Say no with a "because." No, you can't take care of her cats because you're allergic.
3. Say no with a "how about." No, you can't take care of her cats, but how about you give her the phone number of a neighbor who loves cats and would probably be willing to do it.
4. Say you'll get back to her. "I'm right in the middle of something— can I call you back?" That gives you time to make the right decision and, if the answer is no, figure out how to say it. I don't think on my feet quickly, so I use this one all the time.

When this happens, try to calm your mind. Sleep on it. Have a glass of wine. Take a hot shower. Try to shut out all external distractions so you can listen to what your inner wisdom is telling you. You usually know what to do even when you think you don't.

> *I sometimes get stressed out when having to choose something to eat at a restaurant, which is when I really laugh at myself. I'm much better than I used to be, though. When I was in my twenties, I'd have a panic attack trying to choose which socks to wear in the morning—everything had to be perfect. Lately I've become really good at it. Small decisions, big decisions, you name it. I've been running my own life and making all major decisions for myself.*
>
> —Carolyn

# Moving Right Ahead

W hen I was in high school, my sister and I decided to throw a New Year's Eve fondue party. Everyone had so much fun that we gave another party the next New Year's Eve, and the next. It became a tradition that I continued for many years, first with my sister and then, after I got married, with my husband, Dave. We invited new friends and old friends. Over the years the guest list grew longer and longer because we never felt comfortable taking anyone off it, even if the only time we saw them all year was at this party. About ten years ago the crowd became too large for fondue, so we supplied sandwich fixings and desserts and asked each guest to bring a favorite appetizer.

My mother died in late September 2004. When the holidays rolled around, I realized I couldn't possibly plan a party for eighty-five people— I still felt too preoccupied with grief. My husband and I decided not to have our annual New Year's Eve party.

Some of our friends couldn't believe that we were ending this tradition. A few told us that they had spent nearly every New Year's Eve of their adult lives at our parties. Disappointed, they had to look for other ways to celebrate the dawning of the new year.

As the holiday season approached, feelings of perfectionism and guilt made me second guess myself. Did I do the right thing, ending such an established tradition? Should I have pushed myself to have the party for my guests' sakes? Was I letting people down by failing to do what was expected of me? I wasn't sure.

On New Year's Eve, Dave and I spent a quiet evening at a friend's house watching the Times Square celebrations on television and cuddling with our daughters. I thought I might feel sad and lonely without eighty-five people to toast and hug at midnight, but I didn't. In fact, I felt incredibly relieved.

Skipping the party was the best gift I could have given myself—it was such an act of self-nurturance. I didn't realize how much of a burden it had become to throw such a huge party during the craziest time of the year. I laugh when I think about it: If my mother hadn't died, it wouldn't have occurred to me to let go of the party. It was an automatic, unexamined holiday expectation. I had to give the party because I always gave the party. It wasn't a choice, it was a habit.

I learned something that New Year's Eve. It's OK to let go of traditions that don't make sense anymore. You don't have to wait for a major tragedy or life event to give yourself permission. It's also OK to put your own needs first sometimes, even if doing so disappoints eighty-five people. They'll get over it. Changing habits, traditions, and routines is not a sign of weakness or imperfection. It's a way of being happy without being perfect.

## Making Changes

Once you are known as someone who gives 110 percent of your effort to everything, the world expects a lot from you—a pristine house, an unquestioned willingness to work overtime, an automatic yes when the parent-teacher organization needs volunteers to raise money for new playground equipment. Letting go of perfectionist habits can be difficult for the people around you—but don't let that stop you from changing your life for the better.

As you read the advice in this book, you may have felt that your family won't know how to handle it if you start reigning in your perfectionist tendencies. What will they do when you serve a store-bought rotisserie chicken instead of roasting your own? How will they react when you leave a pile of dirty dishes in the sink at bedtime?

It's normal to have a lot of fear about how those around you will respond when you begin to change your habits and behaviors. However, my experience helping women become physically and psychologically healthier is that in most cases, once a woman starts changing for the better, her family is not disappointed—they're relieved. I can't tell you how many women have told me that their husbands were thrilled to see them being less uptight and gentler on themselves. Their husbands are relieved to see them caring less about how the canned foods are arranged in the kitchen cabinets or what color pens should be used to address Christmas

## Resistant Husbands

Some husbands disapprove when their perfectionist wives start lowering their standards. If your husband handles it poorly when you implement some of the suggestions in this book, he could be feeling bewildered and left out of the loop. Sitting down and explaining yourself can help. If that doesn't work, and he continues to resent you for changing your perfectionist habits, you may need to see a couples counselor. Every relationship is a seesaw. If you make a very sudden shift, it can throw the whole relationship off kilter. Counseling may help rebalance your relationship.

Some women find that their husbands cannot accept them when they scale back their perfectionist ways. I've treated patients who have left their husbands because they could no longer stand trying to meet their rigidly perfectionistic ideals. In almost all of these cases, the women were happier without their husbands than with them. It's better to be single and happy than married and trying to live up to pathologically unhealthy expectations.

card envelopes. Even their children respond positively. The people who love you won't care that the coffee table is dusty or the laundry is a little wrinkled. But they will notice if you are smiling more.

Make things easier for your family by telling them what's going on. Explain that you will be making some changes to improve the quality of your life. Describe the changes and share the reasons behind them. This is especially important if you'll be asking them to take on more responsibilities. If you include them in your thought processes, they're more likely to give you the patience and cooperation you need to succeed.

## No Hurry

When people decide to change a negative habit, they often set out to make a huge change all at once: Sedentary people decide to start exercising ninety minutes a day. Overweight people decide to lose a hundred pounds. Perfectionists are even more prone to this because of their tendency to give in to all-or-nothing thinking. Try to resist the temptation to make too many changes at once. Go slowly as you work to move yourself away from perfectionism. Take baby steps, especially in situations that affect other people. Make one small change at a time. Not only will you make the transition easier for your family and friends, but you'll be more likely to succeed: Research shows that small, slow changes tend to be far more successful than big, impetuous ones.

Start with something easy. Go back to the quiz at the beginning of this book and refresh your memory about which area in your life is *least* detrimentally affected by perfectionism. Start in the place where you are least perfectionistic because that's where you'll be able to rack up some easy, confidence-building successes. After a while you can build up to the more difficult challenges in your life.

Don't give up if it's not working. If you try changing one area of your life and fail miserably, move on to another area.

You may need to think about all this for a while before you jump into a less-than-perfect way of life. Researchers who study the process of

Be Happy Without Being Perfect

change have found that acquiring some level of "readiness" for change, which comes after careful thought and planning, boosts success. It's OK to contemplate all this for a while. You've been a perfectionist all your life, so a few extra weeks or months won't make much difference.

## The Joy of No

As you start to let go of your perfectionist expectations, you'll find yourself saying no more often. This can be uncomfortable for you and for the people you're saying no to. Begin small and say no to little things. Notice that the world doesn't fall apart. Then take it up a notch. Soon you'll be saying no like a pro.

Once you feel you've made some progress, you can start encouraging the perfectionists around you to take some baby steps, too. You can't force other people to change their perfectionist ways, but you can be a role model. If you're feeling more relaxed, less stressed, and happier, if you're laughing more, snapping less, and feeling a greater sense of satisfaction with your life, others can't help but notice.

If you get stuck on some old perfectionist habit, ask yourself: How important is this? We do so many things out of habit or because our mothers did them that way. But, as with my New Year's Eve party, we so seldom ask ourselves whether we really need to do something in a certain "perfect" way. You may find, as I did, that letting go of a perfectionist habit will leave you feeling liberated and lighthearted.

Expect some tough transitions while you begin to shed your perfectionism. As you work to become less of a perfectionist, you'll sometimes make mistakes—which will bring out the perfectionist in you! Be patient with yourself and know that slip-ups are part of the normal process of change. Nutritionists say you have to introduce children to a new food ten times before they learn to like it. The same is true with perfectionists—it takes us a while to change our ways. If you struggle, just pick yourself up and keep trying.

Remember—practice makes perfect.

# Index

automatic thoughts (*continued*)
    stopping of, 64–65, 116, 241
    *see also* cognitive distortions;
        cognitive restructuring

# B
baby care, 42–43, 195–96
babysitters, 215, 219, 225
Bailey, Kent G., 206
Bartholomew, John, 106
Baumrind, Diana, 221
Beck, Aaron T., 60
Beecher, Catharine E., 21–22
belittling or minimalization, 61, 167
    body issues and, 100, 101
    decision making and, 255
Benson, Herbert, 68
black-and-white thinking, 39
    body issues and, 99, 102
    decision making and, 246, 254
    parenting and, 222, 234
    work issues and, 170
body and weight issues, 43, 53–54,
        89–123
    aging and, 116–17
    automatic thoughts and, 96–97,
        115–16
    cognitive distortions and, 98–102
    eating disorders and, see eating
        disorders
    gratitude and, 110–11
    illness and, see health problems
    media images and, 91–92, 111–12
    parenting and, 216, 217–18
    quiz on feelings about, 9–10
    rewards and, 114–15
    self-forgiveness and, 115–16
    setting realistic eating goals,
        107–8
    setting realistic exercise goals, 104,
        105–6

setting realistic weight goals, 102–5
    sexuality and, 112–14, 123
Borysenko, Joan, 195
Braiker, Harriet B., 167–68, 199–200
breathing exercises, 68
    mini relaxations, 75–76, 164, 195,
        241
bulimia nervosa, 43
Burns, David D., 60
Byron, Christopher, 137

# C
catalogs and stores, 29, 30
catastrophizing or magnification, 61,
        193
    dieting and, 101, 115
    parenting and, 235
    relationships and, 193
Child, Lydia, 20–21
children, *see* parenting
clothing, 172
cognitive-behavioral therapy, 148–49
cognitive distortions, 59–64
    all-or-nothing thinking, 39, 41, 60,
        100, 130–31, 169, 268
    approval seeking, 62–63, 102, 130,
        142, 179, 193–94, 236, 256
    black-and-white thinking, 39, 99,
        102, 170, 222, 234, 246, 254
    body-related, 98–102
    comparison, *see* comparison
    decision making and, 254–57
    disqualifying the positive, 61, 130,
        192
    emotional reasoning, 61, 101–2
    fallacy of fairness, 63–64, 236
    fortune-telling, 192
    on home and housework issues,
        130–31
    jumping to conclusions, 61,
        100–101, 192–93, 255

Index

home and housework (*continued*)
  and putting yourself first, 133–35
  quiz on feelings about, 10–11
  sharing work with spouse, 145–48
  stay-at-home mothers and, 138
  working women and, 127, 142
housewives, 24–25
humor, 82–83
  disagreements and, 195

## I

illness, *see* health problems
immune system, 77, 201
  humor and, 82–83
individualism, 20
infertility, 218, 226, 250
injunctions, unconscious, 160
Internet, 248

## J

job, see work
journaling, 77–80, 84
  decision making and, 260–61
  family relationships and, 209
  gratitude and, 77, 80–81, 122
  home issues and, 131, 138
  parenting and, 243
jumping to conclusions, 61
  body issues and, 100–101
  decision making and, 255
  relationships and, 192–93

## K

Katie, 81, 106, 259

## L

labeling and mislabeling, 62
  body issues and, 101
  decision making and, 256
  parenting and, 235
  relationships and, 193

LaRoche, Loretta, 83
laughter, 82–83
Legato, Marianne J., 145, 178
LLuminari, 154

## M

magazines, 23, 26–27, 30–31, 111, 112
  *Martha Stewart Living,* 27–28, 136
magnification or catastrophizing, 61, 193
  dieting and, 101, 115
  parenting and, 235
  relationships and, 193
mantras, 69, 70, 87
marriage, 177–89
  arguments in, 180, 181, 194–95
  changing perfectionist habits and, 197–98, 267
  communication style and, 187
  counseling and, 267
  expectations about, 179–81
  gratitude in, 197
  highs and lows in, 182–83
  "my way or the highway" thinking and, 195–96
  nagging in, 187
  needs and, 183–85, 201
  perfectionism's effects on, 185–86
  reality checks in, 198–99
  taking turns in, 199
  and understanding your husband's viewpoint, 196–97
  work required in, 180–82
*Married to the Job: Why We Live to Work and What We Can Do About It* (Philipson), 170–71
*Martha Inc.* (Byron), 137
*Martha Stewart Living,* 27–28, 136
maximizers, 249–50, 257

media, 29, 31
  advertising in, 24, 29, 30
  home and, 135, 136–37
  images of physical perfection in, 91–92, 111–12
  magazines, 23, 26–28, 30–31, 111, 112
meditation, 68, 69–71
mental filtering, 60, 167
  body issues and, 100, 116
  decision making and, 255
  home issues and, 130
  parenting and, 235
  relationships and, 192
mind/body medicine, 51
  *see also* cognitive distortions; cognitive restructuring
mindfulness, 68, 71–72
mindful parenting, 242–43
mindful walking, 72
mind reading, 184–85, 191, 192
minimalization or belittling, 61, 167
  body issues and, 100, 101
  decision making and, 255
mini relaxations, 75–76
  disagreements and, 195
  parenting and, 241
  at work, 164
models, 92, 93, 112, 113
mothering, see parenting
*Mrs. Doubtfire,* 231
"must" statements, 56, 62
"my way or the highway" thinking, 195–96, 234

### N

nagging, 187
Nani, Christel, 209–10, 229
needs, 4–5, 6, 59, 266
  marriage and, 183–85, 201
  of your children vs. yourself, 225–26
Nelson, Miriam, 103, 117
"never" statements, 56, 62
"news and goods" ritual, 81
"no," learning to say, 263, 269

### O

OCD (obsessive-compulsive disorder), 40–41, 45, 244
  perfectionism vs., 39–40
"ought to" statements, 56, 62
overgeneralization, 60
  decision making and, 255
  parenting and, 234
  relationships and, 191–92
oxytocin, 178–79

### P

*Paradox of Choice, The: Why More Is Less* (Schwartz), 248, 257
parenting, 19, 26, 31–32, 213–44
  and anxiety in children, 216, 217
  authoritarian, 221, 222
  authoritative, 222
  baby care, 42–43, 195–96
  babysitters and, 215, 219, 225
  children's needs in, 225–26
  cognitive distortions and, 233–37
  cognitive restructuring in, 243
  counseling help and, 243–44
  criticism in, 215, 223, 224
  disagreements about, 230–31
  empathy and, 237
  expectations and, 215, 216, 220–21, 223, 226, 237, 238, 239–40
  failure and, 228, 237
  and focusing on the positive, 240
  happiness and, 226–27

performance reviews and, 151–52, 160

rewarding yourself at, 164–65

rumination habits and, 166–67

quiz on feelings about, 11–12

separating home life from, 174–75

to-do list at, 173–74

unconscious injunctions and, 160

women's unique challenges at, 154–55

women's vs. men's approaches to, 170–71

working at home, 172

working mothers, 19, 142, 155, 156–57, 165, 175, 207, 219

World War II, 23

writing, *see* journaling

*Writing to Heal: A Guided Journal for Recovering from Trauma and Emotional Upheaval* (Pennebaker), 80

**Y**

yoga, 68, 72–73, 86, 90

*You Just Don't Understand* (Tannen), 187

## About the Authors

**Alice D. Domar, Ph.D.,** is executive director of the Domar Center for Mind/Body Health in Waltham, Massachusetts. She is also an assistant professor of obstetrics, gynecology, and reproductive biology at Harvard Medical School; director of mind/body services at Boston IVF; and senior staff psychologist at Beth Israel Deaconess Medical Center. She lives in the Boston area with her husband and two daughters. Her previous books include: *Healing Mind, Healthy Woman*; *Self-Nurture*; and *Conquering Infertility* (cowritten with Alice Lesch Kelly).

**Alice Lesch Kelly** is a freelance writer specializing in health and psychology. Her work has appeared in many publications, including the *New York Times, Los Angeles Times, Shape, Health, Reader's Digest, Fit Pregnancy, Woman's Day,* and *O, The Oprah Magazine.* She lives in Newton, Massachusetts, with her husband and two sons.

For more information:
The Domar Center for Mind/Body Health
130 Second Avenue
Waltham MA 02451
USA
(781) 434-6578
www.domarcenter.com

Also from Piatkus:

# THE POWER OF WOMEN

## Harness your unique strengths at home, at work and in your community

## Dr Susan Nolen-Hoeksema

Women are transforming the world and transforming the face of power. In *The Power of Women*, leading psychologist Dr Susan Nolen-Hoeksema puts the spotlight on women's man gifts and argues passionately that it is time for society to recognise and make the most of their extraordinary strengths for the betterment of everyone. She inspires women everywhere to recognise and employ their talents and distinctive skill sets so they can reach their full potential. In this important and motivating book you will discover how to:

- Identify and harness your four key strengths
- Enhance your natural skills as an entrepreneur and manager, wife and mother, mentor and community leader
- Develop your inventiveness, resilience and determination
- Pursue your talents and your dreams

'I've been waiting for a long time, for a sensible, non-strident, evidence-based book about the strengths of women. This is it!'

Dr Martin Seligman, professor of psychology, University of Pennsylvania, and author of *Authentic Happiness*

978-0-7499-2883-4

# THE HOW OF HAPPINESS

## A practical guide to getting the life you want

## Sonja Lyubomirsky

The key tenet of *The How of Happiness* is that every human being has a happiness 'set point' which, depending on how high or low it is, can determine how positive or negative they feel. Sonja Lyubomirsky offers a practical approach to help readers increase their set point, and find a level of happiness above that which they would normally feel, and feel more satisfaction in life.

Based on scientific research and trials, this is a groundbreaking book that offers practical steps to achieving a more positive outlook at home, at work and in your personal life.

978-0-7499-5246-4